CONCISE COLLEGE TEXTS

GCSE AND "O" LEVEL LAW

OTHER BOOKS IN THIS SERIES:

"A" Level Law, B. Hogan, P. Seago and G. Bennett
Banking Law, C. Hamblin
Contract, F. R. Davies
Criminal Law, P. Seago
English Legal System, K. J. Eddey
Grant and Levin: Family Law, Jennifer Levin
General Principles of Law, C. R. Newton
Hotel and Catering Law in Britain, David Field
Introduction to Commercial Law, C. Hamblin and F. B. Wright
Labour Law, C. D. Drake
Land Law, W. Swinfen Green and N. Henderson
Law of Arbitration, William H. Gill
Law and Procedure of Meetings, Matthew Moore
Law for Retailers, Jennifer Brave
Patents, Trade Marks, Copyright and Industrial Designs, T. A. Blanco White and Robin Jacob
Press Law, Robin Callender Smith
Sale of Goods and Consumer Credit, A. P. Dobson
Shipping Law, R. Grime
Tort, C. D. Baker

AUSTRALIA AND NEW ZEALAND
The Law Book Company Ltd.
Sydney : Melbourne : Perth

CANADA AND U.S.A.
The Carswell Company Ltd.
Agincourt, Ontario

INDIA
N. M. Tripathi Private Ltd.
Bombay
and
Eastern Law House Private Ltd.
Calcutta and Delhi
M.P.P. House
Bangalore

ISRAEL
Steimatzky's Agency Ltd.
Jerusalem : Tel Aviv : Haifa

MALAYSIA : SINGAPORE : BRUNEI
Malayan Law Journal (Pte.) Ltd.
Singapore and Kuala Lumpur

PAKISTAN
Pakistan Law House
Karachi

CONCISE COLLEGE TEXTS

GCSE AND "O" LEVEL LAW

by

W. J. BROWN
LL.B. (Hons.), F.C.I.S.

THIRD EDITION

LONDON
SWEET & MAXWELL LIMITED
1986

First Edition 1978
Second Edition 1982
Third Edition 1986

Published in 1986 by
Sweet & Maxwell Ltd. of
11 New Fetter Lane, London
and printed in Great Britain by
Richard Clay (The Chaucer Press) Ltd., Bungay, Suffolk

British Library Cataloguing in Publication Data

Brown, W.J.
GCSE and 'O' Level law.—3rd ed.—(Concise college texts)
1. Law—England
I. Title II. Series
344.2 KD661

ISBN 0–421–35250–7
ISBN 0–421–35260–4 Pbk

PREFACE

THE aim of this book is initially to cover the "O" Level English Law syllabuses of the G.C.E. examining boards and, secondly to help candidates prepare for the G.C.S.E. examinations in law, which are planned for June 1988.

At the end of each chapter there is a revision test and a list of examination questions, systematically covering the contents of the book, which may be used by teachers and candidates as class tests, homeworks or assignments.

I wish to thank the Football Association for kindly providing a copy of a professional footballer's contract, and Ken Andrews for his illustration of a Crown Court in session. I also wish to thank friends and colleagues for their helpful comments and advice. And finally I thank Linda for preparing the manuscript.

May 1986 W.J.B.

CONTENTS

TABLE OF CASES

TABLE OF STATUTES

Chapter 1

THE NATURE OF LAW

WHAT IS MEANT BY LAW

It is difficult to be precise as to what law is, but it may be defined as a code of conduct for the people in a given community, which controls their activities towards each other, with respect to their private and business lives, and to their relationship with the State.

It is generally agreed that law must be accepted by the majority of the community. Most road-users recognise the necessity for all drivers travelling on the same side of the road, or stopping at traffic lights when they show red. Even if there was no punishment for these offences, the majority of drivers would still follow the Highway Code because they know it is the sensible thing to do.

Most associations and sports are governed by laws or rules. The laws of cricket are observed by cricketers throughout the world, but they are not "law" in the context we are discussing. To be effective, law must be binding on the whole community and must be enforceable. Members of a community do not have to play cricket, and those who do play may agree to change the rules for their own benefit or convenience, but people in this country may not ignore or change the law to suit themselves. Holidaymakers, for example could play cricket on the beach and ignore the cricket law relating to "leg before wicket," and also create a law that a hit into the sea is "six and out." They could not, however, ignore the criminal law and decide to have gunfights as seen in western films on television most Saturday nights. In a recently decided case two men staged a friendly shooting contest to see who had the faster "draw." Although there was no intention for either to be hurt, one was shot and died. The survivor was found guilty of manslaughter. (*R*. v. *Moloney* - see p. 211). It is against the law to kill or attempt to kill, and members of the community have no choice as to whether the law applies to them or not.

Law often reflects a country's moral values. Generally, it is very difficult to define moral conduct, because one person might consider an act to be moral while another person might consider the same act to be immoral. A person might contribute to a lottery which will result in someone winning a large sum of money and the net profits of the lottery being donated to a charity. Another person, however, may consider the lottery to be gambling and therefore immoral and wrong, although recognising that the aim of benefiting the charity is worthwhile.

The difficulty with a moral attitude to law is that moral values change with time and locality. The country's attitude to homosexuality, prostitution, suicide, censorship of plays and pornography has changed drastically over recent years and the law has changed accordingly. There are many people who still consider such things to be immoral, but Parliament has probably considered that the attitude of a large part of the community has changed and has consequently passed the appropriate legislation to make certain conduct lawful which was previously unlawful.

Until a few years ago public houses in Wales did not open on Sundays, but several counties in the Principality changed this law because the community's attitude had changed. On the Continent most sporting activities take place on a Sunday with little restriction, but in this country it is difficult to ascertain the real position of the law. Horse racing is widely organised on Sundays on the Continent, but as yet not in this country, yet professional cricket and football is played on Sundays. It could be argued that in this respect a previous society's morals are being forced on to-day's society which in the main does not have the same attitude. Although, in 1986 the Government considered changing the law with regard to Sunday trading, Parliament did not pass the Bill.

Moral and religious attitudes do have a great effect on our law. "Thou shall not kill," "thou shall not steal" are not only religious commandments, they are also legal commandments. This is because the community as a whole considers it wrong to steal or to kill, and it would still be against the law for a starving person to steal food or to kill for food (see p. 230).

Since the end of the Second World War, legislation dealing with the community's welfare has been introduced on a huge scale. The State has decided that in many aspects of life, it must provide for the needy. The benefit of this legislation is available to all who qualify. The lowest paid worker and the managing director of the largest company will be entitled to the same State pension when they reach the age of 60 for women and 65 for men. The community has recognised the need to help the less fortunate and Parliament has passed laws to comply with this attitude.

It might be considered that everything a person does is affected by some element of law. If you attend school, college or work, there are Acts of Parliament which govern the condition of the buildings, the hours of attendance, etc. Law affects you when you travel, buy a newspaper, play a radio, enter a football ground, go to the pictures and so on. It is important, therefore, that we should have some knowledge of our law and how it works and is administered.

It should be noted that this book deals with English law, and that it affects the people who live in England and Wales. Scotland has its own system of law.

How good or effective is English law? If you ask a person who has just won a legal case, the answer may be "English justice is the best," but if a person has lost a case on a technical point of law, the reply to the question could be "The law is an ass."

The aim of law should be justice, but as a legal system becomes advanced and sophisticated it is possible that the "letter of the law" becomes more important than the "spirit of the law." It is then possible for a decision of the courts to be legally correct, but not to have achieved justice. In *Re Bravda* (1968) a will had four witnesses, although a valid will only requires two. The last two witnesses were to benefit under the terms of the will and the testator only wished them to be aware of the existence of the will and its contents. However, because the Wills Act 1837 provided that witnesses cannot benefit from the will the court ruled that they could not receive their inheritance.

In this case the letter of the law was followed, but the intentions of the testator were defeated and the outcome for the last two witnesses was certainly not justice. It should be noted that Parliament quickly changed the law to provide for such an occurrence (Wills Act 1968), but it did not help the two persons concerned in the case.

The difficulty in defining law and the nature of law is that it concerns cultural, moral, religious and egalitarian values, together with political policy and philosophy. But whatever the nature of law, if it is to be effective, it must encompass and bind the whole community, and it must be enforceable. A law that cannot, or will not, be enforced, is in effect no law at all.

THE NECESSITY FOR LAW

"Bank Clerk Shot."
"Armed Gang Steal Wage Roll."
"Terrorists Bomb Hotel."
"Soccer Fans Run Wild."
"Hi-jackers Kill Hostages."

Headlines such as these are commonplace and their like can be seen in newspapers most days of the week. If there was no system of law the persons responsible for the above events would be under no fear of punishment or sanction by the State or community in general. Murder is considered by modern society to be a terrible heinous offence, therefore, it is essential that there is an established procedure for providing that murder is a crime and that murderers will be punished. It is essential in a civilised community that there is a clearly defined criminal law which may be enforced, and a system of law for determining commercial and private disputes, and providing a means of compensation for injured parties.

If a community did not have a system of law which was capable of being enforced the strongest person, or group of persons, could dominate with arbitrary and unfair rules, or there could be anarchy, with no form of establishment and individuals following the dictates of their own conscience. If a community is to develop as a fair and free society, law must be present to ensure that an individual's rights and freedoms are protected. As a community develops its industry and business, its law must similarly develop and create a system which will ensure that transactions may take place with reasonable certainty, that disputes will be settled and that breaches of law will be enforced or compensated. It is not a coincidence that as business in the world has developed over the last 100 years, so has mercantile and company law, and the law dealing with insurance, revenue and taxation, consumer protection, industrial relations and similar matters.

Law is not only needed to ensure that offenders will be punished, it creates a code of conduct which a community wishes to follow. The Factories Acts created laws to protect workers from injury by placing a duty on an employer to provide a safe place of work. Drivers of motor vehicles are required to be insured, so that a third party injured in an accident will be compensated for any loss suffered. Shopkeepers have to refund the cost of goods which customers return because they are not of merchantable quality.

A community has its own values and its law should reflect these values. Laws are not made to be broken, but to be followed.

All breaches of civil or criminal law are not necessarily deliberate. The examples mentioned above could result in a breach of law which was not intentional; an employer may have created a dangerous place of work by accident; a motor accident could have been caused by the negligence of the driver, and a shopkeeper may not have known that the goods were unsatisfactory. Yet all three may have committed an offence or a breach of law. There have been breaches of law because the community created the laws and requires individuals to behave or conduct themselves accordingly for the benefit of the community as a whole.

DIVISIONS OF LAW

English law is usually classified as being either public or private law.

1. Public law

Public law is the law which governs the relationship between the State and individual members within the State, and between one State and another. This division of law comprises several specialist classes of law such as:

(a) *Criminal law*

Crime affects the whole community and as offences are considered to be against the State, they are punished by a system laid down and administered by the State.

Criminal law is designed to protect the public from attack on their individual property or person, and to enable any individual or group of individuals to perform their rights and duties under the law. Although a crime is against the State, an individual may suffer from the offence, so, as will be seen below in "Private law," in addition to the punishment laid down by the State, the individual will be able to obtain compensation for personal loss.

(b) *Constitutional law*

This branch of law deals with the method of government within the State. Constitutional Law affects the general public, in that it provides for the structure of the legislature (in this country the Houses of Parliament), the formation of the executive (the cabinet), the courts and legal system (the judiciary), the system of administration both local and central, and the laws created and administered by these bodies affect the rights, duties and freedoms of each individual within the State. Ideally, there should be a separation of the powers of executive, legislature and judiciary, but in this country only the latter exercises a separate power.

(*c*) *Administrative law*

As the government has legislated for the provision of a large number of benefits for individual members of the State (*e.g.* welfare benefits), the courts and administrative tribunals (usually set up by the government) have developed a body of laws and principles to regulate and control the agencies which administer the legislative provisions.

Administrative law is usually concerned with appeals and complaints from individuals against the ministerial agencies. For example, if a person has supplementary benefit withdrawn, an appeal may be made to the Supplementary Benefits Appeal Tribunal.

2. Private law

This division of law is sometimes called civil law and is contrasted with criminal law. The latter deals with offences against the State, while civil or private law concerns the dealing between individual members of the State. When the State starts an action the case is usually called in the name of the Monarch. Regina is used when a Queen is on the throne and Rex when there is a King. For convenience, a case is usually written as *R.* v. *Brown.* In civil cases the names of the individual parties are used: *Smith* v. *Brown.*

Because civil law only affects the individuals involved, it does not mean the State is not concerned or involved. In many instances the State will have created the law which regulates the conduct between the individuals, and will also administer the courts to hear disputes which have arisen. The main distinction may be that in a criminal case, the State brings the action, and stipulates and administers the punishment, while in civil cases the individual starts the action and the courts award the wronged individual the remedy best suited to the situation. For example, in breach of contract or negligence a sum of money called damages may be sufficient compensation but if a trespasser refuses to leave another person's land, an injunction may be needed to enforce the trespasser to leave the land.

Civil remedies are discussed on p. 76.

The main classes of civil law are as follows:

(*a*) *Law of contract*

An agreement between two or more persons which is intended to be legally binding.

(*b*) *Law of tort*

A recognised civil wrong other than a breach of contract or trust. Torts cover such wrongs as trespass, negligence, nuisance and defamation.

(*c*) *Law of property*

The rights of individuals to ownership and possession of their property, both land and personal property (chattels). The law of succession deals with wills and how property is distributed after death.

(*d*) *Family law*

The law concerning marriage, divorce and separation, and the responsibilities, and duties of parents to each other and to their children.

(*e*) *Welfare law*

As administrative law (see above) deals with disputes arising from the provision of State benefits, welfare law is concerned with the rights of individuals to obtain State benefits, and the rights and duties of parties with respect to housing and employment.

HOW THE LAW HAS GROWN

It was the Norman conquest of 1066 which established the basis of the English common law. Before William the Conqueror arrived the laws and courts varied from area to area, and there was no system which applied to the country as a whole. It was not the intention of the Normans to introduce new laws, their aim being to discover the laws that existed and make them uniform and applicable to the whole country.

The Normans set up the *Curia Regis* (the King's Council) which had judicial powers, as well as being the administrative centre for making laws and raising finance. The importance of the *Curia Regis* in the development of English law was that it probably led to the establishment of Parliament, and it allowed the creation and development of the various common law courts.

The court was composed of the tenants-in-chief of the Crown, who were high-ranking persons and barons. All the land of the country belonged to the King, and the tenants-in-chief were those who received the land directly from the King. Other members of the court were the chief officers and officials of State.

The aim of the Normans was to establish a system of law which would cover and apply to the whole country. Common law means that it is the same law for all; that it is shared by and affects all persons alike; common in this meaning does not mean low, cheap or inferior.

Although William I established the *Curia Regis*, it was in the reign of Henry II (1154-1189) that great steps were taken to develop common law.. Judges were sent out to tour the country to settle disputes and administer justice, and eventually to deal with criminal matters. The judges would return to discuss their cases and problems and from these discussions they were able to create a uniform common law. As law developed, the jurisdiction of the *Curia Regis* gradually diminished as new courts were introduced. The principal common law courts were:

(i) The Court of Exchequer. This was so called because the table or bench of the court was covered with a black and white chequer (like a chessboard). This court was usually concerned with financial and revenue matters.

(ii) The Court of Assize. This was concerned with criminal and civil matters, although later it dealt mainly with criminal cases. The country was divided into areas (circuits) and the itinerant judges travelled the country to administer the law.

This court was in existence until 1971, when it was replaced by the Crown Court.

(iii) The Court of Common Pleas. This was a civil court, dealing mainly with cases concerning disputes over land, between subjects other than the King.

The court was established to hear cases in Westminster while the King travelled the country. It was staffed by full-time judges who had been serjeants-at-law (barristers). The cost of legal actions was high and the costs for this court in particular were very expensive, therefore only the wealthy could afford to take legal action, and as the main source of wealth was ownership of land this court was very important. The court was abolished by the Judicature Acts 1873-75 and its jurisdiction was eventually transferred to the Queen's Bench Division of the High Court.

(iv) The Court of King's Bench. This court had criminal and civil jurisdiction and could hear appeals. Originally the court had civil jurisdiction, dealing mainly with the tort of trespass and the law of contract.

The court was the last of the three main courts to leave the *Curia Regis*, and the King's close association with the court gave it jurisdiction to issue the prerogative writs of *mandamus*, prohibition and *certiorari* (see p. 111). The court used a legal "fiddle" to take cases from the Court of Common Pleas by means of the fictitious Bill of Middlesex procedure. The court had power to hear cases when a defendant was in custody, therefore, the Sheriff of Middlesex would arrest a defendant on a fictitious trespass action, and then the court would hear the real cause of action and drop the other. A defendant was usually pleased because it meant the case was not heard in the Common Pleas with its expensive costs. The court was abolished by the Judicature Acts and most of its jurisdiction was transferred to the Queen's Bench Division of the High Court.

(v) The Courts of Exchequer Chamber. The first court of this name was established in 1357 to hear appeals from the Exchequer. A later court was created to hear appeals from the

King's Bench, and in 1830 a court was created to hear appeals from all the common law courts. The court was abolished by the Judicature Acts 1873-75 and its jurisdiction was transferred to the Court of Appeal.

In addition to the above, other courts were established to deal with the growth of trade, both national and international. The Courts of the Law Merchant, the Pie Powder Courts and the Courts of Staple, administered instant justice at markets and fairs, but eventually the work of these courts was taken over by the Common Law Courts.

THE WRIT SYSTEM

Henry II also developed the writ system. A writ was a Royal command to attend court and it had the effect of centralising the jurisdiction of the courts. If a person wished to start an action, it was necessary to obtain a writ from the King's chancellor, which meant that the Royal courts acquired more power. The Judicature Acts 1873-75 abolished the forms of action, but it is still necessary today to obtain a writ to start certain actions, although the wording of the claim is left to the plaintiff, and there is no danger of the case being lost because of a mistake in the format of the claim.

Writs originally began with a statement of the claim which was common for all writs of a similar nature. The wording on the writs was prepared beforehand for only a limited number of actions, and if a plaintiff had a new or different claim it would be difficult to bring an action before the courts. The clerks began to issue new writs for actions not previously covered, thereby widening the scope of the writ system and helping the development of the common law.

Because the barons considered that the issue of new writs took away their power the Provisions of Oxford 1258 was passed which provided that no writs were to issued for any new actions. This statute had the effect of severely restricting the development of the common law. To alleviate the harshness and inconvenience of this law the Statute of Westminster 1285 provided that new writs could be issued which were similar (*in consimili casu*) to existing writs. The effect of this statute was that the common law saw further development, but it could still be very difficult to bring a claim before the court if it was for an action that could not easily be adapted into an existing writ.

In addition to the difficulty of obtaining a suitable writ, an action could fail for a minor or simple mistake in the wording of the claim in the writ.

EQUITY

The writ system became very formal and as previously explained could only be issued for particular forms of actions. If there was no writ for a particular complaint, or one could not be adapted, there was no cause of action and, no matter how justifiable the complaint, an injured party could not obtain a remedy. If there was no writ there was no remedy.

To overcome the harshness of the writ system, appeals were made directly to the King, who made decisions on the facts of the case. As appeals grew in number, the King passed them to his Lord Chancellor. The earlier Chancellors were also the King's chaplain (often referred to as the "Keeper of the King's conscience"), and because of their ecclesiastical calling, their decisions tended to ignore the formal rules of law and were based on conscience and natural justice.

A separate Chancery Court was eventually established to hear the many appeals that were referred to this form of justice. In many instances decisions were contrary to those made in the common law courts and this led to disputes between the two courts. In the early seventeenth century, James I, on the advice of Sir Francis Bacon, ruled that in cases with contrary decisions, equity should prevail. This decision saw an extension of the work of the Chancery Court and new concepts of law were introduced such as the law of trusts (common law would not recognise a trust or the duties of trustees), and new remedies were provided.

Damages was the only common law remedy. Equity offered new remedies such as injunctions, specific performance and rescission (see p. 145). The main problem was that the courts could only award their own particular remedy. If a person bringing an action for trespass was asking for damages and an injunction to stop the other party from continuing the trespass, the litigant would have to go to the common law court for damages, and then start another action in the Chancery Court for the injunction. This situation existed until the middle of the nineteenth century when piecemeal legislation enabled both courts to award each other's remedies.

The main disadvantage of equity was the difficulty of foreseeing with any certainty the result of a case. Decisions varied from judge to judge, and the uncertainty of the outcome of cases led to the opinion at that time that the Chancellors' decisions varied as did the length of their feet.

Equity eventually became a formalised system, but procedure was very slow and, consequently, very expensive, as Dickens highlighted in "Bleak House."

It must be noted that common law was a complete system of law; equity was not. Equity was considered as the polish, "the gloss on the common law," which helped to improve the legal system and fill in any deficiencies. The Judicature Acts 1873-75, whilst confirming that in matters of conflict equity should prevail, fused the administration of the Chancery Court with the common law courts. It is unlikely that any new equitable concepts would be created today.

As a result of the Acts, the common law courts and the Court of Chancery were joined together under the Supreme Court of Judicature, which comprised the Court of Appeal and the High Court of Justice. For convenience, the High Court was divided into three divisions: Queen's Bench; Chancery; and Probate, Divorce and Admiralty. See p. 14 for a diagram of the structure of the courts by 1880.

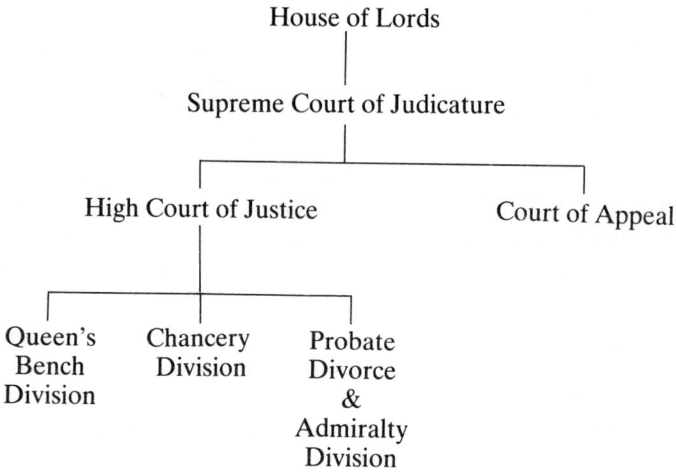
House of Lords
Supreme Court of Judicature
High Court of Justice
Court of Appeal
Queen's Bench Division
Chancery Division
Probate Divorce & Admiralty Division

Revision Test

At the end of each chapter a Revision Test will be set. They usually require short answers of a few words. Answer the questions, preferably on a separate sheet of paper and check your answers from within the pages of the chapter. The correctness (or otherwise) of the answers should indicate your understanding of the chapter. If you find the questions difficult, read the relevant section again.

1. Name two specialist classes of public law.

2. Name three classes of civil or private law.

3. To which class of private law does negligence and trespass belong?

4. Name the system whose harshness lead to the establishment of Equity.

5. Name the Acts which fused the administration of the Chancery Courts with the common law courts.

Specimen Questions

1. What is law? Why do you think it is necessary for a community to have a settled system of law?

2. What were the changes to the legal system introduced by the Judicature Act 1873-75? Draw a diagram of the structure of the courts as a result of the Acts, and compare it with the present day structure.

3. If Parliament did not have the power to make law would we have a system of law?

4. Describe the early writ system and explain how it lead to the growth of Equity.

5. Comment on the statement, "a law that cannot be enforced is in effect no law at all."

Chapter 2

SOURCES OF LAW

Many new students of law have difficulty at first in understanding the meaning of the phrase "sources of law." If asked, however, to locate the source of the River Nile, or the Thames, or the Mersey, most students would realise that the answer would be the place at which the river started.

The phrase "sources of law," has a similar meaning. Where does the law come from? Where does it start? Who makes it? In English law the law comes from two main sources, legislation (Acts of Parliament) and judicial precedent (the decisions of judges), and from subsidiary sources such as custom and books of authority. It must be emphasised that in modern times only very occasionally does law arise from the subsidiary sources.

If a person is accused of breaking the law, it is essential that all interested parties know the source of the law. For example, if a person takes goods out of a supermarket without paying, the shopkeeper, the police, the judge and the shopper will need to know the law that applies if the shopper is to be brought before the court. This particular offence arises from legislation. Parliament passed a law in 1968 (the Theft Act) which makes it a crime for a person to "dishonestly appropriate property belonging to another with the intention of permanently depriving the other of it." The sources of law concerning theft or stealing are the Theft Acts 1968 and 1978 and law reports which record decisions taken in court on the interpretation of these Acts (*e.g. R.* v. *Morris* 1983).

There is a maxim in law "that ignorance of the law is no excuse," which means that everyone is presumed to know the law. Obviously no single person knows all the law of the land.

Even judges, barristers and solicitors have to look up the law, but because of their training they know where the law originated and are able to go to the source.

The details of the different sources of law are as follows:

JUDICIAL PRECEDENT

Judicial precedent, or case law as it is often called, is the source of a large part of common law and equity. The law is "judge-made," in that when a judge makes a decision in a court case on a particular aspect of law, other judges may be bound to follow this decision in subsequent cases. Once the law has been established, the example or the precedent is binding on other judges, who must make a similar decision in cases concerning this aspect of law.

The doctrine of judicial precedent became firmly established by the late nineteenth century, although a system of precedent existed for hundreds of years before that. It was not until a reliable system of law reporting was started in 1866, and the administration of the courts was re-organised by the Judicature Acts 1873-75, that judicial precedent became an established source of law.

STARE DECISIS (THE STANDING OF DECISIONS)

Not all decisions of judges create a precedent. Some courts are more important than others. The higher the court which creates a precedent, the greater the authority the decision will have. A general rule is that lower courts are bound by decisions of higher courts, and some courts are bound by their own previous decisions. The hierarchy or standing of the courts is as follows:

1. The House of Lords

The House of Lords is the highest appeal court in civil and criminal matters, and decisions of this court are binding on all lower courts. Unlike most other courts, the House of Lords is not bound by precedent and may depart from their own previous decisions if they wish to do so, but if a precedent is to be reversed consideration should be given to the effect it would have, particularly on criminal law and commercial and business transactions.

2. The Court of Appeal (Civil Division)

The court is bound by decisions from the House of Lords and, although it has been suggested in court that the position should be otherwise, the court is bound by its own previous decisions. This principle was established by the Court of Appeal in *Young* v. *Bristol Aeroplane Co.* (1944), although it was laid down that the court may depart from its previous decisions under certain circumstances:

(i) where it considers that a decision was made "*per incuriam*," that is, in error,

(ii) where there are two previous conflicting decisions, the court may choose which decision is correct and overrule the other decision.

(iii) when a later House of Lords decision applies, this must be followed.

Decisions of the Court of Appeal (Civil Division) are binding on all other lower courts, but do not bind the Criminal Division of the Court of Appeal.

3. The Court of Appeal (Criminal Division)

Decisions of the House of Lords are binding on the Criminal Division, but unlike the Civil Division of the Court of Appeal, this court is not always bound to follow its own previous decisions. The court will probably follow decisions of its predecessor, the Court of Criminal Appeal, unless that would cause an injustice.

The decisions of this court bind all lower criminal courts and may bind inferior courts hearing civil cases. Decisions of this court are not binding on the Civil Division of the Court of Appeal nor is it bound by decisions of the Civil Division.

4. The Divisional Courts of the High Court

These courts are bound by the decisions of the House of Lords and Courts of Appeal. The civil divisional courts are bound by their own previous decisions, but the Divisional

Court of the Queen's Bench Division (which deals with criminal matters) is not so strictly held to its previous decisions. Decisions of the Divisional Court are binding on judges of the same division of the High Court sitting alone, and on the inferior courts.

5. The High Court

Decisions of cases of first instances, where the judge sits alone, are binding on the inferior courts but are not binding on other High Court judges. A previous decision of a High Court judge will be treated as a persuasive precedent but will not be binding in other High Court cases. It is suggested that this also applies to High Court judges sitting in the Crown Court, but does not apply to Circuit judges or Recorders, and they would be bound by previous decisions of a High Court judge. Decisions of the House of Lords, Courts of Appeal and Divisional Courts of the High Court are binding on these courts.

6. The inferior courts

The county courts and the magistrates' courts are bound by decisions of the superior courts. The inferior courts are not bound by their own decisions as they cannot create a precedent.

BINDING AND PERSUASIVE PRECEDENTS

It is not the entire decision of a judge which creates a binding precedent. When a judgment is delivered the judge will give the reason for his decision (*ratio decidendi*), and it is this principle which is binding and must be followed in future cases.

On occasions, judges make general comments in the course of their judgment to explain a particular point. Remarks made "by the way" are known as *obiter dicta* and are persuasive authority, not binding precedent. If, however, the judge is well known and respected for previous judicial decisions, such comments may be followed as persuasive authority in cases where there appears to be no existing binding precedent. Other sources of persuasive authority are text-book writers and decisions from courts of other countries such as the United States, Australia and New Zealand.

1. Ratio decidendi

Ratio decidendi is the vital part of case law. It is the principle upon which a decision is reached, and it is this principle which is binding on subsequent cases which have similar facts in the same branch of law.

2. Obiter dicta

The second aspect of judgments, *obiter dicta*, are things said "by the way," and do not have to be followed. Decisions of the judicial Committee of the Privy Council are only persuasive authority because the Council is not part of the English legal system. However, because the Privy Council is mainly comprised of the Law Lords, its decisions have great influence on subsequent cases with similar facts.

Court of Appeal cases have three or more judges and the result is given on the decisions of the majority. A judge who disagrees with the decision of the other judges gives a dissenting judgment, which is *obiter dictum* and never binding. If the judge who dissented is respected, the dissenting judgment might be used as a persuasive authority if the case proceeds to the House of Lords. There have been instances of judges giving a dissenting judgment in the Court of Appeal, and later, when sitting as Law Lords in the House of Lords, hearing a completely different case, overrule the precedent created in the earlier Court of Appeal case. In these instances the Law Lords have been "persuaded" by the dissenting judgment to overrule an existing precedent.

3. Distinguishing

Although the facts of a case appear similar to a binding precedent, a judge may consider that there is some aspect or fact which is not covered by the *ratio decidendi* of the earlier case. The judge will "distinguish" the present case from the earlier one which created the precedent.

4. Overruling

A higher court may consider that the *ratio decidendi* set by a lower court is not the correct law, so when another case is argued on similar facts, the higher court will overrule the previous precedent and set a new precedent to be followed in future cases.

5. Reversal

When a court is hearing an appeal, it may uphold or "reverse" the decision of the lower court. For example, the High Court may give judgment to the plaintiff, and on appeal the Court of Appeal may "reverse" the decision and give judgment to the defendant.

6. Disapproval

A superior court may consider that there is some doubt as to the standing of a previous principle, and it may "disapprove," but not expressly overrule, the earlier precedent.

ADVANTAGES AND DISADVANTAGES OF PRECEDENT

1. Advantages

(*a*) *Certainty.* When a precedent has been established the law becomes settled. Lawyers and laymen know and recognise the law and can act accordingly.

(*b*) *The existence of a wealth of detailed, practical knowledge.* All case law arises from a practical situation, and the law reports give detailed information of actual cases. In English law there are never "theoretical cases." The case before the court must be on facts in which one party claims a legal right from the other party.

(*c*) *There is provision for future growth.* We live in a changing world, and a law which was relevant 50 years ago may not be suitable now. The doctrine of precedent allows the law to grow according to the needs of the community. For example, as we will see later (p. 87) a person under 18 is known as an infant or minor. A minor is not bound by contracts for goods which are luxuries. Fifty years ago a motor car or motorcycle would certainly have been considered a luxury, but to-day the court would probably take the opposite view, particularly if a student or young employee lived a long distance from college or work.

2. Disadvantages

(*a*) *Rigidity.* Although it is considered an advantage for law to be certain, a binding precedent may mean that the law is difficult to change. The House of Lords, however, may change a precedent by overruling a previous decision, and Parliament can legislate for a change of the law.

(*b*) *Danger of illogical distinctions.* Judges may look for a justification for not following precedent, particularly if it is considered to be a bad decision, and a case may be distinguished from another for illogical reasons, so that a different decision may be given.

(*c*) *The complexity and volume of the law reports.* Law reports date back many hundreds of years and it may be difficult to find an appropriate case, as there are more than 400,000 reported cases.

THE LAW REPORTS

The basis of judicial precedent is the reporting of cases. Without a reliable system of reporting, it would be impossible for case law to be a source of law.

An extract of a law report, *Re Jones, decd.* [1981] 2 W.L.R. 106 is reproduced on the following pages.

[FAMILY DIVISION]

In re JONES, DECD.

1980 July 17 — Sir John Arnold P.

Will—Soldier's will—"In actual military service"—Soldier shot while on patrol in Northern Ireland—Oral declaration that personal effects to be given to fiancée—Whether noncupative will to be admitted to probate—Wills Act 1837 (7 *Will.* 4 & 1 *Vict., c.* 26), *s.* 11

During a period when the armed forces had been asked by the Northern Ireland authorities to assist the civil power in maintaining law and order there, the deceased, a soldier, was serving in Northern Ireland and, on March 16, 1978, he had been sent out on a military patrol with an officer and a warrant officer. An unknown assailant shot him and, before he died, he made an oral testamentary declaration to the two soldiers with him leaving his possessions to the applicant whom he was to have married the following week. She applied to have the declaration admitted to probate as a privileged will under section 11 of the Wills Act 1837.

On the question whether the soldier was on actual military service within the meaning of the section:—

Held, that it was the nature of the duties a soldier was called upon to perform which determined whether he was on actual military service; that, provided the service was both active and military, it could be either within the United Kingdom or abroad against a force that need not be organised on conventional military lines and, therefore, when the soldier

A was called upon to go out on patrol at a time when there was a clandestinely organised insurrection, he was on actual military service and his oral declaration would be admitted to probate (post, pp. 108E, 110D–E, 111H—112B).

In the Will of Anderson (1958) 75 W.N.(N.S.W.) 334 applied.

The following cases are referred to in the judgment:

B *Anderson, In the Will of* (1958) 75 W.N.(N.S.W.) 334.
Attorney-General for Northern Ireland's Reference (*No. 1 of 1975*) [1977] A.C. 105; [1976] 3 W.L.R. 235; [1976] 2 All E.R. 937, H.L.(N.I.).
Booth, In re, [1926] P. 118.
Drummond v. *Parish* (1843) 3 Curt. 522.
Tweedale, In the Goods of (1874) L.R. 3 P. & D. 204.
Wingham decd., In re [1949] P. 187; [1948] 2 All E.R. 908.

C

The following additional cases were cited in argument:

Hiscock, In the Goods of [1901] P. 78.
Limond, In re [1915] 2 Ch. 240.
Rippon, In the Estate of [1943] P. 61; [1943] 1 All E.R. 676.
Spark decd., In the Estate of [1941] P. 115; [1941] 2 All E.R. 782.
Thorne, In the Goods of (1865) 4 Sw. & Tr. 36.

D

MOTION

The applicant, Anne Mannering, formerly Anne Newport, of Pudsey, West Yorkshire, applied for an order that the oral statement made by David Anthony Jones on March 16, 1978, be admitted to probate as a privileged will under section 11 of the Wills Act 1837. The hearing was in
E chambers. Judgment was delivered in open court.

The facts are stated in the judgment.

Colin Braham for the applicant.

John Mummery for the Attorney-General as amicus curiae.

F SIR JOHN ARNOLD P. This is an application in connection with an alleged will of David Anthony Jones deceased, who was killed in Northern Ireland while on a military patrol on March 16, 1978. He was fired upon by unknown hands and died on the following day. He was in the company of an officer and a warrant officer of his battalion, and to those two men he made a declaration, and it was in these words: " If I don't make it," he said, " make sure Anne gets all my stuff." Anne was his fiancée; Anne
G Mary Newport, as she then was; Anne Mannering, as she has now become; and it is plain enough that if that was an effective will it was one which contained a universal bequest of personalty in favour of Anne. The question whether it was an effective will depends upon whether there extended to the deceased the privilege afforded by section 11 of the Wills Act 1837 to make a nuncupative will in the sense of an oral testamentary declaration;
H and in accordance with the language of the section, that depends upon whether the right view is that the deceased was at the time of making that testamentary declaration in " actual military service."

The evidence in the case includes this authoritative statement emanating from an officer of the Ministry of Defence, that in 1969 a request was made by the Northern Ireland authorities for the deployment of the armed forces to assist the civil power in the maintenance of law and order in Northern Ireland; and it was in pursuance of that request that the deceased's

unit was deployed in that province. The background was something which A
was conveniently described by Lord Diplock in *Attorney-General for Northern Ireland's Reference (No. 1 of 1975)* [1977] A.C. 105, 136:

> "In some parts of the province there has existed for some years now a state of armed and clandestinely organised insurrection against the lawful government of Her Majesty by persons seeking to gain political ends by violent means—that is, by committing murder and other B
> crimes of violence against persons and property."

Now the doubt which has arisen in this case—and which has made the summons necessary—arises from this general circumstance: that for the most part in cases which have been held in the case of soldiers to come within the ambit of the statutory privilege to which I have referred, the background has been the existence or the impending existence or the C
recent existence of something which may conventionally be described as a war, in the sense of hostilities between two sovereign governments, where the deceased in question has been in the service of one of them. That is not a state of affairs which can accurately be characterised as identical with or similar to that which prevails in Northern Ireland. The question therefore was posed whether the state of affairs which does prevail in Northern Ireland is such that a military participant in the aid to the civil power D
which is and was being afforded there was in a state of "actual military service."

The meaning of the words "actual military service" was considered by Bucknill and Denning L.JJ. in the Court of Appeal in *In re Wingham, decd.* [1949] P. 187. There emerges from that authority in my judgment this: that there may be equated with that description that of active military E
operations; that it must be predicated that the deceased was in service at the time that he made his will; that that service was active and of its character military.

In this case, the person who would be entitled either on intestacy or on the basis of an earlier will to the personal estate of the deceased, if the will in question is not effective as a nuncupatory will, is the deceased's F
mother who for understandable reasons has chosen to take no part in the litigation. I have had the advantage of the assistance on the instructions of the Treasury Solicitor of Mr. Mummery as amicus curiae. His submission has been that the answer to those questions is to be derived from a consideration of all the circumstances of the case and to be decided as a matter of fact. With that view of the matter, I wholeheartedly agree. There is ample material in the authorities for saying that this or that or the other G
circumstance is not by itself decisive one way or the other, and that it is the concatenation of circumstances, the totality of the relevant environment which has to be looked at in order to decide the question.

There has been a very large number of cases in which the question has had to be answered against the background of a war, as that phrase is ordinarily understood. These cases have all turned upon the extent to H
which it could fairly be said that at the actual moment of the alleged testamentary act the deceased was already embarked upon activities in connection with that war, or whether at that moment he had ceased to be engaged in activities connected with that war, or in other cases whether his intrinsic connection with the prosecution of that war was sufficiently intimate to justify the view that he was engaged in actual military service.

Those cases help me in my judgment only to the extent that they

The Weekly Law Reports, January 30, 1981

A demonstrate a consistent view of the courts that in the interpretation of this section, and its predecessor, the right view is the expansive view; the view that if there be a doubt, it should be resolved in favour of the validation rather than the invalidation of the alleged testamentary act. But there have been other cases in which either there has been an absence of what could ordinarily be referred to as a war, or the state of the facts has not been spelled out sufficiently to enable one to form any real conclusion on
B that matter and it is really to those cases which one must look for guidance in the circumstances of the present case.

The statute which was the predecessor of the Wills Act 1837 in this manifestation was the Statute of Frauds 1676, passed in the reign of Charles II, and section 23 dealt with a similar subject matter. The earliest case in which any relevant matter has had consideration was *Shearman* v.
C *Pyke*, not itself reported, which was referred to in *Drummond* v. *Parrish* (1843) 3 Curt. 522. The decision in *Drummond* v. *Parrish* is of no great interest or importance to what I have to decide. But there were two matters within it in the judgment in the Prerogative Court of Canterbury of Sir Herbert Jenner Fust which do help. One was a citation from a very old book called *Swinburne on Testaments & Last Wills*, vol. 1, 7th ed. (1803), Part I, p. 95, and Sir Herbert Jenner Fust's comment on that book was
D that it was one which undoubtedly the court would consider a very high authority. The citation was concerned with the distinction between military operations and garrison duty—to use broad and not very precisely defined terms,—which had of course a relevance to the question whether the deceased was or was not on actual military service. The contrast that Swinburne makes is this: when describing those on garrison duty, he
E says, at p. 96:

> " they be such as lie safely in some castle or place of defence, or beseiged by the enemy, only in readiness to be employed in case of invasion or rebellion, and then they do not enjoy these military privileges ":

Swinburne then goes on to look at those who do, and he says:

F

> " or else they be such as are in *expedition* or *actual service of wars*, and such are privileged, at least during the time of their expedition, whether they be employed by land or by water, and whether they be horsemen or footmen."

It is quite plain that what the author is there doing is describing within those two descriptions collectively the totality of those whose position has
G to be considered; and therefore it is plain that when they proceed on expedition or actual service of wars in the course of their employment in case of invasion or rebellion, he regards them as coming within the privileged class. So one can derive from that that the repulsion of an invasion upon which they proceed from their garrison place, their castle or place of defence, or the suppression of a rebellion for which purpose they like-
H wise proceed, in the view of that learned author would put them into the privileged class. So one finds at any rate a strong indication at this stage that the suppression of a rebellion is the sort of expedition or actual service of wars which creates the privilege. This is borne out by a reference a little later on in the judgment of Sir Herbert Jenner Fust when he proceeds to rely upon and describe *Shearman* v. *Pyke* which had been decided in 1724. Whether in the Prerogative Court or in Doctors Commons does not appear with any clarity, but I think it was in the Prerogative

Court at Canterbury. It was a case therefore which had been decided A
under the Act of Charles II, the predecessor section to that of the Wills Act 1837. It is not necessary to deal with the case at very great length.

Shearman v. *Pyke* concerned a cook who was a soldier in the service of the East India Company, and attached in his culinary capacity to one Governor Pyke of St. Helena. In 1719 the governor, with the cook in attendance, left St. Helena to proceed to Bencoolen, a place in India. But B
when they got as far as Batavia they were informed that the factory at Bencoolen was cut off by the natives, and so they proceeded, presumably not alone, to Bencoolen, to re-establish the factory. And that service completed they returned to some intermediate place on the journey called Moco Moro where unfortunately the cook died. It was held in the event that that expedition to relieve the cut-off factory at Bencoolen, which had not been completed when the cook died on the way back, was an occasion C
of actual military service, with the consequence that an informal will of the cook was upheld.

It is true to say, I think, that the state of affairs in which a factory is cut off by the natives could be part of an incident of a conventional war, but it seems to be much more likely that it was a description of some sort of insurrection. At least this is significant: that no consideration D
seems to have been given to the question whether it was the one or the other in the course of the adjudication to the effect that its relief was the subject of actual military service; so that at least that case suggests that provided there is service, provided that it is military, and provided that it is active, it is not of consequence whether its purpose is to fight off a foreign enemy or to suppress a rebellious group of subjects.

That is the first case which is relevant to a consideration of the nature E
of the background against which the service requires to be performed. The next case, which has the same sort of utility, is *In the Goods of Tweedale* (1874) L.R. 3 P. & D. 204. It concerned a testator who was an officer at the relevant time in the 8th Regiment Bengal Cavalry. What had happened was this: in 1842 some disturbances broke out in the district of Bundelcund in India, and evidently, from the report, in British India, and a field F
force was put together for the purpose of suppressing the disturbances. The testator was engaged with his regiment as part of that field force. Sir James Hannen P. said at p. 206:

> "This will is not attested, but it is proved to have been made whilst the deceased was in actual military service on an expedition which was employed in suppressing disturbances in the Bundelcund district." G

So he regarded the suppression of insurrection, or disturbances within the ambit of the area of government, but contrary to the ordinances of that government, as a matter of actual military service where the military were called out to suppress them. The operation was quite local. The field force proceeded from its station in India to the scene of the trouble, and that was, in the eye of Sir James Hannen P., the engaging in actual military H
service.

A less clear case, but one pointing in the same direction, is *In re Booth* [1926] P. 118. This concerned an officer of the 46th Regiment who, when stationed at Gibraltar in 1882, had been posted with his regiment to Egypt; immediately before embarkation he had made a testamentary declaration, and the question in the case was whether that was an effective nuncupatory will. The point which was argued was not whether the service on which

A he was to embark was actual military service but whether the occasion on
which he had made his will was sufficiently proximate to that service to
justify the conclusion that he was already engaged upon it.

Nevertheless, it is the fact that the service in question was regarded as
being actual military service for the relevant purpose; and I have been
given as part of the evidence an official description of what happened in
the Egyptian campaign of 1882. The Khedive of Egypt, who was to an
B extent subject to the Ottoman Empire of the Sultan, had to face an insurrection led by one Arabi Pasha, and in pursuance of certain existing international engagements—as they are called in a letter written by the Secretary
of State for War to Sir Garnet Wolseley who was in charge of the expedition—the British government went to the assistance of the Khedive to
suppress that insurrection. It was very plainly an expedition in aid of the
C civil power—not the British civil power, it is true, but the civil power in
authority in Egypt—for the purpose of assisting it to suppress an insurrection. The instructions to Sir Garnet included specifically an instruction
that while he was at liberty to make any military settlement, or military
convention as it is called, he was not to engage in any act of political settlement. There again the conception of actual military service as including
the suppression of an insurrection is present.

D That is really the extent of what one can derive from English authority;
but the nearest of all cases to the present is an Australian decision called
In the Will of Anderson (1958) 75 W.N.(N.S.W.) 334. That concerned the
death in action of a soldier in the Australian contingent made available for
the assistance of the government of the Federation of Malaya to suppress
what is described in the report as:

E
> " armed and organised aggression and violence against the government
> and the people of Malaya designed to overthrow the government by
> force."

This was the terrorist activity which prevailed in and about the year 1956,
when the deceased was killed; and the very question which arises in this
F case as to how far what is conventionally called and regarded as a state
of war is necessary to the exercise of the jurisdiction was considered by the
judge, albeit on an unopposed application supporting the nuncupative will.
Myers J. said at p. 335:

> " In the present case there was no state of war and it is difficult to
> see how there could have been, for there was no nation or state with
> G which a state of war could have been proclaimed to exist, but in all
> other respects there was no difference between the situation of a mem-
> ber of this force and that of a member of any military force in time of
> war. In my opinion the deceased was in actual military service and it
> would be unreasonable to hold otherwise."

This decision is valuable persuasive authority which in my judgment is not
H distinguishable in any material particular from that which I have to decide.

When the deceased in the present case was ordered to go out on his
patrol, the fatal patrol, he was obliged by the conditions of his service in
accordance with the discipline which prevailed in his military unit so to do.
That the service was military, that the service was active, seems to me to
be beyond contest. The fact that the enemy was not a uniformed force
engaged in regular warfare, or even an insurgent force organised upon
conventional military lines, but rather a conjuration of clandestine assassins

The Weekly Law Reports, January 30, 1981

112

Sir John Arnold P. **In re Jones, decd. (Fam.D.)** **[1981]**

and arsonists, cannot in my judgment affect any of those questions. I have no hesitation in pronouncing this will a valid nuncupative will. It is not the state of the opponent, or the character of the opponent's operations, in my judgment, which affect the answers to the questions which arise. They must be answered by reference to the activities of the deceased and those with whom he is associated; and it is nihil ad rem in relation to the answers to the questions whether there is service, whether it is active, and whether it is military, that the context in which it occurs is that of foreign expedition, foreign invasion, or local insurrection. A B

Order as prayed.
No order for costs.
Legal aid taxation.

C

Solicitors: *Roche, Son & Neale for Wright, Atkinson & Pearson, Keighley; Treasury Solicitor.*

M. B. D.

The Year Books were probably the first kind of law reports. They were compiled in the period from approximately 1272-1535 and dealt with pleading and procedure. It is likely they were used as early text books by young lawyers and were probably written by students as guidelines in procedure and pleadings. In the main they dealt with civil cases.

Abridgements were a collection of cases from the Year Books. They were written by judges and lawyers, and for convenient reference the cases were grouped in subject-matter, rather than in date order. Some Abridgements were published, the most important and best known being by Fitzherbert (1516) and Brooke (1568).

Private reporting came into fashion when the Year Books were no longer written. The most notable of these reports were Plowden's Reports (1550-1580), Coke's Reports (1572-1616) and Burrow's Reports (1756-1772). the last named established a particular reputation for good reporting of judgments. The value of the private reports depends on the reputation of the reporter, and while many of them were regarded highly, others have no standing and judges have refused counsel permission to quote from them. It has been said of one reporter named Barnardiston, that he often slept through court cases and other reporters would write nonsense in his notebook, which he later printed.

Modern law reporting started when the Inns of Court created the Council of Law Reporting in 1865 to ensure a satisfactory standard of reporting of cases of legal significance. In 1870 the Incorporated Council of Law Reporting was established. The reporters, who are barristers, must present a report which is to be published, to the judge of the case who may revise the wording before publication.

The Council publishes the Law Reports and Weekly Law Reports. The latter were first published in 1953 and replaced the "Weekly Notes." The Weekly Law Reports are consolidated for each year and issued in volumes, so that at the end of a year, there are usually about three or four volumes of the reports.

Reporting of cases is not the monopoly of the Council and other companies and private organisations publish reports which have equal authority. The best known are the All

England Law Reports, started in 1936, while reports from *The Times* are frequently cited in court.

Students should known how to refer to a law report. Cases are quoted, for example, as *Rapley* v. *Rapley* [1983] 1 W.L.R. 1069. The reference after the names of the parties means that a student must consult the first volume of the Weekly Law Reports of 1983 and at page 1069 details of the case are reported. It would be an interesting exercise for students to look up some of the cases quoted and listed in this book. If your college or school does not have law reports in the library, you may find them in the nearest large public library. *Rapley* v. *Rapley* is referred to in this book on page 247.

LEGISLATION

Legislation is law enacted by Parliament, and when an Act of Parliament, known as a statute, is passed it becomes the law of the land. (A recent Act is reproduced on p. 36.) A statute is superior to all sources of law and judges must enforce this law in the courts, even if it is contrary to an existing binding precedent. This supremacy of Parliament over all other sources of law is called the "Sovereignty of Parliament," and it means that Parliament may make laws which have to be enforced and cannot be challenged on the grounds that they are illegal. In the United States of America this is not so. The Constitution of the United States is very rigid and not easily changed, and the Supreme Court of the United States may rule that a law passed by the Senate is unconstitutional and illegal.

THE PROCESS OF A STATUTE

Parliament consists of the House of Commons and the House of Lords, and a statute has to pass through a series of debates in both Houses before becoming law.

Approval of the House of Lords is not essential for measures dealing with finance. There is a set procedure which has to be followed and until this has been finally completed the "statute" is called a Bill (see below). The procedure which follows usually starts in the House of Commons before going to the Lords, but it may be reversed.

1. First reading

The Bill is formally presented and there is little debate. The purpose is to inform members of the Bill's existence and to indicate that printed copies will be available.

2. Second reading

There is usually a debate on the general principles of the Bill. If the vote is in favour, the Bill goes to the next stage. It is not necessary to vote at this reading unless 20 members object.

3. The committee stage

The Bill is examined in detail. Each clause is debated and may be amended or even excluded. As the name suggests, the examination may be by a "select" or "standing" committee, or it may be discussed by the entire House acting as a committee. The examination at this stage is very important. Select committees and standing committees (20–50 members) are appointed on the basis of the parties' numerical strength.

4. The report stage

Its purpose is to inform the House of changes that have been made and to give an opportunity for further discussion. The House may make additional amendments.

5. Third reading

Generally only verbal amendments to the Bill may be made at this stage. It now passes to the other House.

6. The House of Lords

The above procedure is repeated in the House of Lords, unless it started in this House, when it would pass to the Commons.

7. The Royal Assent

After a Bill has passed through Parliament, it does not become law until it has been signed or authorised by the Queen. The Assent is a formality, and by convention cannot be refused. Immediately the Royal Assent is given, the Act of Parliament becomes law, unless another starting date has been provided for in the Act.

A Bill lapses if it is has not completed all the above stages by the time a session of Parliament has been ended by Prorogation, or when Parliament is dissolved for a general election. It may be introduced in another session of Parliament but the Bill must pass through all the stages once again.

An Act of Parliament is printed and may be purchased by the general public from Her Majesty's Stationery Office, or its agents.

Bills

A Bill is a draft of the provisions which are proposed to become law and submitted to Parliament.

There are different types of Bills.

1. Public Bill

Public Bills are usually drafted by civil servant lawyers under the control of the Prime Minister. They may be introduced by the government or by a private member, and they alter or amend the law for the country at large.

2. Private Member's Bill

A private member may introduce a Bill, although it is not likely to be successful in passing through the necessary stages, unless it is adopted by the government. The opportunity to present a Private Member's Bill is limited and a ballot is held early in the session to decide the order in which members may introduce a Bill.

3. Private Bill

These are Bills for special interest or benefit of a person or persons. The most common presenters of these Bills are local authorities wishing to widen the scope of their activities or powers.

Codification and Consolidation

Codification entails bringing together all the existing legislation and case law into a restatement of the law. Codification may be of either the complete law of a country or for a particular branch of law. The law of most Continental countries is codified, but in this country and other common law countries (mainly the U.S.A. and Commonwealth countries) there is little codification. At the end of the nineteenth century there was an attempt to codify commercial law, and as a result there were enacted the Partnership Act 1890, the Sale of Goods Act 1893 and the Bill of Exchange Act 1882. It has been suggested that the law of contract would be a suitable area for codification, but is unlikely to be so affected in the near future.

Consolidation occurs when all the provisions of several Acts of Parliament, dealing with a common topic, are brought together into one Act. It is becoming very popular because, although it does not alter the law, it makes it easier for lawyers and laymen to find. Areas of law which have recently been consolidated include company law, marriage, taxation and employment protection. On page 36 is a reproduction of the first page of the Sale of Goods Act 1979, which consolidated the law relating to the sale of goods.

Interpretation of a Statute

It has been explained that Parliament is supreme, and that the courts cannot challenge the legality of a statute. The courts, however, do have some effect on the law created by legislation. An Act of Parliament may have been drafted badly, in that the words used may be ambiguous, or not clear in meaning or may not provide for every eventuality.

For example, if an Act was passed ordering "every dog to be destroyed" by a certain date, what would be the law relating to bitches? An owner of a bitch may contend that the law only concerns male animals of the canine species, and does not affect bitches. In such an event the dispute would go to the courts for the "legal" interpretation of the word "dog," as used in the Act.

It must be noted that it is the courts which usually interpret

Sale of Goods Act 1979

1979 CHAPTER 54

An Act to consolidate the law relating to the sale of goods. [6th December 1979]

BE IT ENACTED by the Queen's most Excellent Majesty, by and with the advice and consent of the Lords Spiritual and Temporal, and Commons, in this present Parliament assembled, and by the authority of the same, as follows:—

PART I

CONTRACTS TO WHICH ACT APPLIES

Contracts to which Act applies.

1.—(1) This Act applies to contracts of sale of goods made on or after (but not to those made before) 1 January 1894.

(2) In relation to contracts made on certain dates, this Act applies subject to the modification of certain of its sections as mentioned in Schedule 1 below.

(3) Any such modification is indicated in the section concerned by a reference to Schedule 1 below.

(4) Accordingly, where a section does not contain such a reference, this Act applies in relation to the contract concerned without such modification of the section.

PART II

FORMATION OF THE CONTRACT

Contract of sale

Contract of sale.

2.—(1) A contract of sale of goods is a contract by which the seller transfers or agrees to transfer the property in goods to the buyer for a money consideration, called the price.

the meaning of statutes, not Parliament, although many Acts include an interpretation section on words and phrases used in the particular Act. In addition, the Interpretation Acts interprets many general words and terms that are used in Acts, unless a contrary intention appears. One example provides that "words in the singular shall include the plural and words in the plural shall include the singular."

When the courts have to interpret the wording of an Act, there are certain rules to follow, but is is left for the judge to decide which rule is appropriate to the particular case. The rules are as follows:

1. The literal rule

If the words used are clear and unambiguous, the judge will interpret the words in their ordinary, plain, grammatical meaning.

2. The golden rule

This principle follows on from the literal rule, in that the plain, ordinary meaning of the words is taken, unless it would be absurd or repugnant to the law. In *Re Sigsworth* 1935, it was held that a man who murdered his mother could not benefit from her estate. The ordinary meaning of the word "issue" would have included the son, but as it would have been repugnant for a murderer to benefit from the estate of the person killed, the court deviated from the ordinary meaning of the word.

3. The mischief rule (the rule in Heydon's Case 1584)

In this rule, the courts try to discover the reason for the Act. The courts look for the defect, or the mischief which the Act was trying to remedy, and they then interpret the words accordingly.

Gardiner v. *Sevenoaks R.D.C.* (1950). An Act required film to be stored in premises under certain conditions. G. kept his film in a cave and claimed that as a cave was not "premises" he was not bound by the requirements of the Act. The court held that the purpose of the Act was the safety of workers or other persons and therefore the cave was "premises" for the requirements of the Act. The court looked for the mischief the Act was designed to protect.

4. The "ejusdem generis" rule

It is a principle of interpretation that where general words follow specific words, the general words must be applied to the meaning of the specific things. If an Act was worded "dogs, cats and other animals," the general words (and other animals) would have to be interpreted in the light of the specific words (dogs and cats). It would be obvious that the Act referred to domestic and not to wild animals.

Evans v. *Cross* (1938). The appellant was charged with ignoring a traffic sign. He claimed that a white line on the road was not a traffic sign for the purposes of the Act, which read, "... warning signposts, direction posts, signs or other devices." The court held that the general words (or other devices) must relate to the preceding words and in this case they did not.

5. The express mention of one thing implies the exclusion of another

If specific things are mentioned and not followed by general words, only these specific things are affected by the Act. A statute referred to "quarries and coal mines," and it was held that as there were no general words, the Act did not cover any kind of mine other than a coal mine.

If we look back at our hypothetical case of the dogs (see above), it can be seen that the literal rule and the golden rule would be unsuitable as the word dog has an ambiguous meaning.

If the mischief rule was applied, and it was shown that the reason for the Act was to stop dogs fouling the footpaths or pavements, or to stop the spread of rabies, then the interpretation might be all dogs of the species, whether they be male or female.

DELEGATED LEGISLATION

1. What is delegated legislation?

Parliament may give ministers, government departments and other bodies the power to make laws which are binding on the community and the courts. Generally, Parliament lays down the framework of the law, and then delegates to subordinates the authority to make laws and rules for specific purposes within the Act. This form of legislation is increasing every year and has become a very important source of law.

2. Why is there a need for delegated legislation?

(a) Because of the increasing volume of legislation, Parliament does not have the time to consider and debate every small detail needed for the routine administration of an Act.
(b) In an emergency, Parliament may not have the time to deal with the situation, or in fact may not be in session.
(c) Although Parliament has passed a statute, the members may not have the technical expertise or local knowledge to deal with the necessary details, so they are delegated to experts.
(d) It is a difficult procedure for Parliament to amend a statute. Delegated legislation is more flexible and elastic, and if experience shows that a regulation or procedure is not achieving its purpose, or is inappropriate to the aims of the statute, it can easily be amended or revoked.

3. Who has the power to make delegated legislation?

(a) Orders in Council
The government, usually in times of emergency, may be given the power to make laws in this way. Such an Order requires a meeting of the Privy Council and the signature of the Queen.

(b) Ministers of the Crown
Ministers are given the power to make rules and Orders under statutes which affect their own departments. For example, the minister responsible for transport has the power to change the maximum speeds allowed on motorways and roads.

(c) By-laws
Parliament gives power to local authorities and certain other public and nationalised bodies to make laws within the scope of their own areas of activity. These laws have to be approved by central government.

4. Publication

All delegated legislation is technically made public by "statutory instrument," but this term usually refers to rules and Orders made by ministers of the Crown.

Control of Delegated Legislation

There are certain safeguards which ensure that delegated legislation is controlled.

(1) Parliament has the right to inspect every statutory instrument, and has a select committee to scrutinise certain legislation considered likely to be oppressive. Parliament also has the ultimate safeguard, in that it may revoke or rescind the delegated power.

(2) The courts may declare a statutory instrument to be *ultra vires* and void. *Ultra vires* means "beyond the power," and if a court considers that the statutory instrument has gone outside the scope of the Act under which it was issued, it may make such a declaration. In *Att.-Gen.* v. *Fulham Corpn.* (1921) an Act allowed the Corporation to build a wash-house, but the Corporation decided to open a laundry. The court held that it was "*ultra vires*" the Act, and issued an injunction restraining the Corporation. In *Bromley L.B.C.* v. *Greater London Council* (1982), the Transport (London) Act 1969 provided that the G.L.C. had a general duty for the provision of integrated, efficient and economic transport facilities and services for Greater London. The G.L.C. reduced fares by 25% and required London boroughs to increase rates to pay for the cost. Bromley L.B.C. claimed that this was invalid and the House of Lords agreed that the action of the G.L.C. was *ultra vires* the 1969 Act.

(3) Before certain delegated legislation may be put into effect, it is necessary to have a public enquiry, so that public opinion may be tested, and an opportunity given to those who wish to object to the proposed legislation to air their misgivings.

EUROPEAN COMMUNITY LAW

A completely new source of English law was created when Parliament passed the European Communities Act 1972. Section 2(1) of the Act provides that:

> "All such rights, powers, liabilities, obligations and restrictions from time to time created or arising by or under the Treaties, and all such remedies and procedures from time to time provided for by or under the Treaties, as in accordance with the treaties are without further enactment to be given legal effect or used in the United Kingdom shall be recognised and available in law, and be inforced, allowed and followed accordingly. . . . "

The effect of this section is that English courts (and all United Kingdom courts) have to recognise EEC law, whether it comes directly from treaties or other Community legislation.

As soon as the 1972 Act became law, some aspects of English law were changed to bring them into line with European Community law. For example, certain principles of our company law were immediately amended, and certain sections of the Companies Act 1980 were the direct result of an EEC directive (see below).

Community legislation is enacted in the form of regulations, decisions and directives.

1. Regulations

A regulation is of general application in all Member States and, in theory, it is binding in this country without reference to Parliament. It is usual, however, for there to be some legislative action, if only to repeal law which is contrary to the regulation.

Re Tachographs: EC Commission v. *United Kingdom* (1979)

A Council Regulation provided that tachography (mechanical recording equipment) should be installed in all road vehicles used for the carriage of goods. The United Kingdom government decided not to implement the regulation but left the road haulage industry to introduce the equipment on a voluntary basis only. The Commission referred the matter to the European Court of Justice and it was held that:

(i) the Regulation provided that the Member States shall adopt the law, and
(ii) the Treaty provides that a regulation shall be binding in its entirety on the Member States.

2. Decisions

A decision has a more specific application, in that it may be addressed to a state or corporation, and is binding only on that state or corporation. They come into effect immediately, but may need legislative action by the Member State.

3. Directives

A directive is binding on all Member States, but the states must bring it into being by whatever means they wish. In the United Kingdom they are usually issued by statutory instrument.

European Community law has also had an effect on the courts and on case law. Any court from which there is no appeal (House of Lords) dealing with a case requiring an interpretation of a European treaty must suspend the case and submit it to the European Court for a ruling. Decisions of the European Court must be accepted, but it is the Member States' courts which must enforce them.

It is also probable that European law affects precedent, in that if the law is contrary to a binding precedent of English law, a lower court may ignore precedent and give a decision based on the Community law. In a Court of Appeal case Lord Denning discussed the effect of the Treaty of Rome upon English law.

> "The Treaty does not touch any of the matters which concern solely England and the people in it. They are not affected by the Treaty. But when we come to matters with a European element the Treaty is like an incoming tide. It flows into the estuaries and up the rivers. It cannot be

held back. Parliament has declared that the Treaty is henceforward to be part of our law. It is equal in force to any statute. . . . "

SUBSIDIARY SOURCES OF LAW

As was explained earlier, the following sources have little impact in modern times, but are still, technically, sources of law.

LOCAL CUSTOMS

Custom is the origin of common law. From the earliest days of William the Conqueror's reign, judges have tried to discover existing customs and absorb them into the common system of law. Although custom has now become part of the formal legal system, in certain areas of England customs are still recognised and enforced by the courts. These exceptional cases only apply to the particular area in which the custom exists, and a person claiming the right of custom (usually the defendant) will have to prove that the following conditions apply:

1. The custom existed since "time immemorial"

"Time Immemorial" is fixed at 1189, which is the end of Henry II's reign. It is only necessary to claim that the custom existed beyond living memory, but if the other party can show that the custom was first used after 1189, or could not have reasonably existed at that date, the claim will not be upheld. In *Bryant* v. *Foot* (1868) a clergyman claimed that by custom he should be paid 13 shillings (65p) for every marriage he performed. He proved that the fee had been paid for nearly 50 years, but the court held that the fee would obviously have been unreasonable in 1189, and would not have existed.

2. It must be reasonable

3. It only applies to the particular locality

Fishermen in Grimsby could not claim a custom established

for the fishermen of Walmer, in Kent.

4. It must not be contrary to a statute, or any basic principle of common law

5. It must have been exercised continuously

The custom does not have to have been exercised at all times, but it must have been possible to exercise the custom had the inhabitants of the locality wished to do so.

6. It must be exercised as a right

The custom must be used peaceably and openly. This means it must not be exercised with force, or in secret, or by permission.

BOOKS OF AUTHORITY

If a precedent cannot be found to cover an aspect of law, judges may refer to legal text books for help. In the past, only works of dead writers carried the requisite authority but in recent years judges have taken notice of the opinions of living writers. Examples of old works which have been accepted as books of authority are:

Glanvill, *Tractatus de legibus et consuetudinibus regni Angliae*;
Coke, *Institutes of the Laws of England*;
Blackstone, *Commentaries on the Laws of England*

Works of modern authors which have been quoted or discussed in court include:

Cheshire, *Modern Law of Real Property*;
Cheshire and Fifoot, *Law of Contract*.

Revision Test

1. Name the two main sources of English Law.
2. Is the House of Lords bound by its own previous decisions?
3. What is the *ratio decidendi* of a judges decision?
4. Name three advantages of judicial precedent.
5. Name the stages of a Bill's passage through Parliament.
6. Name the three types of Bills.
7. Name three bodies which have the power to make delegated legislation.

Specimen Questions

1. What are the main modern sources of law in the U.K. and how have they been affected by membership of the EEC?
2. Explain the doctrine of judicial precedent.
3. Explain the meaning of the following:
   (a) *ratio decidendi*
   (b) *per incuriam*
   (c) *stare decisis*
4. What is meant by delegated legislation and outline the advantages and disadvantages of such legislation.
5. Explain the different ways by which Bills are introduced to Parliament and outline the stages of a Public Bill's passage through Parliament before it becomes an Act.

6. (a) Have the courts any control over the abuse of delegated legislation?
   (b) How has Parliament attempted to control any such abuse?

Chapter 3

THE ADMINISTRATION OF THE LAW

THE COURTS

It is now necessary to examine the structure of the courts and to consider their constitution and the jurisdiction which they exercise. The civil courts will be dealt with first, followed by the criminal courts and, finally, by courts which lie outside the English system.

THE CIVIL COURTS

The House of Lords

As a court of law, the House of Lords is the highest and final court of appeal in civil cases for the whole of the United Kingdom. In theory an appeal is to the whole House, but it is only the "Law Lords" who hear appeals. The ordinary lords or peers of the realm do not take part in this process of the law.

1. Jurisdiction

The House of Lords hears appeals from the Court of Appeal and, in certain cases, direct from the High Court. Appeals from the Court of Appeal may only be made by leave of either that court, or the House of Lords. The Administration of Justice Act 1969 provided that, if all parties agree, in cases concerning the interpretation of a statute (or on a point of law) which was subject to a binding precedent, the appeal could go direct from the High Court to the House of Lords, thereby "leap-frogging" the Court of Appeal.

2. Constitution

Appeals are heard by a committee of not less than three from the following:

(i) The Lord Chancellor.
(ii) The Lords of Appeal in Ordinary - the "Law Lords." They are life peers who have been barristers for at least 15 years. They are usually appointed after sitting as Lords Justices of Appeal in the Court of Appeal.
(iii) Peers who have held high judicial office (*e.g.* previous Lord Chancellors).

The Court of Appeal (Civil Division)

1. Jurisdiction

The court may hear appeals from the county court and the High Court on matters of law or fact. Appeals may also be heard on questions of law from the many administrative tribunals, such as the Restrictive Practices Court and the Lands Tribunal.

Appeals may be allowed or dismissed, or the court may order a new trial. The majority of appeals are on points of law, but appeals may dispute the judges' awards of damages or costs.

2. Constitution

Appeals are heard by a court consisting of not less than three of the following:

(i) The Lord Chancellor.
(ii) The Lord Chief Justice.
(iii) The President of the Family Division of the High Court.
(iv) The Lords of Appeal in Ordinary (the Law Lords).
(v) The Master of the Rolls.
(vi) The Lords Justices of Appeal.

As a general rule the appeals are only heard by a court consisting of the Master of the Rolls and the Lords Justices of Appeal. The usual number of judges for each case is three, but several divisions of the court may sit at the same time. In cases of great importance, five or more judges may sit in what is called a full court.

A Lord Justice of Appeal is appointed by the Queen on the advice of the Prime Minister. He must have been a barrister for

15 years, and usually a High Court Judge for many years.

High Court of Justice

This court has unlimited civil jurisdiction and hears appeals from inferior courts (civil and criminal) and tribunals. The work of the High Court is divided amongst the following three divisions:

(i) The Queen's Bench Division.
(ii) The Chancery Division.
(iii) The Family Division.

Each division has jurisdiction to hear any High Court action, but for administrative convenience the divisions specialise in specific areas of work.

Constitution

The divisions consist of a head or president and High Court judges or puisne judges (pronounced pewny). In addition, cases may be heard before a judge or former judge of the Court of Appeal, a circuit judge, a recorder or a former High Court judge. The judges are appointed by the Queen on the recommendation of the Lord Chancellor, and must have been barristers for at least 10 years. The judges usually sit alone but in the divisional courts there must be at least two judges. The usual or ordinary High Court cases have original jurisdiction, which means that it is the first time the case has appeared before the courts. The divisional courts, in the main, have appellate jurisdiction and hear appeals from inferior or lower courts.

The Queen's Bench Division

1. Jurisdiction

(*a*) *Ordinary court*

This division hears more cases than either of the other divisions, and it has the widest jurisdiction, dealing with all matters not covered by the other divisions, the majority of them being actions in tort and contract.

The Administration of Justice Act 1970, created two courts as part of the Queen's Bench Division.

(i) The Admiralty Court hears cases concerned with the Admiralty, and acts as a Prize Court.

(ii) The Commercial Court hears cases on commercial matters, such as banking and insurance.

(*b*) *Appellate court*

Appeals are heard by the Divisional Court from certain administrative tribunals, and from solicitors on appeal from the Disciplinary Committee of the Law Society.

The Queen's Bench Divisional Court also has jurisdiction to hear applications for the writ of *habeas corpus*, and the orders of *certiorari, mandamus* and prohibition (see p. 111).

2. Constitution

The head of the Queen's Bench Division is the Lord Chief Justice, although his work is mostly concerned with hearing criminal appeals. The majority of the work is heard by approximately 50 puisne judges.

The Chancery Division

1. Jurisdiction

(*a*) *Ordinary court*

It hears cases concerning trust, property, company law, partnerships, winding up of companies and bankruptcy, mortgages, taxation, administration of estates of deceased persons and contentious probate cases.

(*b*) *Appellate court*

Appeals from the Commissioners of Inland Revenue are heard by a single judge.

The Divisional Court may hear appeals from the county court on certain bankruptcy and land registration matters.

2. Constitution

The nominal head of the Chancery Division is the Lord Chancellor, but he never sits. The Vice-Chancellor is the working head of the division and there are 12 puisne judges.

The Family Division

1. Jurisdiction

(*a*) *Ordinary court*

It hears cases dealing with:

(i) the validity and the breakdown of marriage and all relevant matters, such as the custody of children and the distribution of property.
(ii) non-contentious probate matters.
(iii) applications in respect of guardianship and wardship of minors, legitimation, adoption and disputes between spouses over title to property.

(*b*) *Appellate court*

The divisional court of the Family Division hears appeals on matrimonial and family matters from the county court and the magistrates' courts.

2. Constitution

The Family Division is headed by a President, and there are approximately 16 puisne judges.

The County Court

The county courts were set up in 1846 to provide an opportunity for claims to be settled cheaply, although it is still likely to prove expensive if a person engages the help of lawyers. It is not expensive to start an action if you conduct your own case and, with straightforward matters for small amounts, the ordinary lay person is encouraged to do so, particularly where consumer goods are involved. For claims under £500 the court fees would probably not exceed £25 and the person winning the case is allowed to add these fees to the amount claimed.An excellent booklet and pamphlets are available from the offices of the county courts which explain the necessary steps which must be taken to sue and defend actions without a solicitor.

There are about 400 county courts in England and Wales in which approximately three-quarters of all civil actions start. These figures give some indication of the courts' importance within the administration of civil cases.

Each court has a registrar responsible for the administration and day-to-day running of the court and its office. In addition to this administrative function, the registrar has a judicial role, in that he may hear claims for less than £500, and for other amounts if the parties both agree. Where the amount of a claim does not exceed £500 the registrar may refer the action to an arbitrator, if requested to do so by one of the parties. If the amount exceeds £500 the registrar may still refer the case to arbitration if both parties agree, or by order of the judge.

The registrar usually acts as arbitrator, although it may be the judge, and procedure in these cases is very informal. The registrar or judge will wear normal dress (not in robes or wig) and the hearing may be in private. If one party fails to appear the arbitrator may make an award upon hearing the other party.

1. Jurisdiction

The county courts deal with most civil disputes, but their jurisdiction is governed by two factors:

(*a*) *Locality*

Actions should be started in the county court for the district in which the defendant lives or carries on business.

(*b*) *Finance*

The jurisdiction of the court, in most matters, is limited to the size of the claim. The amounts shown below may change, particularly in times of inflation, so check for the current amounts if you intend going to court, or before taking an examination in law.

The court deals with all sorts of claims and disputes, with the majority of its work in the following areas:

(i) Actions in contract and tort not exceeding £5,000. The courts have no jurisdiction to hear cases of defamation, unless the parties agree.

(ii) Equity matters such as trusts and mortgages for claims

less than £30,000.

(iii) Actions concerning the title to land or possession of land, where the rateable value does not exceed £1,000.

(iv) Winding up of companies with a paid-up capital of less than £10,000.

(v) Bankruptcy matters. This jurisdiction only applies to certain courts outside London.

(vi) Admiralty matters for claims not exceeding £5,000. Salvage cases may not exceed £15,000.

(vii) Probate disputes where the estate is not valued at more than £30,000.

(viii) Undefended divorce cases.

(ix) Matters concerning the adoption, guardianship and legitimacy of children.

(x) Actions with respect of extortionate credit agreements under section 139 of the Consumer Credit Act 1974, not exceeding £5,000.

The above list is not complete, but covers the principal areas of the court's work. The court may hear claims in excess of the amounts stated above, if both parties agree.

2. Constitution

County court judges are appointed by the Queen on the recommendations of the Lord Chancellor. The county is divided into 64 circuits in which there are approximately 400 county courts. Each circuit has one or more judges. The circuit judge, as he is designated, travels around hearing cases in the county courts in the circuit or district.

In addition to the circuit judges, recorders and judges of the High Court and Court of Appeal, if they agree, may sit in any circuit as directed by the Lord Chancellor.

A circuit judge may also hear criminal cases in the Crown Court. As was stated earlier, each circuit has a registrar who acts as clerk to the court. The registrar, who must be a solicitor of at least seven years' standing, is appointed by the Lord Chancellor.

Magistrates' courts and the Crown Court also have civil jurisdiction as will be shown when these courts are discussed later.

System of Appeal through the Civil Courts

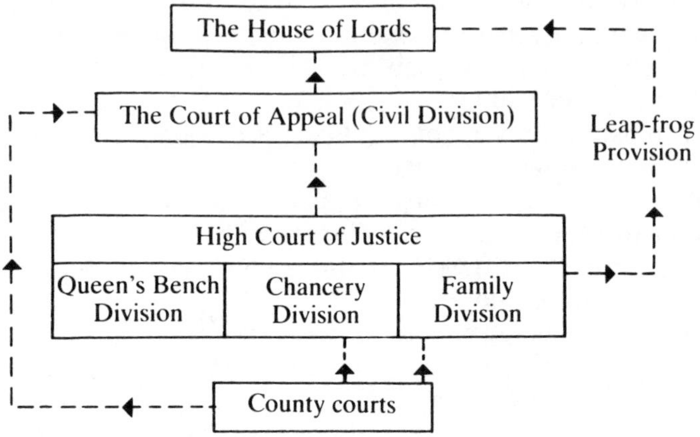

THE CRIMINAL COURTS

The House of Lords

The court hears appeals from the Court of Appeal (Criminal Division) and the Divisional Court of the Queen's Bench provided that these courts certify that a point of law of general public importance is involved, and leave to appeal has been granted by these courts or by the House of Lords.

The Court of Appeal (Criminal Division)

1. Jurisdiction

The court hears appeals against decisions of the Crown Court by persons convicted on indictment, or by persons convicted by a magistrates' court but sentenced by the Crown Court. Appeals against conviction on matters of law may be made as of right, but only with leave of the court for other reasons.

Appeals against sentence may only be made by leave of the court. Should the Court of Appeal refuse to grant leave to hear an appeal, the convicted person may appeal to the Home

Secretary, who has the power to refer the case back to the Court of Appeal.

The court has the power to:

(i) dismiss ("quash") the decision,
(ii) vary the sentence by making it smaller. The court has, at present, no power to increase the sentence,
(iii) order a new trial.

2. Constitution

The Lord Chief Justice is the head of this court, and in addition to the Lords Justices of Appeal, judges of the High Court (in practice, judges of the Queen's Bench Division) may sit if asked by the Lord Chief Justice.

The court must consist of at least three judges, but may consist of higher odd numbers (*e.g.* five or seven).

The Crown Court

The Courts Act 1971 abolished the courts of assize and quarter sessions, the Crown Courts at Liverpool and Manchester, and the Central Criminal Court in London, and established the Crown Court as a single court to carry out the work previously administered by these courts. The Act, however, provided that when the Crown Court sits in London, it shall be named the Central Criminal Court, or as it is traditionally called, "The Old Bailey."

The old courts, in the main, heard cases which were committed in the towns or districts in which the courts were situated, but the jurisdiction of the Crown Court is not so limited and its business may be carried out anywhere.

1. Jurisdiction

The Courts Act 1971 which created the Crown Court, provided that it shall be a superior court of record and will deal with:

(i) all cases on indictment, wherever committed,
(ii) hear appeals from the magistrates' court against conviction or sentence
(iii) pass sentence on cases where the accused has been found guilty by the magistrates but the lower court considers

The Crown Court. *From left to right*, the judge, clerk of the court, jury, senior counsel, junior counsel, solicitors, defendant, public gallery. *Foreground*, the Press.

considers that they do not have the jurisdiction to pass the appropriate sentence,

(iv) conduct certain civil work, previously carried out by the quarter sessions, such as dealing with appeals over licencing.

2. Constitution

Judges of the Crown Court are as follows:

(*a*) *All judges of the High Court*

The Lord Chancellor may request a judge of the Court of Appeal to sit in the court, when he shall be regarded as a judge of the High Court.

(*b*) *Circuit judges*

They are appointed by the Queen, on the recommendation of the Lord Chancellor. The latter may remove them from office on grounds of incapacity or misbehaviour. Circuit judges are appointed from recorders of at least five years' standing, or from barristers of at least 10 years' standing. It should be noted that solicitors may be appointed as recorders and therefore, this Act provides for the appointment of solicitors as High Court judges.

In addition to the above appointments, many persons holding judicial offices, such as all county court judges, recorders and chairmen of certain quarter sessions, became circuit judges when the Act came into operation on January 1, 1972. Circuit judges are full-time appointees, but they must retire at the age of 72, although the Lord Chancellor may allow them to continue in office until the age of 75. The jurisdiction of circuit judges is both criminal and civil (see the county courts, p. 53).

(*c*) *Recorders*

They are appointed by the Queen on the recommendation of the Lord Chancellor, who may remove them from office on grounds of incapacity, misbehaviour or failure to satisfy the requirements of the terms of appointment. Recorders must retire at the age of 72.

Recorders who are part-time judges, must be barristers or

solicitors of 10 years' standing. Their appointment, which is on a temporary basis, states the period and frequency of their duties. Although recorders are primarily concerned with criminal cases, they have authority to sit as county court judges.

(*d*) *Justices of the peace*

Not less than two, and not more than four justices of the peace must sit with the judge when hearing appeals, or when a convicted person has been committed to the Crown Court for sentence. The same constitution of judge and justices has jurisdiction to hear any case before the Crown Court.

The Distribution of Crown Court Business

Cities and towns (known as court centres) in which the High Court and Crown Court sit are divided into three tiers.

First Tier

There are 24 court centres which deal with criminal and civil work, and the cases are tried by High Court judges and circuit judges.

Second Tier

There are 19 court centres which deal with criminal work only, and the cases are tried by High Court judges and circuit judges.

Third Tier

There are 46 court centres which deal with criminal work only, and the cases are tried by circuit judges.

The work of the Court has been distributed amongst the various judges on the basis of the class of offence. For the purpose of the trial, offences have been divided into four classes.

Class 1 contains serious offences, tried by a High Court judge, and includes offences which carry the death sentence, treason, murder, genocide, and offences against the Official Secrets Act 1911, s.1.

Class 2 offences are tried by a High Court judge, unless the case is released by the authority of a presiding judge for trial by a circuit judge or recorder. A presiding judge is a High Court judge who has the responsibility for the distribution of the judges in a given circuit. The offences in this class include, manslaughter, rape, sexual intercourse with a girl under 13, sedition, mutiny and piracy.

Class 3 offences may be tried by a High Court judge, a circuit judge or recorder. The class includes all indictable offences, other than those allocated as Class 1, 2 or 4. (An indictment is a written accusation that a person has committed a crime. Indictable offences are generally the more serious crimes.)

Class 4 offences may be tried by a High Court judge, circuit judge or recorder, but cases are usually listed for trial by a circuit judge or recorder. Offences in this class include, causing death by dangerous driving, causing grievous bodily harm and burglary, as well as all offences which may be tried either summarily or on indictment.

All cases, with the exception of appeals and persons committed for sentence, are tried by a judge sitting alone, and before a jury.

The Magistrates' Court

The magistrates' courts deal with about 99 per cent. of all criminal cases. This percentage gives an indication of the volume of work of the court and its importance in the legal system. There is a magistrates' court in every county and in most boroughs.

1. Jurisdiction

The court has three main criminal functions:

(*a*) *A court of petty sessions*. This deals with minor offences that may be tried summarily, and carry a maximum penalty of not more than six months' imprisonment and a fine of £400. With offences that may be triable either way (summarily or on indictment) the limit is £2000. A summary offence means that the magistrates have power to hear the case without sending it for trial to the Crown Court. Examples of summary offences are drunkenness, minor motoring offences such as speeding, not obeying road signs and unauthorised parking, and riding a bicycle without lights after dark. A defendant in such cases may plead guilty by post, and need not attend the court.

(*b*) *A court of preliminary hearing or examination.* Persons accused of indictable offences are subject to an enquiry by the court to see if there is a case to be sent to the Crown Court for trial by jury. The court does not try or prejudge the case, but considers if the prosecution's evidence is sufficient for the court to decide that there is, on the face of it, a case to answer. If the court decides there is no evidence to support the prosecution's claim, the defendant is dismissed, but if the court considers otherwise, the defendant is committed for trial to the Crown Court.

(*c*) *A juvenile court.* When children (10–14 years) and young persons (14–17 years) are charged with a crime (other than homicide) they are brought before this special magistrates' court. The procedure is not as formal as in the usual court, and the purpose is to keep the young offender away from ordinary criminal proceedings. A juvenile court must not take place in a court where other sittings have taken place, or will take place within one hour. The court is not open to the public and the press may not publish the names of the charged persons.

Magistrates have the usual powers when passing sentence on a juvenile, in that they may fine or place the juvenile on probation. The Children & Young Persons Act 1969, however, limits other forms of punishment to a care order, in which the offender is committed to secure local authority accommodation, hospital or guardianship orders, and the payment of compensation by parents. Detention will only be ordered if it is necessary to protect the public. The court cannot send a juvenile to prison, but the magistrates may commit an older child to the Crown Court for a sentence of borstal training.

Civil Jurisdiction

It should be noted that the magistrates' court does have civil jurisdiction, which may be summarised as follows:

(i) recovery of civil debts, such as income tax, rates, gas and electricity charges.

(ii) family and matrimonial matters, such as applications for separation and custody of a child, maintenance and affiliation orders, and adoption.

(iii) granting licences for premises for showing films, for the sale of alcohol or for gambling.

2. Constitution

A magistrates' court is presided over by at least two and not more than seven justices of the peace (magistrates). In England and Wales there are about 20,000 lay-magistrates and 50 stipendiary magistrates.

Stipendiary magistrates are full-time paid magistrates. They have to be barristers or solicitors of seven years standing.

Justices of the peace are appointed by the Lord Chancellor, using a document called the "Commission of the peace." There are committees in counties and boroughs to advise the Lord Chancellor on appointments. Justices may be removed from the Commission by the Lord Chancellor, without him giving the reason for this action. Usually, removal from office is caused by the justices' refusal to recognise and enforce certain laws. Generally a magistrate retires at 70.

A single magistrate may sit alone:

(i) in minor cases involving very small fines or periods of imprisonment, or

(ii) when conducting a preliminary hearing, or

(iii) when appointed as a stipendiary magistrate,

but generally, there must be two or more magistrates.

There is no jury in a magistrates' court. When a juvenile court is in session there must be a quorum of at least three magistrates, comprising women and men (*i.e.* there must be at least one woman or one man in the quorum).

Every magistrates' court has a justices' clerk, who is paid, usually legally qualified, and helps the justices on matters of law and procedure. Although they may only preside in the magistrates' court in the area of their commission, justices may sit in any Crown Court when required (see p. 58). Appeals from the magistrates' court go to:

(*a*) *Crown Court*

The defendant may appeal against the sentence.

(*b*) *Divisional Court of the Queen's Bench Division*

The prosecutor or defendant may appeal on points of law by means of "a case stated."

System of Appeal through the Criminal Courts

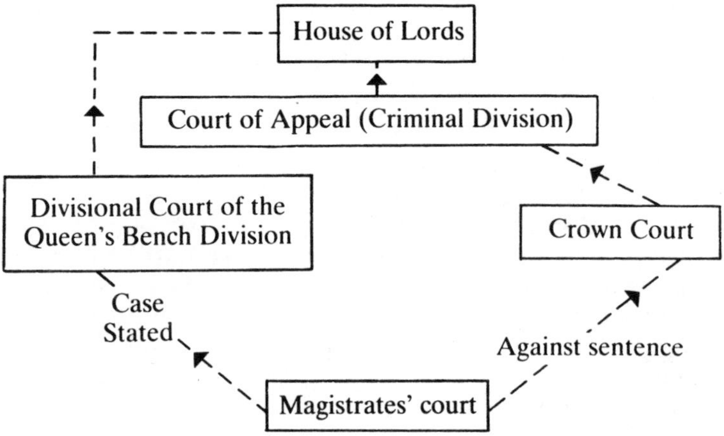

OTHER COURTS

The Judicial Committee of the Privy Council

The Committee does not make a decision but advises the Queen of its opinion, which is then implemented by an Order in Council. This Committee is outside the court system and its findings are not binding precedent on a lower court (see p. 21), but because of the constitution of Committee, it has immense persuasive authority.

1. Jurisdiction

The main work of the Committee is to hear appeals as set out below, but it is sometimes required to advise on other matters of law, such as the validity of certain legislation.

The Committee hears appeals from:

(*a*) *Outside the United Kingdom*
The Privy Council may hear appeals from the Channel Islands, the Isle of Man and certain Commonwealth countries.

(*b*) *Ecclesiastical courts*
It is the final court of appeal on ecclesiastical matters. Appeals are heard on matters concerning church buildings or the clergy.

(*c*) *Queen's Bench Division of the High Court*
Appeals are heard from the Admiralty Court when acting as a Prize Court.

(*d*) *Medical tribunals*
Appeals are heard from doctors who have had their names removed from the medical register for disciplinary reasons.

2. Constitution
The Committee consists of not less than three, but usually five members from the following:
- (i) The Lord Chancellor;
- (ii) The present and previous Lord President of the Council;
- (iii) Privy Councillors who hold or have held a high judicial office;
- (iv) The Lords of Appeal in Ordinary (the Law Lords);
- (v) Persons who hold high judicial office in Commonwealth countries.

The Committee is usually formed from the Law Lords and, therefore, the constitution in practice is similar to the House of Lords.

Coroners' Courts

1. Jurisdiction
The main work of the court is concerned with inquests on persons who died a violent or unnatural death, or died from an unknown cause, or died in prison. A coroner may only enquire

into deaths that occur in the district for which he is appointed.

If the verdict of the court is murder by a named person, the coroner may commit that person for trial. In this respect the court is similar to the preliminary hearing of the magistrates' court.

The court also has jurisdiction for disputes over treasure trove. Treasure trove is gold, coin, etc. which has been deliberately hidden and the owner of which is unknown. If the coroner finds that the property was not hidden, but lost or misplaced for some reason, the finder acquires a good title, next to the real owner. Treasure trove belongs to the Crown, but it is often the practice for the Crown to pay a reward, based on the value of the property, to those who have not concealed the find.

2. Constitution

A coroner must be either a barrister, solicitor or medical practitioner of five years' standing, and is appointed by county, and certain borough councils to act within the district of the county or borough, but may be removed from office by the Lord Chancellor for misbehaviour. The coroner may, and sometimes must, summon a jury of between seven to 11 members. The jury's verdict need not be unanimous.

The Court of Justice of the European Communities

The Court of Justice of the European Communities ensures the observance and recognition of community rules with regard to legal interpretation and application. It is concerned with disputes between Member States over community matters. It hears appeals from Member States, individuals and the Community institutions on matters relating to the treaties, and its rulings are binding. The court is the final arbiter in all matters of law that lie within the scope of the treaties. It has an important function in creating Community case law and its decisions can have an effect on case law in the English courts (see p. 42).

There are nine judges and four advocate-generals appointed for six years. One judge and one advocate-general are from the United Kingdom. Decisions are made by a majority vote but dissenting opinions are not made public.

TRIBUNALS

ADMINISTRATIVE TRIBUNALS

For a long period of time Parliament has delegated a judicial function to bodies or boards outside the usual system of the courts. Since 1945 this practice has grown, in the main due to the advent of nationalisation and the increase in social and welfare services provided by the State.

Instead of disputes being settled in court, certain Acts of Parliament have provided for the creation of tribunals to decide problems that have arisen within the particular scope of those Acts. In 1957, the Franks Committee (which reported on tribunals) estimated that there were over 2,000 tribunals, and it can be expected that this has increased. It is therefore impossible to give a complete list of the tribunals in existence, but the following will give some indication of their nature:

(i) National Insurance Tribunals which hear disputes on such matters as claims for unemployment and sickness benefits;

(ii) Rent Tribunals which hear disputes between landlords and tenants;

(iii) Industrial Tribunals which hear matters concerning unfair dismissal, redundancy payments and the like;

(iv) Land Tribunals which hear disputes over the amount of compensation to be paid when land is compulsorily purchased by the local authority.

The main benefit of tribunals is that they help in administering Acts quickly and inexpensively. Procedure is less formal than in court and in many instances there is no need for the parties to be legally represented. The constitutions of tribunals vary, but certain tribunals must have members who are lawyers, and the chairman of some tribunals may only be appointed by the minister of the department concerned, from a list of persons nominated by the Lord Chancellor. Generally, a tribunal will have several members, usually a lawyer will be chairman, with the other members representing organisations likely to be affected by the dispute.

DOMESTIC TRIBUNALS

Certain professional organisations have their own tribunals to settle disputes between members of their organisations. Conditions of membership will usually stipulate that disputes between members, and between members and the organisation, will be governed by a tribunal, and therefore, members have mutually agreed beforehand how their differences will be settled.

In some cases Parliament has created a tribunal for a particular organisation. For example, the Medical Act 1956, created the Disciplinary Committee of the General Medical Council. Tribunals set up by statute are usually subject to a right of appeal, and provided that the tribunals do not go beyond the agreed powers, and follow the rules of natural justice, the courts have no jurisdiction.

MEANS OF CONTROL

1. By the courts

(i) Making prerogative orders of *mandamus*, *certiorari* or prohibition (see p. 111). This method of control only applies against tribunals created by statute.

(ii) By awarding an injunction to prevent a tribunal statutory or domestic) performing against the rules of natural justice, or acting "*ultra vires*" (beyond its powers).

(iii) Decisions from tribunals created by statute may be subject to appeals as provided by the statute.

2. By the Council of Tribunals

The Council was established by the Tribunals and Inquiries Act 1958.

It has an advisory function to review the working of statutory tribunals and makes reports when necessary to the Lord Chancellor who has the responsibility of appointing the members of the Council.

ARBITRATION

It is often the practice in commercial contracts to refer disputes to arbitration, instead of starting court actions. If you look at the booking conditions in some holiday brochures, you will find that disputes are referred to arbitration. Therefore, if there is a dispute between a holidaymaker and the travel company, the parties will not go to court, but to arbitration.

Arbitration means that the two parties agree to allow a third party to decide the dispute. The arbitrator does this by making an "award," and giving the reasons for doing so. When an award has been made, neither party may start a court action in relation to the same dispute. The courts will not interfere with the decision unless the arbitrator acted improperly, or unless fresh evidence is introduced.

A different form of arbitration was established when the Advisory Conciliation and Arbitration Service (ACAS) was created by the Employment Protection Act 1975, to help in trade disputes and to improve industrial relations.

THE JUDICIARY AND THE LEGAL PROFESSION

Judges are appointed by the Queen and, except for the newly created circuit judges and recorders, may only be removed on an address from both Houses of Parliament. Circuit judges and recorders may be removed by the Lord Chancellor for misconduct.

When assuming office all judges take an oath, " . . . to do right to all manner of people after the laws and usages of this realm without fear or favour, affection or ill-will."

JUDICIAL OFFICERS

The qualifications and functions of most judges have been detailed in the section discussing the constitution of the courts. This section will deal with the senior judicial appointments. Students should make themselves aware of the names of the present holders of these offices.

The Lord Chancellor

The Lord Chancellor is appointed by the Queen on the advice of the Prime Minister. The office is the highest in the legal profession, but, strange as it may seem, it is a political appointment. The Lord Chancellor is a member of the Cabinet, and as with any other minister, may be removed at any time, or when there is a change of government. In the role of politician, the Lord Chancellor is speaker of the House of Lords, where he sits on the Woolsack. He does not, as one examination candidate stated, "sit on a sack of wool."

As a judge, he is head of the House of Lords, the Court of Appeal and the Chancery Division of the High Court.

The Lord Chief Justice

This appointment is also made by the Queen on the advice of the Prime Minister. The Lord Chief Justice is head of the Queen's Bench Division of the High Court, but his principal duties are as head of the Court of Appeal (Criminal Division) and the Queen's Bench Divisional Court. On appointment he is made a peer, but, although entitled to hear House of Lords' cases, in practice he rarely does.

The Master of the Rolls

The Master of the Rolls is appointed by the Queen, on the advice of the Prime Minister, and is made a peer on appointment. The holder of this office is the virtual head of the Court of Appeal (Civil Division); organising the work of the court, and deciding the composition of the divisions to hear appeals. As Master of the Rolls he supervises the admission of qualified solicitors to the rolls of the court, which then allows them to practice.

President of the Family Division of the High Court

This appointment is made by the Queen on the advice of the Prime Minister. The president is head of the Family Division and, in addition to organising the work of the Division, sits in the High Court and in the Divisional Court.

THE LAW OFFICERS

The Attorney-General and Solicitor-General are usually members of the House of Commons, and their appointment, by the Queen on the advice of the Prime Minister, is political. In addition to being Members of Parliament, they are also experienced barristers.

1. The Attorney-General

The Attorney-General has the following duties:

(i) Advising the government on legal matters;
(ii) Representing the Crown in civil cases and acting as prosecutor in important criminal cases;
(iii) Certain prosecutions may only take place with the authority of the Attorney-General. The House of Lords recently upheld this right, after a private person had sought an injunction against postal workers;
(iv) Is Head of the English Bar;
(v) Supervises the work of the Director of Public Prosecutions.

2. The Solicitor-General

The Solicitor-General is the deputy of the Attorney-General, and has similar duties. Any act or function that may be discharged by the Attorney-General may also be carried out by the Solicitor-General, when the former has so authorised, or is ill or absent, or the office of Attorney-General is vacant.

THE LEGAL PROFESSION

Unlike most countries, the legal profession in England and Wales has two bodies of lawyers that have different functions in the legal system. Barristers are mainly concerned with advocacy before the courts, while solicitors carry out many aspects of legal work. Most countries have one legal profession that has the right to deal with all legal work, although lawyers in these countries may tend to specialise in one aspect of the law.

Not all lawyers publicly practise law. Many are employed by companies or the Civil Service as legal advisers, while others lecture or teach law. A large number of Members of Parliament are either barristers or solicitors.

Solicitors

The functions and duties of solicitors are very wide and varied. They deal with most aspects of legal work, such as giving advice, making wills, conveyancing (transferring) the ownership of houses, drafting partnership agreements and forming companies, preparing litigation, interviewing witnesses and so on. Solicitors have the right to appear before the magistrates' courts, county courts, Crown Court (on appeal or sentencing from the inferior court) and have a limited right of audience before the High Court. They may, however, concentrate on drafting documents such as wills, conveyances, etc., and never appear in court.

Solicitors may work by themselves or in partnership with other solicitors. Although solicitors do practise in all aspects of law, it is probable that in large partnerships individual partners will specialise in certain branches of the law. Solicitors may now, subject to certain rules, advertise their practice.

Clients may sue solicitors for negligence in carrying out their professional functions, and solicitors may sue clients for non-payment of fees.

Solicitors qualify by serving articles, with a solicitor of at least five years' standing, for two to five years, depending on whether the entrants into the profession are graduates or non-graduates, and attending certain courses and passing the examinations. The number and length of time of each course again depends on whether the entrant is a law graduate, a non-law graduate or a non-graduate.

When a person is qualified as above, his or her name will be entered on the Roll of Solicitors (maintained by the Master of the Rolls) and the Law Society will issue a certificate to practise, which certifies that the requirements of articles and examinations have been satisfied and the solicitor is morally fit to be an officer of the Supreme Court. In 1982 there were nearly 42,000 solicitors with practising certificates.

Legal Executives

The Institute of Legal Executives holds examinations for staff who work in a solicitor's office but do not hold a legal qualification. A Fellow of the Institute may later qualify as a solicitor, and the Law Society makes provision for this category of entrant, similar to the requirements for a non-law graduate.

Barristers

A barrister's main function is to conduct a case in court. Barristers may appear before all courts and have exclusive right before superior courts, with certain exceptions (see p.70). Besides their advocacy work, barristers will also draft legal documents, such as pleadings and "counsel's opinion" on legal problems submitted by solicitors.

Clients cannot approach a barrister directly. A meeting has to be arranged by a solicitor and this means that, to a certain extent, barristers rely on solicitors for their work. It also means a client pays two fees. A prisoner in the dock may instruct any robed barrister in court for a small fee. Because of legal aid a "dock brief" is a dying practice. The possibility of clients having a right of direct approach to a barrister is under consideration.

Barristers tend to specialise in one branch of law. They cannot enter a partnership, but must act alone, although in practice they share chambers with other barristers and the "barristers' clerk," who acts as secretary and arranges meetings between the clients, solicitors and the barristers, and also settles the amount of the fees.

Barristers are not liable in negligence for their advocacy in court and for matters which occur beforehand which are intimately connected with how the case will be conducted and managed in court. This principle is based on public policy (*Rondel* v. *Worsley* (1969)). The House of Lords, however, in *Saif Ali* v. *Sydney Mitchell & Co.* (1978) held that in certain circumstances a barrister could be liable in negligence for matters not within the area of work mentioned above. Barristers may not sue for their fees.

A barrister of 10 years' standing may apply to become a Queen's Counsel. A Queen's Counsel wears a different gown from other barristers. Originally it was made of silk, hence the expression when a barrister becomes a Q.C. that he "takes silk." It has been the practice that in cases conducted by a Q.C., a junior barrister also had to be engaged. As a result of recent discussions between the Director General of Fair Trading and the Bar Council, all existing provisions that restricted the freedom of Queen's Counsel to appear alone have been abrogated, and the Bar Counsel permits Q.C.s to appear alone if they wished to do so. It must be noted that the change gives a Q.C. the option to decide in the client's best interests whether or not a junior should also be instructed.

With the exception of circuit judges, all judges of the superior courts are appointed solely from the ranks of barristers. Barristers qualify by joining one of the four Inns of Court. Lincoln's Inn, Gray's Inn, Inner Temple and Middle Temple, are the Inns of Court. Students must keep "terms," which means attending the Inn and dining a required number of times. They must also pass the examinations set by The Council of Legal Education. Students who wish to practise at the Bar must spend one year studying at the Inns of Court School of Law before taking the final examination, and on passing the final examination a student must spend an additional year in pupillage under a barrister of five years' standing.

In 1983 there were 5,000 barristers, including Q.C.s.

Complaints against the Legal Profession

As shown above, solicitors may be sued for negligence when their conduct is not of a reasonable minimum standard. This may be difficult, however, as other solicitors, particularly those practising in the same locality, are often reluctant to take such an action.

In cases where negligence is not alleged, clients may complain about the conduct of their lawyers by writing, in the case of barristers, to the General Council of the Bar, and with regard to solicitors, to the Law Society, either to London or to the local society.

Generally, complaints to the professional associations do not help the client directly because if the complaint is upheld the association will take disciplinary action against the member. The Law Society may, however, pay compensation if a client has been defrauded of money by a solicitor. There is a proposal to change the present code of disciplinary procedure, which would provide more suitable remedies for the client.

SANCTIONS AND REMEDIES

Sanctions is the word used to indicate the sentence passed by the criminal courts, and remedies refers to awards of the civil courts to remedy the cause of complaint or compensate for an injury.

Criminal Sanctions

The purpose of criminal sanctions is, in the main, to punish the offender. As criminal offences are considered to be against the State, it is the State which provides and administers the following punishments:

Death

The death penalty may still be imposed on persons found guilty of treason or piracy.

Imprisonment

The purpose of imprisonment may be to (i) punish the offender, (ii) protect the public from further crimes (a thief in prison cannot steal from the public) and (iii) act as a deterrent (the prospect of a prison sentence may stop a would-be criminal from committing a crime).

A sentence of imprisonment may vary from life to one day. Most crimes have maximum sentences, but they are rarely used. The length of the maximum sentence also varies from crime to crime and it is difficult at times to appreciate why similar crimes have different maximum sentences. For example, an indecent assault on a man or boy carries a maximum sentence of 10 years, while it is two years for an indecent assault on a woman.

A sentence of imprisonment for life or less does not mean the prisoner will spend that length of time in prison. Most sentences are reduced by one third for good behaviour in prison and a prisoner may also be released on parole after serving one third of the original sentence. A person sentenced to life imprisonment may be released at any time on licence by the Home Secretary.

A suspended sentence may be imposed. This means that the sentence is not put into effect during the period of the sentence, unless the offender commits another offence within this time. The offender would then have to serve the original sentence as well as the punishment for the second offence.

Fines

Any court may fine an offender for any offence other than one for which the penalty is fixed by law (*e.g.* murder). Many offences carry a fine as the punishment or as an additional punishment or as an alternative to prison, *e.g.* a £10 fine; or six months' prison and £10 fine; or six months or a £10 fine.

Probation

Instead of awarding one of the punishments above, the court may make a probation order if the offender is willing to be bound over. The order may make conditions as to the offender's movements during the order, and it will involve regular meetings with a probation officer. An offender who breaks the conditions of the probation is liable to receive a sentence for the original offence.

Absolute or conditional discharge

If the court considers any punishment to be inappropriate, the offender may be discharged absolutely or conditionally. A conditional discharge means the offender must not commit an offence during a period of time between one year and not more than three years. Breach of this condition may also mean that the offender will be sentenced for the original offence. An absolute discharge means the offender leaves court without a stain on his character. It is awarded when a law has been broken, but the offender was not, in the court's opinion, at fault.

Borstal and detention centres

Persons aged between 15 and 20 years who have committed a crime punishable by imprisonment may be sentenced to a period of borstal training lasting six months to two years. After leaving the institution the offender is subject to supervision for up to two years and may be required to do a further period of borstal training during this period. A young offender of at least 14 years, guilty of an offence for which an adult would be sent to prison, may be sent to a detention centre. The order is to detain the offender for a period of three to six months.

Compensation

The court may, in addition to other sanctions, order a convicted person to pay compensation to the victim for loss or damage resulting from the offence.

In addition to compensation paid under an order from a criminal court, a victim of a crime of violence may apply to The Criminal Injuries Compensation Board for a payment. Widows and other close relatives of a person who received fatal injuries may also apply. Compensation from the Board will be reduced by any damages received in a civil claim and by any compensation awarded by a criminal court.

Rehabilitation of offenders

The Rehabilitation of Offenders Act 1974 aims to restore the reputation of convicted persons who have not committed another crime for a specified period afterwards. Any convicted person who received a sentence of not more than two-and-a-half years in prison and has not offended again within the "rehabilitation period," has the advantage of not having to reveal the conviction when applying for jobs; an employer cannot refuse to employ a person because of the conviction; and the conviction may not be mentioned in civil court proceedings. There are some exceptions to the above, and if a person commits another serious offence the benefit may be lost.

As an example of how the Act works, a sentence of six months to two-and-a-half years would require a rehabilitation period of 10 years free of trouble and, for sentences of under six months, the period would be seven years before the offender could benefit from the Act.

Civil Remedies

The purpose of civil remedies is not to punish but, generally, to compensate.

Damages (payment of money)

This is the common law remedy, and is available for all civil actions as of right. In the law of contract the aim of damages is to place the injured party in the same financial position as if the contract had been completed. In tort, the aim may be to place the injured party in the financial position enjoyed prior to being wronged.

Damages may be nominal (*e.g.* 1p), substantial or aggravated. Nominal damages may be awarded when a person has a legal right, but has suffered no financial loss. Substantial damages are the actual amount needed to compensate the injured. Aggravated damages are more than the actual loss, and are awarded where the injury suffered was aggravated by the malice or wrong conduct of the defendant.

Specific performance

This is an equitable order, granted at the discretion of the judge. Its purpose is to force a party to perform the contract (see p. 145). It is usually awarded in contracts for sale of land.

Injunction

This is also an equitable order, granted at the discretion of the judge. It has the effect of making a party perform an act (a mandatory injunction, *e.g.* an order to knock down a wall), or preventing a person from acting in a certain way (a prohibitory injunction, *e.g.* stopping an actress under contract from making a film for another company). Sometimes an injunction is granted to stop a person doing an act pending a court action (an interlocutory injunction, *e.g.* the county cricketers who joined the "Packer" organisation could not be dismissed by the counties until the case was brought before the court).

For other civil remedies see the section on the law of contract (p. 145).

LEGAL AID

Legal Aid is a scheme administered by the Law Society, which pays or contributes to the cost of legal fees. It has often been said "the law is for the rich," meaning that people with low incomes could not afford to pay the cost of taking legal action. The aim of the scheme is to help people to obtain their legal rights without the worry of the possible financial burden.

The financial aid available depends on the income and capital of the client, and the maximum amounts of income and capital vary with the different types of legal aid required (figures quoted below applied in November 1984). The types of legal aid available are as follows:

(*a*) *Legal advice and assistance* (*the Green Form scheme*)

A person needing legal help may go to a solicitor for advice. The solicitor may help by writing what is known as "a solicitor's letter," which informs another party of the legal rights of the client, and that legal action will be taken if the third party does not recognise them.

Help may also be given in writing or made orally by advising clients of their rights on legal problems, such as unfair dismissal from work; or the right to redundancy pay; disputes with landlords; dissatisfaction with goods and the shopkeeper's reluctance to help; obtaining a barrister's opinion and matrimonial problems concerning divorce, claiming and collecting maintenance, and custody of children. Most solicitors are in the scheme and it is common to see the legal aid sign outside solicitors' offices.

Application for legal advice and assistance is made to a solicitor, who will help with the application form (the Green Form).

To be eligible for this form of advice or help, the client's disposable weekly income or disposable capital must not exceed £108 or £765 respectively. Applicants who are in receipt of supplementary benefit or family income supplement will obtain the service free of any contribution. Disposable income is the gross weekly income, less income tax, national insurance contributions, allowances for dependants, housing costs and work expenses.

Should the net disposable income be less than £51 the legal advice and assistance will be free. If the figure is between £51 and £108 the contribution paid by the client is on a sliding scale; £60 is the maximum contribution.

In cases where the weekly disposable income exceeds £108 the client will not be entitled to legal advice and assistance.

Disposable capital is calculated on the total amount of savings and investments, and possessions of value (such as jewellery). The value of a house is usually not included, nor are items of furniture, clothes and tools of trade. In addition, allowance is made for dependants. To qualify for legal advice and assistance, the disposable capital must not exceed £765.

(*b*) *Civil court proceedings*

Legal Aid is provided for most civil court actions, although it is not generally available in litigation for defamation or tribunals, with the exception of the Land Tribunal and the Employment Appeal Tribunal. In addition to the services of a solicitor to help with a case, it may also include the services of a barrister, if necessary for the case to go to court. Application is made, usually through a solicitor, on a prescribed form to the Legal Aid office.

In order to qualify for aid a person has to show that it is reasonable to bring or defend the action, and that the amount of both disposable income and disposable capital does not exceed the figures allowed by the scheme. A local Legal Aid office will decide if the legal grounds for a case are reasonable. It is usual for the Local Committee to consist of solicitors and barristers. If an application is refused, an appeal may be made to an Area Committee. The Department of Health and Social Security assesses whether or not an applicant qualifies financially.

Disposable income is the amount expected to be received during the year after application. From this yearly income, deductions may be made for mortgage or rent, rates, income tax, national insurance, pension contributions, allowances for dependants and other payments deemed necessary.

Disposable capital for legal aid is calculated on the same basis as legal advice but there is no deduction for dependants.

A person with a disposable yearly income of more than £5,155 will not qualify for legal aid for civil proceedings. If the figure is less than £5,155, but exceeds £2,145 legal aid will be granted, but a contribution will have to be made from income. A person with a disposable income of less than £2,145 is eligible for legal aid without making a contribution.

A disposable capital in excess of £4,710 does not usually qualify a person for legal aid, but with an amount between £4,710 and £3,000 a person would have to make a contribution to the cost. Below £3,000, a person is eligible without contribution.

When a certificate for legal aid is granted, it specifies the contribution to be made (if any). Contribution from income is one-quarter of the excess by which the disposable income exceeds the minimum figure. The contribution from capital is the amount by which the disposable capital exceeds the minimum amount.

(*c*) *Criminal court proceedings*

A person charged with a criminal offence may obtain legal aid which may include the services of a solicitor to help with the case, and a barrister if the case goes to the Crown Court. Application is usually made to the magistrates' court, who will decide if it is in the "interests of justice" that legal aid be granted, and that the applicant requires financial help. It is generally considered to be in the "interest of justice" if the accused is in danger of losing his liberty or job, or is mentally ill, or if there is a substantial question of law to be discussed.

As with civil cases an assessment of disposable income and capital is made and the basis of assessment is similar. Legal aid would be free if the weekly disposable income is £44 or less. If it was more than £44 a week, an accused would have to contribute each week a quarter of the excess over £44 for a period of six months. In addition, an accused would be required to pay, in one lump sum, any excess of disposable capital over £300. For example, if a person applied for legal aid with a disposable capital of £4,000 and a disposable weekly income of £48, his contribution would be, £1,000 lump sum from capital and £1 each week (a quarter of £4) for six months from his weekly income.

In 1984 more than 90 per cent. of all accused in the Crown Court were represented under legal aid.

(*d*) *A fixed fee interview*

Although not technically legal aid, many solicitors give legal advice for a period of 30 minutes for a fee of £5. This service is available regardless of income or capital.

In addition to legal aid, there is a right of every person at any stage of an investigation at a police station to communicate and to consult privately with a solicitor. This means that a person in custody should be allowed to telephone a solicitor or friends or have letters sent by post with the least possible delay.

A national scheme started in 1985 which will provide a 24 hour duty solicitor scheme for suspects held in police stations. It is intended that the scheme will apply to all police stations.

It should be noted that the figures shown above apply as at November 26, 1984 and that they are likely to change year from year. A pamphlet "Financial Conditions for Legal Aid" gives details of current rates and contributions, and is available with other pamphlets from Citizens Advice Bureaux, Consumers Advice Centres, and other places which distribute public information. Students are advised to obtain the latest copy of the pamphlet. Free legal advice may also be available from these centres as well as Law Centres or Legal Advice Centres which operate on a voluntary basis in certain areas.

Recovery of legal aid costs

The costs of legal aid may be deducted from the damages and/or costs received by a successful applicant. In criminal cases, it is likely that any contribution would be returned if the accused was acquitted.

JURY

Juries are used in civil and criminal cases. Trial by jury in civil cases is not common and is usually restricted to actions involving defamation, malicious prosecution, fraud, and false imprisonment. Any party to one of these actions has the right to trial by jury. A jury will be ordered for other cases when the court considers it necessary, which it rarely does. A county court jury consists of eight jurors and a High Court jury has 12.

In criminal cases, juries of 12 persons are used in all trials in the Crown Court. There are seven to 11 jurors in a coroner's court. It is the duty of the judge to decide all matters of law, while the duty of the jury is to decide matters of fact.

Qualifications of jurors

It is the responsibility of the Lord Chancellor to prepare the panels of jurors and issue the summonses. Most people aged 18 to 65 are eligible to serve on a jury. The only qualifications are that persons:

(i) must be on the electoral register, and
(ii) have been resident in the United Kingdom for the last five years or more.

The Juries Act 1974 and the Juries (Disqualification) Act 1984 provide that certain persons are disqualified from jury service.

A person will be disqualified:

(i) if, at any time in the last 10 years he has served any part of a prison sentence, youth custody or detention, Borstal detention, or has been given a suspended sentence of imprisonment, or
(ii) if, at any time in the last five years, he has been placed on probation.

A person sentenced to prison for five years or more is disqualified for life.

The following persons are ineligible for jury service: Judges, persons concerned with the administration of justice, the clergy and persons who have, or are still suffering from, a mental illness.

Certain classes of persons such as doctors, full-time members of H.M. Forces, and Members of Parliament, may be excused from duty by claiming "excusal as of right." Other persons may be excused service if they show good reason, or if they have a physical disability, or their knowledge of English is not good enough for them to act as competent jurors. It is possible to request a temporary deferment if a person can show good cause. A student, for example, would be justified in making such a request if summoned for duty on, or immediately before, the day of an examination.

Unless a person is disqualified, ineligible or excused from duty, he or she must attend or risk a penalty, usually a fine. Summons to jury duty does not mean that a person will automatically serve on a jury. It is possible to turn up every day for a week or more and never actually be called upon. In addition, either party may challenge any juror and request a replacement. A person charged with a criminal offence may challenge up to three jurors without showing cause and may make further challenges provided an explanation is offered in every case.

Verdicts

The verdict of a jury in criminal cases does not have to be unanimous. The Juries Act 1974 provides that majority verdicts are acceptable:

(i) (a) where the jury consists of 11 or 12 jurors and a majority of 10 jurors are in agreement.
(b) Where the jury consists of 10 jurors, nine must agree, and

(ii) The jury have deliberated for what the court considers to be a reasonable length of time. In the Crown Court, the period must be at least two hours.

(iii) The foreman of the jury in the Crown Court states the number of the jurors who agreed and disagreed with the verdict.

In *R.* v. *Pigg* (1983), the foreman only stated the number of jurors agreeing with the verdict, and did not state the number dissenting. The House of Lords held that it was sufficient if the words used by the foreman of the jury made it clear to ordinary persons how the jury was divided.

Advantages and Disadvantages of Trial by Jury

Advantages

(1) A verdict from a jury of ordinary lay persons appears to be more acceptable to the public, than if it came from a single judge.

(2) Ordinary lay people take part in the administration of law.

(3) A jury is impartial and has no direct interest in the result.

(4) There is an impression that not only has justice been done, it has been seen to be done.

Disadvantages

(1) Jurors may not be competent to understand the evidence presented and the issues involved.

(2) Jurors may be easily convinced by the manner and presentation of the barristers during the trial, or be persuaded by a forceful or belligerent foreman when locked in the jury room.

(3) In some trials, say motoring offences, juries have a sympathy with the accused. They may be fellow motorists and think, "There, but for the grace of God, go I."

(4) Although jurors receive payment for travelling expenses etc. and an allowance for loss of earnings, it is probable that many people suffer financial loss.

(5) The period of jury service may take many weeks and this may place a strain on certain jurors, such as mothers with very young children or the more elderly. There is a danger that jurors may "agree" with a verdict to bring an end to the trial.

(6) Jurors may experience frustration in having to wait in a court building for many days before being called to serve, and possibly never being called during the period of their service.

Lay Assessors

Lay assessors are qualified persons with expert knowledge, who are called to help or assist a judge in a case which needs special technical knowledge or expertise. They are mainly employed in the Admiralty Court and here they are known as nautical assessors.

Revision Test

1. Name the judges who may hear appeals in the House of Lords.

2. Who is head of the Queens Bench Division of the High Court?

3. May a justice of the peace hear a case before the Crown Court?

4. Name the three main functions of the Magistrates' Courts.

5. State the titles of the two Law Officers.

6. Name two civil remedies.

7. What are the two qualifications to serve on a jury?

8. Name the persons who are ineligible for jury service.

Specimen Questions

1. What is the jurisdiction of the county court?

2. Explain the work of a magistrates' court. How are magistrates appointed?

3. Explain the Crown Court system, its judiciary and jurisdiction.

4. Explain the system of civil appeal courts. Which judges sit in these courts?

5. Describe the jurisdiction and purpose of the Juvenile Courts.

6. Why have administrative tribunals been established? What are their advantages over the courts of law?

7. (a) Describe the work of solicitors and barristers.
   (b) Should the legal profession, barristers and solicitors, be fused into a single profession?

8. Explain the legal functions of the following:
   (a) the Lord Chancellor;
   (b) the Lord Chief Justice;
   (c) the Master of the Rolls;
   (d) the Attorney-General.

9. (a) Explain in general terms the principle of legal aid.
   (b) What legal aid is available for a person accused of a crime.

10. How is a jury formed? Explain the advantages and disadvantages of the jury system.

Chapter 4

LEGAL PERSONALITY

A legal system exists for the subjects or persons within the State; in English law, there are two classes of persons; human or natural beings, and corporate beings. The latter, called corporations, are artificial persons but they are recognised as having a legal status within the legal system. A corporation is comprised of human persons but has a legal existence separate from them.

Although all persons in Britain have a legal status, not all persons within the community have the same status. As will be explained later in greater detail, in many aspects of law children are treated differently from adults, and the mentally ill are treated differently from normal, sane persons. Generally, the legal status of a human person starts at birth and ends at death, but an unborn child has certain rights, and certain intentions and rights of a person are protected after death (*e.g.* ensuring that provisions in a will or trust are carried out).

CHILDREN

The age of majority is 18 when, generally, full legal status is acquired. Below 18 the age limit for legal responsibility and rights varies according to the particular section of law in question. The reason that young people do not have full legal status is not to prevent or curb their activities, but to protect them. Students will come across many names used to describe persons under 18, infants, minors, young persons, juveniles, children etc., but in the main they all mean the same thing, a person who does not have full legal capacity.

1. Crime

A child under 10 is deemed to be incapable of committing a crime. Between 10 and 14 a child is deemed incapable of forming the intention of committing a crime, unless it can be clearly shown that the child knew that the offending act was seriously wrong and criminal. Over the age of 14, a young person is fully liable for criminal prosecution, but as previously shown (p. 60) special procedures are taken with regard to the trial and punishment.

2. Legality

(a) Legitimate children

A child is legitimate if the parents were married at the time of conception or birth, even if the marriage was later declared void, provided that either of the parents reasonably believed the marriage to be valid.

(b) Illegitimate children

A child born of parents who were not married to each other at the times stated above is illegitimate. If the mother is married, there is a presumption that her husband is the father, but this may be rebutted by evidence, such as the husband being out of the country for more than a year before the birth. An illegitimate child has the same rights as a legitimate child to an intestacy of either parents, and may claim as a dependant within the provisions of the Inheritance (Provision for Family and Dependants) Act 1975. Furthermore, if a will makes a bequest to "my children," illegitimate children are included. A legal disadvantage for illegitimate children is that they cannot succeed to a title or any property attached to the title.

(c) Legitimation

An illegitimate child may be legitimated by the subsequent marriage of the parents and is then considered to be a legitimate child with the same rights.

(d) Adoption

Children who have been legally adopted have all the legal rights as if the adopters were the natural parents.

3. Contract

A contract between an adult and a minor is binding on the adult, but it is not binding on the minor, unless it is for necessaries (food, clothes, etc.) or for the minor's benefit (training, education, etc.). A minor may make contracts to own moveable personal property (records, cars, etc.), but a minor cannot legally own land.

4. Tort

Minors are not so well protected in tort and the age of the person is not as important as the mental understanding of the specific individual. Obviously a young child cannot be expected to show the same standard of care in negligence as an adult, and conversely, an adult may have to show greater care with respect to children than with other adults.

5. Marriage

Minors cannot marry under 16, and may only do so between 16 and 18 if they have the written consent of their parents or a magistrate.

6. Litigation

A minor may not personally bring a civil action, but must do so through a "next friend" (usually a parent) and defend an action through a "*guardian ad litem*." Minors under 17 may not apply for legal aid, although their parents or guardians may do so on their behalf.

7. Other restrictions on the rights of minors

(*a*) *Voting and jury service*

Young persons cannot vote at a local or parliamentary election, or be selected for jury service until they are 18 and their names appear on the electoral role.

(*b*) *Wills*

Generally, persons under 18 cannot make a valid formal will, although they may be competent to sign as a witness to a will.

(*c*) *Passports*

A British passport may be obtained at the age of 16, although children under this age are usually included on their parents' passports.

(*d*) *Driving*

A person must be 17 to obtain a licence to drive a car or motorcycle, although a person of 16 may obtain a licence to drive a moped.

(*e*) *Drinking*

Persons under 14 are not allowed in bars of licensed premises, and persons over 14 and under 18, although allowed to enter a bar may not be served with, or drink, alcohol. Persons over 16 may consume certain drinks if served with a meal.

(*f*) *Guns* (*including airguns*)

The police must not issue a certificate to possess a firearm to a person under 14. Above this age the granting of the certificate depends on the type of gun and the purpose for which it is acquired.

(*g*) *Gambling*

Persons under 18 are not allowed in betting shops, gambling clubs or casinos, and they may not gamble in bars of licensed premises. A person under 18 may attend a club licensed to play "bingo" only, although they may not play or take part in the activity.

(*h*) *Cigarettes*

Although it is not an offence for persons under 16 to smoke, shopkeepers may not sell cigarettes or tobacco to persons apparently under this age, whether or not they are for their own use.

(*i*) *Fireworks*

A shopkeeper may not sell fireworks to persons under 16.

(*j*) *Tattooing*

Persons under 18 may not be tattooed.

(*k*) *Films*

Persons under 18 may not see films certified as "18" and persons aged 14 and under may not see films certified as "15" (see page 106).

It is interesting to note that with many of the above restrictions the law has placed a duty on other persons not to help with, or to provide the activity.

BANKRUPTS

A person who owes another person or corporation more than a fixed amount may be sued for bankruptcy. If the debt cannot be paid the courts will make a bankruptcy order, by which an outsider (a trustee in bankruptcy) or the official receiver will find out the total amount of the bankrupt's debts and the total amount of assets. The assets, nearly everything owned privately or in business, are then distributed to the creditors in a laid down order of preference. The first to claim are any employees for wages, etc., then the Inland Revenue, then the Department of Health and Social Security for any national insurance contributions, followed by the local council for rates, any creditors who secured their loans against a particular asset (*e.g.* the house) and lastly, the unsecured creditors. When there is sufficient cash to settle all but the unsecured creditors, the latter receive a share of what is left, which is usually 10p to 15p for every pound owed. If, for example, it was 10p in the pound, a creditor for £500 would only receive £50. If there are no assets left for the unsecured creditors, they receive nothing.

When adjudicated bankrupt, the bankrupt is disqualified from certain rights which were previously exercised:

(i) He cannot sit or vote in Parliament, either the House of Commons or House of Lords.

(ii) He cannot be a member of a local council or be a justice of the peace.

(iii) He may not be a director of a limited company or take part in its management.

(iv) He may not obtain a loan over a certain figure or make a contract without declaring his bankruptcy. It is a criminal offence to ignore this requirement.

Previously, some of these restrictions could last during a bankrupt's entire lifetime, but from October 1, 1977, the Insolvency Act 1976 provided that anyone who has been a bankrupt for 10 years is automatically discharged. In future, the bankruptcy courts will review the position after five or 10 years and will make suggestions with the aim of restoring more people to their full constitutional rights.

PERSONS OF UNSOUND MIND

The legal capacity of the mentally ill varies with the different branches of law and, in many ways, it is similar to the capacity of children.

1. Crime

A person who can show that he did not understand, or did not know that he was doing wrong may plead insanity, and the court will find that he is "not guilty by reason of insanity" (see p. 228 for the M'Naghten Rules and the defence of diminished responsibility).

2. Contract

A person of unsound mind will be liable on contracts for necessaries but other contracts may be avoided, if it can be shown that the other party was aware of the mental illness.

3. Tort

Unless mental intent is necessary, a person of unsound mind would be liable in tort because the aim of tort is to compensate the injured person, not to punish the person who committed the tort.

4. Litigation

Actions on behalf of a person of unsound mind must be brought in the name of the next friend, and defended by a *guardian ad litem.*

THE CROWN

Monarchy exists when the power of government rests in one person. The United Kingdom is a Monarchy but the Queen is a constitutional Monarch, which means that the powers and duties conferred on her may only be exercised on the advice of her ministers.

The Queen has two distinct legal personalities. She is a natural person in her personal capacity, and she is a corporation sole in her public capacity.

(i) The Queen in a personal capacity "can do no wrong." This means that the Queen cannot be brought before a British court, because technically the courts are the Queen's courts and the judges are appointed by her.

(ii) The Queen in her public capacity is usually referred to as the Crown. The legal person is the corporation sole, which evolves to each person wearing the Crown. When there is a change of Monarch all Crown property is vested in the new Monarch. Although the Queen in her personal capacity may not be sued in court, the Crown and its agents may be sued. The Crown Proceedings Act 1947 permits the Crown to be sued for breach of contract, and for torts caused by Crown agents and servants in the course of their employment.

CORPORATIONS

Corporations are artificial persons that have a corporate legal existence completely separate from the human beings that created and administer them. There are two types of corporations, (i) corporation sole and (ii) corporation aggregate.

(i) A corporation sole consists of one human person at any one time, but when the human member loses office the title passes on to a successor. It is, therefore, the title or office which is the legal person, and the human holds the property and carries out the duties while in office. When the holder dies, resigns or retires from office, the corporation sole continues and the property and powers are vested in the new holder of the office.

(i) A corporation aggregate consists of more than one person, who are usually called members. As with a corporation sole, it is the corporation that has the legal existence separate from the membership. The human membership may change from day to day, but the corporation is unaffected. The Institute of Chartered Secretaries and Administrators, borough councils, British Rail and all limited companies are examples of corporations aggregate.

Ways by which Corporations are Created

1. By Royal Charter

The Monarch has the power to create corporations by Royal Charter, and in the past, trading companies such as the Hudson Bay Company and the East India Company were formed in this way. The British Broadcasting Corporation was granted its Charter in 1926. The power is used mostly these days to create professional bodies, which usually have the word "Chartered" in their title. For example, the Institute of Chartered Accountants, and the Chartered Insurance Institute.

2. By special statute

A specific Act of Parliament creates a specific or particular corporation. Most of the early railway companies were created in this way and it is now used to create the nationalised industries, such as the National Coal Board and local government councils.

Corporations sole are now created by special statute, as are corporations aggregate which in the past would have been created by Royal Charter.

Unlike the B.B.C. the Independent Television Authority was established in 1964 by the Television Act.

3. By registration under the Companies Acts

The Companies Acts provide the means for a group of persons to create a corporation. This method is used as an alternative to the ways mentioned above. Most registered corporations are trading companies wishing to acquire the advantages of limited liability, and they are easily recognised by the last word of their name being "Limited." For example, "Smith & Jones Limited." The Companies Act 1985, s.25 requires all new public companies and existing public companies to include at the end of their names "public limited company" or the abbreviation p.l.c. If a public company has its registered office in Wales, the ending will be "cwmni cyfyngedig cyhoeddus," or the initials c.c.c.

It is not only trading companies which take advantage of this method of incorporation, many charitable organisations and professional bodies, not created by Charter, are registered under the Companies Acts to acquire perpetual existence. An example of this kind of body is the Associated Examining Board which is a company limited by guarantee.

Effect of Incorporation

(a) A corporation has a distinct existence separate from the persons who are its members.

In *Salomon* v. *Salomon & Co. Ltd.* (1897) Salomon had for many years been in business as a boot manufacturer and leather merchant. The firm was solvent and he formed a limited company; the memorandum of association was signed by Salomon, his wife and five children, each holding one share. The boot business was sold to the company for £30,000; 20,000 £1 fully paid-up shares, which were allotted to Salomon, and £10,000 secured by a debenture.

The company failed and went into liquidation. The company's assets of £6,000 were insufficient to repay the debentures and the unsecured creditors, who were owed £8,000. The liquidator claimed that the company and Salomon were the same person and that the debenture held by Salomon should be set aside.

It was held that the company was a separate legal entity, different altogether from the members, and although after incorporation the business was exactly the same as before, the company in law was not the agent of the members. Therefore, as the company was properly registered, Salomon, as the debenture holder, was entitled to the available assets.

(b) A corporation may carry on business as an ordinary person, but its activities may be limited by the Charter or statute.

(i) Chartered corporations have the rights and duties of ordinary persons and may carry on any activities that are not specifically forbidden, or are against the spirit of the Charter.

(ii) Statutory corporations must limit their activities to the powers expressed in the creating statute. Any act outside the scope, or beyond the powers of the statute is said to be *ultra vires*, and void.

(iii) Registered companies' activities are regulated by two documents; The Memorandum of Association, and the Articles of Association.

The Memorandum of Association governs the company's external activities and its main clauses provide information on the name and address of the registered office of the company, the objects of the company, the members' limited liability and the company's share or capital structure.

The objects clause states the purposes for which the company was formed and lays down its powers to attain them. It is this clause which restricts a company's activities and if a company makes a contract which is outside the objects clause and the other party is aware of this, the contract is *ultra vires* and void. (For example, a company formed as a travel agency makes a contract to buy a pig farm.) The purpose of the objects clause is to protect shareholders so that they know how their money may be spent, and it protects persons dealing with the company who will know the extent of the company's powers. It is the modern practice to draft the objects clause in very wide terms so that a company may carry out almost any activity it wishes. The Articles of Association govern the internal administration of the company, on such matters as procedures of meetings, the appointment of directors, etc.

(c) Although a corporation cannot physically commit a crime

or act in a tortious manner, it may be liable for the wrongs of its human agents. Therefore, a corporation may be prosecuted for breach of duty under the Health and Safety at Work, etc., Act 1974, or for defective motor vehicles on the highway. A company may be vicariously liable for the tortious wrongs of its agents and the employees in the ordinary course of their employment (see p. 201). A company could be liable if its van driver was negligent while on company business and caused damage to another person's motor vehicle. A corporation may sue and be sued in its own name.

(d) A corporation has perpetual succession, which means that it continues to function until definite steps are taken to end its existence. The changing membership does not affect its existence, and the corporation will remain although a member or members have died, resigned, retired or transferred their interest to other persons.

UNINCORPORATED ASSOCIATIONS

There are many forms of unincorporated bodies, *e.g.* cricket clubs, darts clubs, chess clubs. All sports and pastimes will probably have a club of some size, small or large. They consist of groups of people joined together to follow their common interest. Unincorporated associations differ from corporations in that they do not have a legal entity separate from their members, and the law regards the associations as a group of individuals who all share the legal responsibility.

When a member of a club makes a contract on behalf of the club, that individual is personally liable to the other party, although the whole committee who authorised the contract may be jointly liable. Generally, a member who commits a tort is personally liable, but a committee who authorised an act which leads to a tort may be liable.

In addition to sporting and social clubs, there are large professional associations which are treated legally in a similar way.

PARTNERSHIPS

The Partnership Act 1890, defines a partnership as a "relationship which subsists between persons carrying on a business in common with a view of profit." It is the aim of making a profit which is important, and it is this which distinguishes a partnership from the clubs and societies just mentioned.

A partnership has no separate legal entity and although the courts do allow a firm to sue and be sued in the name of the partnership, all partners are liable, both individually and collectively, for the legal liabilities of the firm.

Principal Differences between Partnerships and Registered Companies

1. Profit

A partnership must have the intention of making a profit. This is not necessary with a company, and many charitable organisations are registered companies.

2. Perpetual succession

A company, being a legal person, continues to exist regardless of its changing membership. A partnership may end with the death or resignation of a partner.

3. Membership

A partnership may not have more than 20 members (banking partnerships, only 10), although certain professions, such as accountants, solicitors and members of the Stock Exchange, may apply to the Department of Trade to have more than 20. A limited company must have a minimum of two members, but there is no maximum number.

4. Transfer of shares

Generally, shares in a company may be easily transferred to another person, but a partner may not introduce another partner in his place without permission of the other partner or partners.

5. Limited liability

A member of a company is liable for company debts only to the extent of the unpaid amount of the shares. If the shares are fully paid, the member has no further liability. A partner is personally liable for all partnership debts, and any private assets outside the partnership may be used to settle the partnership's liability.

6. Termination or dissolution

A company is wound up either compulsorily, when creditors ask the courts to end the existence of the company because it may be the only way of recovering the debts; or voluntarily, when the company decides to discontinue its existence. A partnership may end by death or bankruptcy of a member, or by agreement, or at the end of an agreed period of time for which the partnership was created. The court may also terminate a partnership if it considers it "just and equitable" to do so.

TRADE UNIONS

A trade union is a group of persons who join together to better their working conditions by collective bargaining. Originally, trade unions were considered unlawful organisations in restraint of trade. In modern times they have legal recognition and are a very necessary and powerful part of the country's labour force.

A union may be sued for contract in its own name, but the liability rests with the members, similar to other unincorporated associations. The Trade Union and Labour Relations Act 1974 provides that collective agreements are presumed not to be legally binding unless they are in writing and expressly provide for such an intention.

NATIONALITY

British nationality gives a person the right to vote; to be a Member of Parliament; to travel to and from the country and all other rights bestowed on a citizen. The British Nationality Act 1981 provided that United Kingdom citizenship may be acquired:

1. Acquisition by birth or adoption. A person born or adopted in the United Kingdom after the commencement of the Act shall be a British citizen if at the time of the birth or adoption the father or mother is:

(a) a British citizen, or
(b) settled in the United Kingdom.

2. Acquisition by descent. A person born outside the United Kingdom shall be a British citizen if at the time of the birth the father or mother is a British citizen (other than by descent).

3. Acquisition by registration. The following persons may apply to the Secretary of State to be registered as a British citizen:

(i) a minor whose mother or father was a British citizen by descent and that parent's mother or father was a British citizen other than by descent.
(ii) a British Dependent Territories citizen or British Overseas citizen who has been in the United Kingdom for five years prior to the application for registration.
(iii) Acquisition by naturalisation. The Secretary of State may grant British citizenship to a person of full age and capacity if he is satisfied that he is of good character, has a sufficient knowledge of the English or Welsh or Scottish Gaelic language, has lived in the United Kingdom for more than five years and his home, after being granted British citizenship, will be in the United Kingdom.

Section 11 of the Act provides that a person who immediately before commencement of the Act was:

(a) a citizen of the United Kingdom and colonies, and
(b) had a right of abode in the United Kingdom under the Immigration Act 1971, as then in force,

shall at commencement of the Act become a British citizen.

It is normally the domicile (where a person permanently lives) that decides the jurisdiction of the civil law, regardless of nationality. Therefore, the laws of marriage, contract, tort, taxation, etc., depend, not on citizenship, but on domicile.

Revision Test

1. Name the two contracts which are binding on a minor.

2. May a child under 10 be found guilty of committing a crime?

3. Name two ways by which citizenship of the United Kingdom may be acquired.

4. Which letters or words must end the name of a registered public company?

5. Name three ways by which a corporation may be created.

Specimen Questions

1. The names of many businesses end with the abbreviations Ltd. or p.l.c. What do they mean and what legal effect do they have?

2. State differences between a limited company and a partnership.

3. "The Queen can do no wrong." Explain the meaning of this statement. Are there any occasions when the Queen or the Crown may be subject to the law?

4. (a) Why is it important to distinguish between domicile and nationality?
   (b) How may British nationality be acquired?

5. What is the legal personality of a trade union, and how does it differ from other unincorporated bodies?

6. Explain the position of minors with respect to marriage, criminal liability and making a formal will.

7. (a) "In law persons are classed as

(i) human or natural; or
(ii) juristic or artificial."

Explain what is meant by this sentence.

(b) John Doakes sold and delivered goods to
(i) E.F.G. Ltd.,
(ii) H.J.K. Social Club,
(iii) Jane Jones, aged 17, and
(iv) the L.M.N. Trade Union.

Explain the legal position if each of the above "persons" refused to pay for the goods, and clearly state who would be liable for the debt and how it may be recovered.

Chapter 5

CIVIL LIBERTIES

RIGHTS AND DUTIES OF THE INDIVIDUAL

It is often said that we live in a free society and, therefore, individuals in the United Kingdom have freedom of speech; are free to choose where to live; may vote for whom they wish and associate with whom they wish. These freedoms are denied to citizens of some countries. It must be noted, however, that they are not absolute rights in this country, because most freedoms of the individual are subject to some restriction, large or small.

It is also contended that all rights of the individual have a corresponding duty. You have the right of freedom of speech, and the rest of the community has a duty not to prevent you from speaking.

On occasions the freedoms or liberties of the individual may conflict with the needs of the community as a whole, and in such cases the right will be restricted by Parliament or the courts.

FREEDOM OF THE PERSON

The liberty of an individual is presumed to exist in this country unless a specific law dictates otherwise. This means that a person is entitled to be free from arrest or detention unless there are justifiable reasons, or the individual agrees to the loss of freedom.

Reasons justifying loss of liberty would include (a) arrest by warrant, (b) imprisonment following conviction in court, or (c) detention of a person in need of care (a child, or person of unsound mind).

It is also possible to arrest a person without a warrant where it is reasonable to suspect the person has, or is about to commit an arrestable offence (see p. 224).

Sometimes the police or armed forces are given special powers by Parliament to intern people, as happened during the recent troubles in Northern Ireland. Subject to such provision, however, a person is arrested with the intention of being brought before a court, and if this does not happen the prisoner has the right to apply for a writ of *habeas corpus*. The effect of this writ is that the prisoner must be brought before a court or judge immediately in order to see if the detention is justified, or whether the prisoner should be released.

FREEDOM OF SPEECH

This freedom is probably the best known and most frequently quoted. The right covers all forms of communication, speech and writing. In many cities and towns, there are areas set apart for individuals to talk about matters of public interest; the most famous is "Speakers' Corner" in Hyde Park, London.

Although we are chiefly concerned with the individual's rights, the importance of freedom of speech in newspapers and broadcasting must not be forgotten. In certain countries the news media are controlled by the government, and therefore, these countries do not have a "free press."

In this country the press has freedom of speech and may even be politically biased, but broadcasting must have no political bias and programmes should give a balanced argument.

Like other rights, freedom of speech is restricted. An individual may say or write what he wishes provided he does not break the civil or criminal law. Examples of the restrictions are as follows:

1. Defamation

An individual has the right to protect his reputation and the tort of defamation provides the legal means of stopping another individual from making false statements to third parties (see p. 196). Defamation may be a crime (criminal libel) if the statement is likely to cause, or lead to, a breach of the peace. Slander, which is the spoken word, may also be a crime if the statement would create an offence such as treason or sedition.

2. Censorship

Certain Acts of Parliament restrict the absolute right to perform plays and films. There is no censorship of plays, but the Theatre Act 1968 makes it a criminal offence to present an obscene play which is likely to corrupt or deprave any individual in the audience. The Attorney-General must consent to the prosecution, and defendants may claim as a defence that the play has artistic or literary merit.

There is no such protection for the showing of films, and at present anyone may start an action in respect of an alleged obscenity. Many people consider that the film industry should have the same rights as the theatre in this matter. Local authorities decide if a film is suitable for showing to the public, and they also have the responsibility of granting licences for premises used for showing films. A local authority may (but is not bound to) rely on the grading given by the British Board of Film Censors. You will have noticed at the start of every film that a form of certificate is shown with the name of the film and one of the following grades:

"*U*" Permits admission of any child of not less than 5 years, accompanied or not.
"*P.G.*" The same conditions apply, but with parental guidance as to the possibility that some scenes may be unsuitable for young children.
"*15*" Permits admission of children not less than 15 years, accompanied or not.
"*18*" Restricts admission to persons less than 18 years of age.
"*Restricted 18*" Films that may only be shown to adults in licensed cinemas or film clubs.

3. National security

Certain persons (mostly civil servants) who by the nature of their employment have acquired knowledge which if made public would jeopardise the safety of the State, are forbidden by the Official Secrets Acts from disclosing this information, and are subject to prosecution if such information is disclosed.

The mass media (broadcasting and the press) are similarly liable for prosecution for publication of information in breach of the Official Secrets Acts. Although there is no direct censorship of the press, the issue of a "D" notice informs the press that the information in the notice should not be published.

4. Obscenity

It is an offence to publish any obscene material which is likely to deprave or corrupt persons who have read, seen or heard the material. It is a good defence to show that the publication was for the public benefit, in the interests of science, literature, art or some other area of public interest.

5. Horror comics

The Children and Young Persons (Harmful Publications) Act 1955 makes it an offence to publish stories (in words or pictures) which show violence, crimes, cruelty, etc., which would be harmful to the minds of young readers.

6. Indecent photographs of children

The Protection of Children Act 1978 makes it an offence to take or show indecent photographs of children. The aim of the Act is to protect children against exploitation by the taking of indecent photographs or making indecent films.

FREEDOM OF ASSOCIATION

As a general rule an individual in the United Kingdom is free to associate with other individuals for any reason, whether it be social, political, business or concerning trade unions. It is the right of individuals to form an association in direct opposition to another association. For example, employers in a particular industry or trade may join together for their common good, and their employees may form a trade union for the collective strength to bargain with the employers' organisation.

Similar to the other rights, this freedom only exists if an association's objectives and aims, and methods of achieving them, do not break the law. Examples of illegalities are:

(i) It is the right of employees to withhold their labour (go on strike) but certain workers are subject to Acts of Parliament which make it an offence to strike. The police may not strike and workers in certain nationalised industries, such as those in the gas industry, are similarly affected if their action would cause danger to the public.

(ii) It would be a breach of contract to strike without giving the proper period of notice. Although technically an employer could sue employees for such a breach, in reality it is very unlikely.

(iii) An association which is a secret society and has illegal objectives and administers unlawful oaths is not permitted.

It is possible that there may be a change of law, so that, although membership of a certain association was legal, a later change of law could make membership illegal. For example, in 1984 the Government decreed that civil servants at the General Communications Headquarters at Cheltenham had to resign from their union. The purpose was to stop strikes which it was contended could jeopardise national security.

FREEDOM TO WORSHIP

An individual in the United Kingdom may follow any religious creed, and it is generally illegal to discriminate against a person because of a religious belief. It is possible for some aspects of a religion to be opposed to the law. In some countries a Moslem man may have four wives (polygamy) but in this country a man, regardless of his religion, may only marry one (monogamy). A sikh is required by his religion to wear a turban, and the law of the United Kingdom requires a motorcyclist to wear a safety helmet; therefore it can be seen that a conflict between religion and law arose whenever a Sikh rode a motorcycle. After many protests by the Sikh community in this country the law was changed to grant an exception from wearing a helmet to drivers who object on this religious ground.

It may appear strange, but an exception to the principle of freedom of worship is the Monarch, who must be a member of the Church of England.

FREEDOM OF MEETING AND PROCESSION

Members of the public are free to meet and demonstrate, unless in doing so they break the law. The following are examples of meetings which would be illegal.

(i) If two or more persons meet to perform an illegal or unlawful act, this is known as conspiracy to commit a crime.

(ii) Unlawful assembly occurs when three or more persons assemble with the intent to commit a breach of the peace, or actually commit a breach of the peace with or without intent, or their behaviour causes reasonable people to fear that a breach of the peace will happen.

(iii) A common law riot exists when three or more persons meet without lawful authority for a common purpose, and there is an intention to use force, if necessary, to help one another against any opposition, and force is applied in such a manner as to alarm at least one person of reasonable firmness and courage.

(iv) It is an unlawful assembly if more than 50 persons meet within one mile of Westminster when Parliament is in session.

(v) The Public Order Act 1936 provides that a local authority, with consent of a chief constable, may prohibit processions and marches, for three months, or, if the police consider that a procession may cause a public disorder, they may impose conditions, such as refusing the use of banners, or stipulating the route of the march.

(vi) Unlawful meetings also exist when torts are committed. If a meeting obstructed the highway this would be a tort of nuisance. Similarly if a meeting involved invading another person's land this would be a tort of trespass. Breach of the rules and regulations of meetings may mean that a chairman has to adjourn or end the meeting, and persons who continue to stay after the meeting has been lawfully ended, may be trespassers if they refuse to leave.

PROTECTION OF RIGHTS AND FREEDOMS

The protection of an individual's rights is provided by many Acts of Parliament and by the courts. In addition, there are societies and agencies whose aims are to ensure that the individual's rights are maintained and preserved.

Protection by Parliament

In the United Kingdom there is no guaranteed protection from Parliament, as any Act of Parliament can be repealed, and there is no safeguard that a law will not be changed. Some countries, such as the United States of America, have a written constitution where a Bill of Rights lays down the individual's rights, and which is difficult to change. Parliament is not bound by any such restriction and may legally change the law by passing an Act. In practice, however, it is very unlikely that any British government would repeal any law which protected an individual's rights if it did not have the support of the majority of the country. The writ of *habeas corpus* was created by Parliament in 1679, and it is inconceivable that this safeguard would be repealed unless replaced by another Act protecting the liberty of the individual.

While there is no Bill of Rights in the United Kingdom, the European Convention on Human Rights was signed by the U.K. in 1950, and, to a certain extent, this country is bound by the rights provided in the Convention. (see p. 114).

Protection by the Courts

The decisions of judges in court have created precedents on constitutional matters, and unless they are overruled by a superior court or by Parliament, they are binding and protect the rights of individuals.

A person's rights may also be protected by application to the High Court for a prerogative order.

The prerogative orders control courts and tribunals by compelling them to exercise their powers according to the law, or by restraining them from over-reaching their jurisdiction. The orders are:

(i) Mandamus. This orders or commands a court or public body to carry out its duty. The order could, therefore, be to a court, a local council or Minister of the Crown. It should be noted that this order, unlike the following two, is not confined to judicial proceedings.

(ii) Certiorari. This requires the proceedings of an inferior court to be brought before the High Court, to consider whether the decision of the lower court should be quashed (made invalid).

(iii) Prohibition. This is an order to an inferior court or tribunal to stop proceedings which would be in excess of its jurisdiction.

Rule of Law

In addition to judicial precedent and the prerogative orders, a subject's rights are protected in the courts by the Rule of Law, which has been defined as "A principle or rule of conduct so established as to justify a prediction with reasonable certainty that it will be enforced by the courts if its authority is challenged."

The Rule of Law was first explained by A. V. Dicey in 1885. The phrase implies the following concepts which are essential and basic to the constitution of a free society.

(i) No man shall be punished unless he has been convicted in an ordinary court of law for a definite breach of law. This concept eliminates arbitrary arrest and conviction.

(ii) All men are equal before the law, whatever their rank or station, and are subject to the ordinary law and procedures of the courts. For example, in 1977 Princess Anne was fined for a motoring offence.

(iii) If there has been a breach of law, there is a certainty of enforcement of justice.

(iv) The constitution concerning the private rights of the individual exists as the result of judicial decisions made in the ordinary courts. It is the fact that every subject has a right to appear before the courts which safeguards the liberties and freedoms.

Natural justice

In addition to the Rule of Law, the courts, tribunals and public authorities have a duty to act in a judicial way to ensure justice for all parties. This is achieved by following the rules of natural justice, which are basically, that the judicial body shall not be biased, and that each party must have an opportunity to be heard.

1. Bias

The Latin maxim "*nemo judex in causa sua*" (no one can judge his own cause) means that a person in a judicial role must not have an interest in the result. In *R.* v. *Sussex Justices*, the following phrase was first used and has since been quoted over and over again, "... that justice should not only be done, but be manifestly and undoubtedly seen to be done." If only one member of a board or tribunal is "interested" the decision will be invalid, even if the financial interest is very small. In *Dimes* v. *Grand Junction Canal Co.* (1852), the Lord Chancellor awarded the decision to the company. He was a shareholder in the company, and the House of Lords later set aside his judgment.

In local government, councillors and committee members must declare their financial interest on any item of an agenda, and will not take part in the discussion on the item.

2. Audi alteram partem

The principle of *audi alteram partem* (hear the other side) ensures that when a body is exercising a judicial function both parties must be allowed to explain their point of view.

THE OMBUDSMAN

In 1967 the Parliamentary Commissioner Act created the post of Parliamentary Commissioner for Administration (the Ombudsman). His responsibility is to investigate grievances, referred to him by members of the House of Commons, from the general public who claim to have suffered injustice through maladministration by central government departments and agencies. In 1973, the Commissioner was given the additional responsibility of Health Service Commissioner, and complaints against all sections of the health service (hospitals, doctors, dentists, chemists, etc.) could also be investigated. The present Parliamentary Commissioner is Anthony Barraclough. Examples of complaints made to the Commissioner are:

(i) A teacher from overseas, complaining that the Department of Education and Science refused to award him qualified teaching status.

(ii) A boy hurt at school, admitted to hospital, and not examined by a senior doctor for four days.

(iii) A man who had to wait four-and-a-half years to have his tax problem solved.

(iv) A 60-year-old invalid whose request for a supplementary heating allowance was dealt with by the Department of Health and Social Services in a manner ". . . far short of an acceptable standard."

In addition to the Parliamentary Commissioner, there is a local "Ombudsman." The Local Government Act 1974 established a Commission for Local Administration in England, and another for Wales, to investigate complaints about injustices suffered as a result of maladministration in local government, or by a police or water authority.

The complaints of maladministration by local authorities are similar to the complaints that the Parliamentary Commissioner has to investigate, concerning such matters as neglect, bias, prejudice and delay. The Commissioner looks into the manner in which the authority has carried out its functions, not into the actual merits of the decision. It must be stressed that complaints must concern the maladministration of the authorities and not action taken by the authorities.

If a Commissioner decides to investigate a complaint, a report is presented to the authority which then opens it to inspection by the press and public. If the report indicates that a person has suffered an injustice, the authority must inform the Commissioner of the action it intends to take.

The Commissioner may not investigate complaints into:

(i) court proceedings,
(ii) investigation or prevention of crime,
(iii) matters dealing with the appointment, dismissal, etc., of personnel,
(iv) certain educational matters.

England is divided into three areas with a local commissioner in charge of a particular area. Wales has a separate commissioner.

INTERNATIONAL CONVENTIONS AND COURTS

There are organisations outside British jurisdiction which endeavour to attain human rights for all subjects regardless of a country's own laws. The United Nations has a Declaration of Human Rights which aims at a common standard of achievement for all peoples and all nations and lays down that,

> ". . . every individual and every organ of society . . . shall strive by teaching and education to promote respect for these rights and freedoms and by progressive measures, national and international, to secure their universal and effective recognition and observance."

The European Convention on Human Rights was signed in Rome in 1950, and the document followed the pattern of the United Nations, in declaring the individual rights and freedoms which should be protected in all the European countries. Many countries have incorporated the convention into their own law, but although Britain has not done so, other nations and nationals as well as British subjects may bring a complaint against her before the European Court of Human Rights. For example:

(i) The Irish government complained of British torture on prisoners in Northern Ireland.

(ii) A prisoner in an English gaol was prevented by prison rules from bringing an action against a prison officer. He complained to the court that it was in contravention of his human rights, and when his claim was upheld the Home Office changed the prison rules to bring them in line with the Convention (*Golder's Case* 1975).

As a result, or in anticipation, of the findings of the Court, in these and other cases, our law has been changed accordingly.

The Court of Justice of the European Communities, in the main, deals with actions concerning the Community or its institutions, but recently the issue of protection of human rights was discussed and, while there is nothing in the Treaty of Rome on the matter, the court declared that "Fundamental rights form an integral part of the general principles of law the observance of which it ensures . . . "

Revision Test

1. Name three restrictions on free speech.

2. What is another name for the Parliamentary Commissioner for Administration?

3. Name the European court which hears complaints when an individual's rights or freedoms have been violated.

4. Name the two basic principals of natural justice.

Specimen Questions

1. Is the United Kingdom "a free country?"

2. How far is it true that we have freedom of speech and association?

3. How does the law protect the liberty of a subject?

4. Write notes on:
   (a) Natural justice, and
   (b) The rule of law.

5. What are the Royal prerogative orders, and how do they protect citizens?

6. Are subjects of the United Kingdom protected by a Bill of Rights or other similar convention?

Chapter 6

CONTRACT

A contract may be defined as an agreement between two or more parties which is intended to be legally binding. It is the last few words which are important.

All contracts are agreements but there are many agreements which are not contracts. If a friend promised to pay for the petrol in return for a lift home from college on your motor-bike, and later refused to do as promised, you would not expect to take the matter to court. This is because there probably was no intention by you or your friend that there should be a legal relationship. There was an agreement between you, but it was not a contract.

ESSENTIALS OF A CONTRACT

The following elements are considered to be essential to the formation of a legally binding contract:

A. (1) Offer and (2) Acceptance.
B. Consideration.
C. Capacity.
D. Legal Relationships.
E. Legality.
F. *Consensus ad idem* (agreement).

A. (1) OFFER

Every contract must start with an offer by one person to another. An offer is a declaration by which the maker (offeror) intends to be legally bound by the terms stated, if accepted by the offeree.

I may offer to sell my car to you for £1,000 and if the offer is accepted, I am legally bound by the terms of my offer. I may not later increase the price, nor change the agreed terms.

The following points must be considered when making an offer.

1. It may be made to an individual or to a large number of people

Carlill v. *Carbolic Smoke Ball Co.* (1892). In an advertisement, the company promised to give £100 to anyone who purchased their smokeball remedy for influenza, and caught the illness within 14 days. To show good faith, the company deposited £1,000 with a bank to meet any claims. Mrs. Carlill bought the remedy, caught influenza and claimed £100. The court awarded Mrs. Carlill £100 and held that:

(i) an offer may be made to the world, it does not have to be to a specific person.

(ii) although the general rule is that advertisements are not offers, the fact that £1,000 had been deposited with a bank showed it was a firm offer and legal relations were intended. (See page 131).

(iii) communication of acceptance may be implied by the conduct of the acceptor. (see below p. 122)

2. It may be made in writing, by words or by conduct

Many people think of contracts as a written document, because they read and hear of footballers or T.V. stars "signing a two year contract." Although it is sometimes desirable to have written evidence of what was agreed, it is not essential for most contracts, and an oral contract is just as legal. On occasions the parties may not contract verbally, but may communicate their intentions by conduct. For example, a taxi may be hired by raising a hand; or a nod at an auction may make a bid for the item on sale. (A written form of contract is reproduced on p. 146.)

3. It must be communicated to the acceptor

A person who, not aware of an offer, acts in a certain way, cannot later, when aware of the existence of the offer, claim that this action was the acceptance. It is of no avail to claim that he would have conducted himself in the same way, had he known at the time that the offer had been made. Such situations arise in reward cases. Suppose, for example, a reward was offered for returning a lost dog, and a person unaware of the offer returned the dog to the owner. The finder could not later claim the reward, because at the time of returning the dog, he did not know that there was an offer to be accepted.

4. Revocation

An offer may be withdrawn at any time before acceptance, but the revocation of the offer must be communicated to the offeree. In *Dickenson* v. *Dodds* (1876), the offeree was informed by a reliable third party that the property, which was the subject of the offer, had been sold. It was held that this communication, although by an outside party, was good notice of the revocation of the offer. An offer may not be revoked if consideration (see p. 125) was given to keep the offer open for a certain period of time.

5. An offer must be distinguished from an invitation to treat

It is important to know which party makes the offer and which accepts. In the case of goods on display in a shop, it has long been decided that it is the customer who makes the offer and the shopkeeper who accepts. The price displayed on goods is not the offer, it is only an invitation for the customer to make an offer and the amount shown is an indication of the acceptable price.

After the Second World War, many self-service shops were opened in this country for the first time and there was doubt whether this law would apply. The goods were individually priced and the customer took them off the shelf and placed them into a basket. When was the offer made, when was it accepted? In *Pharmaceutical Society of Great Britain* v. *Boots Cash Chemists Ltd.* (1953), it was held by the Court of Appeal that the customer makes the offer when the goods are presented for payment at the cash desk, and acceptance takes place when the cashier accepts the money. The law gives a cashier the right to accept or reject a customer's offer.

In a more recent criminal case, *Fisher* v. *Bell* (1961), the defendant was charged with offering for sale an offensive weapon. He had displayed a flick knife with a price in his shop window. The court followed the law of contract and held that a priced article in a shop window is an invitation to treat and is not an offer for sale. The defendant, therefore, was not guilty of "offering for sale" the flick knife.

The above rule has been applied to some advertisements. In *Harris* v. *Nickerson* (1873) it was held that an advertisement giving details of an auction to take place, was not an offer but an invitation to come and make an offer. In *Partridge* v. *Crittenden* (1968), Partridge was charged with illegally offering for sale wild live birds. He had placed an advertisement in a paper offering birds for sale but the court held that he had not made an offer for sale, as the advertisement was only an invitation to treat.

An offer must also be distinguished from an intention to make an offer. An interesting point of law was made in *Harvey* v. *Facey* (1893), in which Harvey sent a telegram asking Facey if he wished to sell Bumper Hall Pen, and asked him to state his lowest price. Facey replied by telegram that the lowest price would be £900. Harvey accepted at that price but Facey refused to sell. The court held that there was no contract. Facey's telegram was not an offer but a mere invitation to treat, and £900 was the lowest price he would consider if he decided to sell in the future.

The law stated above has been decided by cases but there are many similar "offers" which have still to be decided by the courts.

For example, is the wording on a slot machine the offer or is it an invitation to treat so that the customer makes an offer when he places the coin in the slot? Is a bus making an offer when it stops, or is it inviting the passengers to make an offer which the conductor accepts when he takes the money? It is my opinion that the customer in each case makes the offer, but until such a case is decided by the courts the law is not certain.

A. (2) ACCEPTANCE

Once a valid acceptance of an offer has been made and all the other factors are present, a contract is in existence and neither party may escape from the terms expressed, unless both parties agree. As it is important to know when an offer is made, it is equally important to know the exact time an acceptance is made, because from that moment all the duties, obligations and liabilities of the contract are binding on the parties. The following rules of acceptance have been decided by the courts over many years, but are still subject to change by the introduction of new techniques of communication.

1. Acceptance may only be made by the person to whom the offer was made

An offer made to a specific person may be accepted by that person only (*Boulton* v. *Jones* (1857). Otherwise there could be some odd situations, such as A offering C, a famous painter, £1,000 for a portrait, and D, a housepainter who was standing nearby, accepting the offer. The rule only applies when the offer is made to a specific person and not to the world at large.

2. Acceptance must be absolute and unqualified

The offeree must accept the offer as made, and not add any conditions or terms. If a counter-offer is made the offer is terminated and the offeror is under no obligation to honour the offer, even if at a later date the acceptor wishes to accept the original terms. In effect, when a counter-offer is made the acceptor is saying "I do not accept your offer, will you accept my offer?" In *Hyde* v. *Wrench*, the defendant offered to sell his land for £1,000. Hyde counter-offered to buy at £950 but after Wrench had refused this offer, Hyde "accepted" the original offer and sued for the land. It was held by the court that the counter-offer terminated the original offer.

Generally a seller would probably be prepared to sell at the price in the original offer but circumstances may change, for example another party may wish to buy at a higher price.

It must be noted, however, that a request for further information (*e.g.* an inquiry as to whether or not credit would be granted) is not a counter-offer. *Stevenson* v. *McLean* (1880).

3. Acceptance must be communicated to the offeror

Generally, this must be actual communication, either orally

or in writing, but in *Carlill* v. *Carbolic Smokeball Co.* (see p. 118) the Court of Appeal considered that acceptance may be implied from the conduct of the acceptor. In this case, Mrs. Carlill's action in buying the remedy implied her acceptance of the terms of the offer, and it was not necessary to actually communicate her acceptance.

A person making an offer may not stipulate in the offer that no communication will be deemed an acceptance. In *Felthouse* v. *Bindley*, the plaintiff wrote to his nephew offering to buy a horse for £30, and "if I hear no more I consider the horse to be mine." The nephew did not reply but ordered Bindley, the auctioneer, to withdraw the horse from sale. In error the horse was auctioned and Felthouse sued for his loss. The court held that as the nephew had not communicated his acceptance of the offer, no contract existed and Felthouse had no right of action.

4. Acceptance must generally be in the mode specified in the offer

If a particular method of acceptance is not specified in the offer, any reasonable method of communication may be used, but if the offeror stipulates a specific mode of acceptance, it must be carried out in this manner. In *Eliason* v. *Henshaw* (1819), the plaintiff offered to buy flour from Henshaw. The offer stipulated that acceptance must be given to the waggoner who delivered the offer. The acceptance was sent by post and arrived after the return of the waggoner. It was held that as the specific mode of acceptance was not followed there was no contract.

This rule may be relaxed if it is shown that a different method of acceptance places the offeror in a no less advantageous position. (*Manchester Diocesan Council of Education* v. *Commercial & General Investments Ltd.* (1970).)

Termination of an Offer

An offer is terminated by the following events, and is no longer capable of being accepted:

(*a*) *Refusal*

The other party refuses to accept the offer.

(b) Counter-offer

The offeree does not accept the offer as made, but changes the terms or conditions. (See *Hyde* v. *Wrench* above.)

(c) Revocation

The offeror may revoke or withdraw the offer at any time before acceptance, unless consideration to keep the offer open has been given (see p. 119). *Dickenson* v. *Dodds* (1876).

(d) Lapse of time

If no fixed time is allowed for acceptance, the offer is only effective for a reasonable time. What is a reasonable time depends on the circumstances of each case. Therefore, if a person made an offer to buy perishable goods, such as fresh tomatoes, it would be reasonable to expect an immediate or fairly prompt acceptance, but when more durable goods are the subject matter of the offer, a longer period of time may be considered reasonable.

Ramsgate Victoria Hotel v. *Montefoire* (1866). Montefoire offered to buy shares in the company. Nearly six months later the company accepted the offer but Montefoire refused to take the shares. It was held that the period between the offer and acceptance was unreasonable and the offer had lapsed before the company's acceptance was made.

(e) Death

Death by either party before acceptance terminates an offer, unless the acceptor does not know of the offeror's death and the dead person's personal representatives are capable of performing the contract. Obviously, this would not apply if the dead person's personal services were needed to perform the contract. (*Bradbury* v. *Morgan* (1862).)

Offer and Acceptance by the Postal Services

Provided that the post is considered a reasonable means of communication between the parties, the following rules apply:

(*a*) *An offer is effective when it actually arrives*

An offer in a letter posted on July 1 and delivered on July 6 because of a postal delay, becomes operative on July 6 and not when it would be expected to be delivered. *Adams* v. *Lindsell* (1818).

(*b*) *Acceptance*

The general rules of acceptance apply when using the post, that is, the acceptance must actually be received by the offeror. *Holwell Securities* v. *Hughes* (1974). However, if it can be clearly or reasonably shown that the offer intended that it be sufficient for acceptance to be posted, acceptance is effective as soon as it is placed in the post-box, provided the letter is correctly addressed and properly stamped (*Henthorn* v. *Fraser* (1892)). It would be considered a good acceptance if the letter was lost in the post and not delivered to the offeror. In *Household Fire Insurance Co.* v. *Grant* (1879), the defendant applied for shares in the company. The company accepted the offer and posted the letter of allotment, but it was never delivered to Grant. The Court of Appeal held that acceptance took place as soon as the letter was posted, because the post was considered the agent of the offeror. A possible reason for this reversal of the general rule is that it is easier to provide proof of posting than to prove actual receipt.

When Telex is used as a means of communication, the rule established by the Court of Appeal in *Entores Ltd.* v. *Miles Far East Corporation* (1955) is that acceptance takes place when the telex is received. Telex is considered similar to using the telephone and not the post. However, in *Brinkibon Ltd.* v. *Stahag Stahl* (1982) the House of Lords held that this is not a universal rule and would not apply in every case. For example, if the telex was sent at night and was not read until next morning when the office staff arrived at work.

(*c*) *Revocation*

Revocation takes place when actually received by the offeree, not when posted. *Byrne* v. *Van Tienhoven* (1880).

B. CONSIDERATION

Unless it is clearly stated otherwise, all that follows in this chapter concerns the formation of a simple contract (see p. 146).

Consideration is merely the price in a bargain. The price does not have to be money, but it must have a monetary value. In a simple contract a party must promise to give consideration in return for a promise of consideration from the other party. A bookseller promises to give you sole ownership of a book, if you promise to pay him the cost of the book. The bookseller's consideration is the promise to give you the book, and your consideration is the promise to pay the price. The promise for a promise (*quid pro quo*) is essential, because in English law a promise by only one party is not enforceable (unless made by deed).

If a person promised to give you a £100 as a gift at the end of the month, the promise would not be enforceable, because it is a gratuitous gift. It has not been supported by a promise from you.

Consideration may, therefore, be defined as the price, although not necessarily a monetary one, which induces a party to enter into a contract. Over the hundreds of years in which the doctrine of consideration has developed, the courts have ruled whether or not the following promises are sufficient to be valuable consideration:

(*a*) *The position of a third party*

A plaintiff bringing an action must show the court that he made a promise of consideration. If my father and my uncle promise each other to pay me £100 if I pass an examination, I will not be able to enforce the contract if my uncle refuses to pay, because I gave no consideration for his promise. The contract was between my father and uncle, and I was not a party to the agreement. My father could sue my uncle because he gave consideration. In *Tweddle* v. *Atkinson* (1861) William Guy and John Tweddle each promised the other to pay a sum of money to William Tweddle. Guy died before paying and William Tweddle sued Guy's executor. His action failed because he had not provided any consideration and he had not

(b) Value and adequacy

Although consideration must be valuable, it need not be adequate. The courts will not consider the merits of the bargain, provided that each party received what was promised. For example, a football fan may consider paying £100 for a £10 ticket for a cup final. In *Chappell & Co. Ltd.* v. *Nestlés Co. Ltd.* (1960) the House of Lords held that the wrappers off three bars of chocolate were good consideration.

(c) The promise must be more than a duty

It would not be good consideration for a school teacher to promise a class that in return for extra money he would teach to the best of his ability, because it is his duty to teach in such a manner. It may, however, be good consideration if the teacher promised extra lessons after school hours, because this would be outside his duty. In *Stilk* v. *Myrick* (1809) two seamen deserted their ship, and the captain offered to share their wages between the rest of the crew if they brought the ship back to London. Stilk sued for his share, but the court held that he had not provided consideration as it was his duty to work the ship back to London.

In a similar case, *Hartley* v. *Ponsonby* (1857) the ship was in a dangerous situation, and because of this the court held that the promise to bring the ship home was good consideration because of the new danger.

(d) Promises involving debts

A promise to pay a smaller sum to be released from paying a larger sum already owing, is not good consideration.

A promise to pay £50 as payment in full settlement of a debt of £100, is not consideration, and the other party may sue for the balance. This is known as the Rule in *Pinnel's case* (1602), and applies because in promising to pay £50 the debtor is doing nothing more than he is already legally obliged to do. (*Foakes* v. *Beer* (1884).)

(e) Consideration must not be past

The promise must be to do something in the future. A party may not offer an act previously carried out as consideration for a future promise.

In *Roscorla* v. *Thomas* (1842) a horse was bought at an auction. As the purchaser was leading the horse away, the previous owner promised that if the horse was vicious he would return the price. The horse was in fact vicious, but the court held that the promise by the original owner was not supported by consideration from the plaintiff. His action in paying the purchase price was before the second promise of the seller, and therefore his consideration was past.

In a more recent case, *Re McArdle* (1951), a widow had a life interest in a house and she repaired and decorated the property at a cost of £488. The person who would eventually become the owner of the property, after the widow's death, later promised to pay the cost of the work. The Court of Appeal held that as the promise to pay was made after the work was completed the consideration was past and there was no legal obligation to pay.

If, however, a party acts at the request of another and it is inferred that payment is intended, the consideration may be good to support a later promise for payment. This is known as the Rule in *Lampleigh* v. *Braithwaite* (1615). Braithwaite asked Lampleigh to obtain a King's Pardon for him, which he endeavoured to do, and later Braithwaite promised £100 for his efforts. The court held that there had been consideration for Braithwiate's promise because Lampleigh had acted on Braithwaite's request. Further exceptions to past consideration, are bills of exchange and the revival, in writing, of a statute barred debt.

C. CAPACITY

Generally, any person may make a contract, but the law sometimes protects certain classes. In the main, where a person is denied full contractual capacity, the aim is to protect and not to prohibit, and difficulty in enforcing the contract is usually experienced by the party with full contractual capacity.

This section will deal with persons, both natural (minors, drunks, mental patients) and legal (corporations), who have slightly less than full capacity.

Minors (or Infants)

Since the Family Law Reform Act 1969, the age of majority is attained on the first moment of the eighteenth birthday. It must be understood that minors may enter into contracts and do so most days. They buy chocolate, papers, clothes, records, travel on buses and trains, pay to watch films and football, etc., etc. The law does not stop a person under 18 from making a contract, but it aims to protect the minor from certain types of contract. Contracts with minors come into three categories (i) binding contracts, (ii) void contracts and (iii) voidable.

1. Binding contracts

These are contracts for which the minor has full contractual capacity and may be enforced against, as well as by, the minor. There are two types:

(a) contracts for necessaries, and
(b) beneficial contracts of service.

(*a*) *Necessaries*

These may be defined as "goods suitable to the condition in life of such a minor, and his actual requirements at the time of sale and delivery."

It has been considered that a luxury cannot be a necessary, but it must be borne in mind that what might be considered a luxury for a person of small income might be a normally accepted part of life for the more fortunate.

In addition to the nature of the goods supplied, consideration must be given to the actual requirements at the time of sale. A pair of shoes would be necessaries if the minor was barefooted, but they would not be necessaries if the minor had several pairs of shoes.

In *Nash* v. *Inman* (1908), a Cambridge undergraduate, who was a minor, ordered 11 fancy waistcoats from a tailor, but refused to pay the bill. It was held by the court that the tailor's action failed because the minor already had a sufficient supply of clothing and therefore the waistcoats were not necessaries. The minor did not have to pay the bill.

However, in *Chapple* v. *Cooper* (1844), an infant widow contracted with an undertaker to arrange for the funeral of her deceased husband, and later refused to pay the cost. It was held she was liable, as the funeral was for her private benefit and a necessary service.

It is the responsibility of the party supplying the goods to prove that they are necessaries, and where goods are considered necessaries, a minor need not pay the contract price, but must pay a reasonable price.

(*b*) *Beneficial contracts of service*

Included under this heading are contracts for training, education, apprenticeship and other similar contracts. They are binding if, taken as a whole, they are for the minor's benefit.

In *Doyle* v. *White City Stadium* (1935) Doyle was a professional boxer and he entered into a contract which provided a clause that if disqualified he would lose the prize money. He was disqualified, but claimed that as a minor the contract was not binding on him. It was held that although this particular clause appeared onerous, the contract taken as a whole was for his benefit.

This case must be contrasted with *De Francesco* v. *Barnum* (1890), in which a minor became apprenticed as a dancer, on the terms that she would not marry, would receive no pay and would not dance professionally without the plaintiff's consent. When she made a contract to dance for the defendant, the plaintiff sued for damages and the court held that the terms of her contract of apprenticeship to be unreasonably harsh and would not enforce the contract against the minor.

2. Void contracts

The Infants Relief Act 1874, s.1., provided that the following contracts made by a minor shall be void.

(i) Contracts for money lent or to be lent.
(ii) Contracts for goods supplied or to be supplied (other than necessaries).
(iii) Accounts stated.

The effect of the Act is that a minor cannot be sued on the contract, and goods or money which have been transferred to a minor cannot be recovered by the other party. If, however, a minor obtained a loan or goods by fraud, *e.g.* claiming to be over 18, the courts may order the property to be returned, or if sold to a third party, order the proceeds of the sale to be returned (*Stocks* v. *Wilson* (1913)).

3. Voidable contracts

All other contracts which are not binding or void on a minor are voidable at the minor's option. This means that the minor may force an adult to perform the contract but it cannot be enforced against the minor. If, however, a minor repudiates a contract which has been partly performed by the other party, the minor will have to pay for the benefit received. For example, if a minor contracted to rent a flat for six months at £100 per month, and after three months wished to end the contract, he would be able to do so, but would have to pay £300 for the three months in which he lived in the flat. A minor who pays a deposit on goods may not, after returning the goods, claim back the deposit unless there has been a total failure of consideration (*Steinberg* v. *Scala* (*Leeds*) *Ltd.* (1923)).

Drunks and Mental Patients

Drunks and mental patients are liable on contracts for necessaries, and, similarly to minors, must pay a reasonable price. Other contracts are voidable at the option of the drunks or mental patients if they can prove that at the time of making the contract:

(i) they were so drunk or ill that they did not know what they were doing: and

(ii) the other party knew of their condition.

Mental patients will be liable on contracts made during a lucid period, and contracts made while the patient was of unsound mind may be ratified during the lucid period. A mental patient whose property is under the control of the court may not make a contract and any contracts purported to be so made are void.

Corporations

The legal position of corporations is covered in Chapter 4 (p. 93). The limitations placed upon corporations to make contracts arise from the manner in which they are created.

Chartered Corporations (*e.g.* The Institute of Chartered Secretaries and Administrators) are created by a Royal Charter, which lays down the purpose and objects of the corporation. The corporation is not restricted and may make any contract, but the Charter may be withdrawn if contracts are persistently made against the spirit of the Charter.

Statutory Corporations are usually public bodies, created by Acts of Parliament (British Rail). Contracts may only be made within the scope of the creating statute, and any contract outside of the Act is "*ultra vires*" (beyond the power of) and void.

Companies registered under the Companies Acts have their powers specified in the objects clause of the Memorandum of Association, and contracts should not be made which go beyond these objects. If a person makes a contract with the company, knowing it to be outside the powers of the memorandum, the contract is "*ultra vires*" and void. The European Communities Act 1972 provides that if a person deals with the company in good faith (*i.e.* does not know the powers of the objects clause) any contract is valid, whether or not it is outside the powers of the objects clause.

D. LEGAL RELATIONSHIPS

As was shown when dealing with offer and acceptance, it is essential to a contract that the parties intend to create legal relations. The courts presume that with business contracts the parties intend legal relations, and if the parties intend otherwise it must be clearly expressed.

In *Rose and Frank Co.* v. *Crompton* (1925) a written agreement between the parties stipulated that it was not a formal or legal agreement and should not be subject to the legal jurisdiction of the courts. The House of Lords held that the agreement had no legal effect.

The most common case of a contract in which legal relations are excluded occurs on football pools coupons. The contract is made "binding in honour only," and several court actions have been unsuccessful because the courts have held that the intention to create legal relations was expressly excluded (*Appleson* v. *Littlewoods Pools* (1939)).

With social or domestic agreements the courts are reluctant to hold that a contract exists and will look at the relationship of the parties and facts of the agreement before declaring the intention of the parties.

In *Balfour* v. *Balfour* (1919) the husband went to work in Ceylon and agreed to pay his wife £30 per month. He did not pay the money and the wife sued. It was held that there was no contract because the parties did not intend to create a legal relationship.

However, in *Merritt* v. *Merritt* (1970) a married couple separated and the husband agreed to make over the ownership of the house to the wife when she had completed paying all the mortgage repayments. The court held that there was an intention to be legally bound, because the parties were apart and consideration had been provided.

E. LEGALITY

There is a rule of law that no court action will arise from an illegal act. If the contract requires either party to act against the law, the courts will not help the guilty party. A contract may be illegal because it is (i) forbidden by statute, or (ii) against public policy.

The first type is easy to understand. If A made a contract with B to steal C's motorbike for £50, the court would not award A a remedy if B later refused to carry out the contract.

The second type is more difficult, because in this instance the courts consider that in the public interest the contracts should not be enforced. Examples of contracts considered to be against public policy are as follows:

1. Contracts to commit a crime

In *Alexander* v. *Rayson* (1936) the rent for a flat was reduced to avoid paying rates, but the difference was charged as "services." The contract was illegal, because one of its purposes was to defraud the local council.

2. Contracts to corrupt public life

It is considered illegal for a person to make a contract to purchase a public honour. In *Parkinson* v. *College of Ambulance* (1925), the plaintiff donated £2,000 on condition of obtaining a knighthood. When no honour was awarded Parkinson sued for the return of his money. The court held the contract was against public policy and illegal, therefore no money was recoverable.

3. Immoral contracts

Contracts which are against public morals or against the sanctity of marriage are considered illegal.

In *Pearce* v. *Brook* (1866), a prostitute hired a coach to help her acquire clients. The coach owner sued for the hire charge when she refused to pay, but the court held that the contract was illegal, and, as the coach owner knew the purpose of the contract, he could not recover the charge.

4. Contracts where damages are claimed for the birth of a health child

It has previously been considered that, as a matter of public policy, damages should not be awarded when, as a result of a breach of contract (sterilization, etc.) a healthy baby was born. In *Thake* v. *Maurice* (1984), a vasectomy operation was performed, but the operation was ineffective and a healthy child was later born to the parents. The parents sued for breach of contract and the court held that although damages could not be claimed for pain, distress and suffering by the plaintiffs (the parents), damages should be awarded for the costs of the birth and the upkeep of the child until she was 17.

5. Contracts in restraint of trade

The courts are reluctant to enforce a contract which stops a person from carrying on employment or a business, even if only for a limited period of time. The courts' attitude varies according to the nature of the contract, as follows:

(*a*) *Contract between employer and employee (contract of employment)*

An employer may make it a condition of employment that if the employee leaves his job, he will not work for a competitor for a period of time, and/or within a stated distance. Generally the courts will not enforce such agreements unless it is protecting a proprietary interest, such as a trade secret.

In *Attwood* v. *Lamont* (1920), Attwood employed Lamont as a tailor on the condition that if he left, he would not work as a tailor within 10 miles. The court held the agreement to be illegal, because Attwood had no trade secrets to protect.

Fitch v. *Dewes* (1921) was a contrasting case in that a solicitor in Tamworth employed his managing clerk on the agreement that if the clerk left his employment he would not practice as a solicitor within seven miles. The court held that this was reasonable and legal because it protected the interests of the master's clients.

The Court of Appeal, in *Oswald Hickson Collier and Co.* v. *Carter-Ruck* (1984), held that a partnership agreement which restrained a retiring partner from advising previous clients of the firm, to be, as a general rule, contrary to public policy, as it would deny a client the right to choose his own solicitor.

(*b*) *Contracts for the sale of a business*

A business may be sold on condition that the seller will not carry on a similar business within a fixed time and/or distance. The courts are more likely to uphold such agreements if they are considered reasonable between the parties.

In *Nordenfelt* v. *Maxim Nordenfelt Guns & Ammunition Co.* (1894), Nordenfelt was known throughout the world as an inventor, and a maker of machine guns and similar weapons. He sold his business on condition that he would not, for 25 years, engage in similar work anywhere in the world. It was held that because of his reputation, the restriction was reasonable.

It was held in *British Reinforced Concrete* v. *Schelff* (1921) that a similar agreement was not binding on a small local company, because it was not reasonable between the parties.

(*c*) *Solus agreements*

Traders agree to be supplied by only one company. For example a garage may agree to be supplied for the next 21 years by only one particular petrol company. The courts consider such restraints as illegal unless reasonable. In *Esso Petroleum Co. Ltd.* v. *Harpers Garage Ltd.* (1967), the House of Lords held that an agreement for 21 years was too long, but an agreement for five years was reasonable. The Court of Appeal in *Alex Lobb (Garages) Ltd.* v. *Total Oil (G.B.) Ltd.* (1985), held that an agreement to purchase the defendant's petrol exclusively for 21 years, with a provision for a mutual break after 7 and 14 years, was a reasonable restriction on trading.

F. *CONSENSUS AD IDEM (AGREEMENT)*

If a party agreed to enter into a contract because of fraud, misrepresentation or mistake, the contract may be void or voidable. What may appear to be a valid contract, may be invalid because consent was affected by one of these elements. There is no *consensus ad idem*, no real agreement, if one party enters into a contract believing that certain facts, important to the contract, are different from what actually exists.

Mistake

Mistake, as a general rule, does not avoid a contract, unless the mistake was such that there never was a real agreement between the parties.

Raffles v. *Wichelhaus* (1864). A contract was made for the sale of cotton aboard the S.S. "*Peerless*" sailing from Bombay. Unknown to the parties, there were two ships of this name, one sailing in October and the other in December. The buyer thought he was buying cotton on the first ship, but the sale was for cotton on the second ship. The court held that there was no contract.

Mistake as to the quality of goods will not avoid the contract. A mistake of judgment which results in making a bad bargain will not avoid a contract if all relevant facts are revealed.

The courts have avoided the following contracts for mistake:

1. Mistake as to the subject matter

Where one party sells goods, but the other party thinks he is buying something different (*Raffles* v. *Wichelhaus*).

2. Mistake as to the existence of the subject matter

Couturier v. *Hastie* (1856). A contract was made for the sale of corn which was being shipped by sea. Unknown to the parties, the corn had begun to perish and had been sold at a port en route. The court held that at the time of making the contract the corn was not really in existence, having already been sold.

3. Mistake as to the nature of the contractual document

(*Non est factum*: not my deed.)

A contract will be avoided if it can be shown that the party who signed a document:

(i) thought the document to be of a completely different nature, and

(ii) was not negligent in signing the other document.

In *Foster* v. *McKinnon* (1869). An old man of feeble sight thought he was signing a guarantee, but a bill of exchange had been substituted. It was held that he was not liable on the bill.

In *Saunders* v. *Anglia Building Society* (1971) an old lady signed a deed of gift of a house to her nephew. She had not read the document but a rogue had substituted his own name for that of her nephew, and later mortgaged the house to the building society. The House of Lords held that the contract was valid and the plea of "*non est factum*" could not be used because the lady had signed the kind of document she intended to sign, it was the contents which were different.

4. Mistake as to the identity of the other party

As a general rule, where parties are in a face-to-face position, the courts consider the identity of the parties unimportant, because it is presumed that the parties intended to contract with each other.

In *Phillips* v. *Brooks* (1919) a rogue purchased jewellery and paid by cheque. The jeweller would not allow him to take the jewellery until the cheque was cleared by the bank, but when the rogue claimed he was "Sir George Bullough," he was allowed to take a ring from the shop. The rogue pawned the ring. It was held by the court that the contract was not void, because the jeweller's mistake was not the customer's identity, but his financial position. The pawnbroker thereby acquired a good title.

This decision was followed by the Court of Appeal in *Lewis* v. *Averay* (1972). The facts were similar to the case above and the rogue, when buying a car, purported to be Richard Greene, a well-known film and T.V. actor (Robin Hood), and signed a cheque for the price as agreed. The court held there was a presumption that the seller intended to deal with the person in his presence, although he was mistaken as to this identity. As a third party had acquired the car in good faith, the seller could not avoid the contract.

Where the parties do not meet, but negotiate at a distance, say by using the post or telephone, identity is important, and a contract is more likely to be avoided for mistake.

Cundy v. *Lindsay* (1878). A person named Blenkarn ordered goods by post and signed his name on a letter-head so that it appeared that the order came from Blenkiron, a well-known and reputed company. The rogue also used a similar address. Goods were sent to Blenkarn and he resold them to Cundy. When the fraud was discovered, Lindsay (the supplier) sued Cundy in the tort of conversion, claiming that the goods were sent to Blenkarn by mistake. It was held that the contract was void for mistake, because the supplier never intended to deal with the rogue.

Misrepresentation

A misrepresentation is a false statement of fact, which induces the other party to enter into a contract and as a result suffers damage. The statement may be made orally, in writing or by conduct, but, generally, silence will not be considered a misrepresentation.

Misrepresentation must be a statement of fact, not opinion, so that if a salesman claims a car to be "free of rust" it would be misrepresentation if, in fact, the car was rusty. However, if he claimed he only "thought it free of rust," this would not be so. It is a general rule that, "the buyer beware" (*caveat emptor*), and with the second statement it would be the buyer's responsibility to check for rust.

Misrepresentation must also be distinguished from manufacturers' boasts or "puffs." Claims such as "our butter is best" or "we give the best service" are really only the manufacturers' opinions and are not intended to be the basis of a contract.

Misrepresentation may be either:

1. Fraudulent. This is defined in *Derry* v. *Peek* as a false statement made:

(i) knowingly, or
(ii) without belief in its truth, or
(iii) recklessly, not caring whether true or false.

2. Innocent. This is a false statement which the maker believed to be true.

3. Negligent. This is a false statement which the maker had no reasonable grounds for believing it to be true.

As a result of the Misrepresentation Act 1967, remedies available to the injured party are rescission or damages. In cases of fraudulent misrepresentation the remedy may be rescission *and* damages (for the tort of deceit).

Rescission means that the parties are no longer bound by the contract and goods or money which changed hands are returned to the original owner. This is an equitable remedy, granted at the discretion of the court and will not be awarded where:

(i) The injured party was aware of the misrepresentation and carried on with the contract.
(ii) The parties cannot be returned to their original position (*e.g.* the goods which changed hands have been consumed).
(iii) Another party has acquired an interest in the goods.
(iv) The injured party waited too long before claiming this remedy.

Undue Influence

Where a party makes a contract because of undue influence by another, the contract is voidable and may be set aside by the court, at the option of the party influenced.

Undue influence can arise where a "stronger" person has some special or fiduciary relationship over another, and uses this power to gain an advantage.

In *Re Craig* (1971) an 84 year old widower engaged a secretary until he died six years later. During this time he made gifts of large amounts of money to the secretary, which were later set aside by the court, because it was considered the relationship raised a presumption of undue influence.

This doctrine also applies to business contracts and in *Lloyds Bank Ltd.* v. *Bundy* (1975), the Court of Appeal set aside a guarantee which an old man had given to cover his son's bank balance. The son's business was in danger of failing and the court considered the bank had used undue influence to obtain the guarantee.

In *O'Sullivan* v. *Management Agencies Ltd.* (1984), Gilbert O'Sullivan when young and unknown, entered into contracts to further his song writing and singing career. He later applied to the court to have the contracts set aside. The Court of Appeal held that the contracts were unenforceable as a restraint of trade (see p. 133) and as the defendants had been in the position of a fiduciary relationship, the contracts had been obtained through undue influence.

DISCHARGE OF A CONTRACT

A contract is discharged (when it imposes no further legal responsibilities on the parties) by:

1. Performance
2. Agreement
3. Breach
4. Impossibility (or frustration)

1. Performance

A contract is discharged when the parties carry out their promises. If Jones Ltd. agrees to paint Mrs. Smith's house for

£150, the contract is performed when the house is painted and payment made.

Generally a party must do everything promised in the contract, and part-performance is no performance. If performance is not complete, payment for work done may not be recoverable, unless the other party was responsible for non-performance or accepted the work done. Time is not of the essence (that is, the date of performance is not important) unless it is a term of the contract, or becomes a term after agreement.

2. Agreement

The parties may agree to discharge the contract in the following ways, even though it has not been performed:

(*a*) *Discharge by deed and accord and satisfaction*

When one party has performed the contract, the other party may be released from the promise to perform, either

(i) By deed, where no consideration for the release is given, or

(ii) By accord and satisfaction. The parties agree to fresh consideration, by giving and accepting something outside the original contract.

(*b*) *Discharge when neither party has performed*

Where neither party has performed, they may agree to waive their rights and release each other from their obligations.

(*c*) *Discharge on occurrence of specific events*

The parties may agree beforehand that the occurrence of some specific event may discharge the contract. For example a charter-party contract for the hire of a ship may contain a term that a dock strike will discharge the contract.

3. Breach

If one party will not perform the contract as promised, the other party may sue in the courts for breach of contract. Breach of contract may occur when one party fails to perform or does not perform as agreed (*e.g.* a manufacturer supplying sub-standard goods.) When a party gives notice of intention not to perform the contract at a future date, there is no need for the injured party to wait until the agreed time of performance as the action may be started immediately. For example, if in January you contract to start work in six months' time as a hotel courier, and in February the employer informs you that he will not honour the agreement, you may sue for breach of contract in February; there is no need to wait until July, the agreed date of performance, before starting the action (*Hochster* v. *De La Tour* (1853)).

4. Impossibility or frustration

It may be no excuse that performance is impossible because of an event which occurred after the contract was made. The old common law view was that the parties should have foreseen all eventualities, and this rule to some extent still applies, as in *Davies Contractors* v. *Fareham U.D.C.* (1956) where the plaintiffs agreed to build 76 houses for a cost of £92,000. There were difficulties with labour and supplies, and when the houses were completed, the cost was £17,000 more than the agreed price. The builders contended that because of the difficulties the contract was frustrated, and claimed the actual cost. It was held that the contract was not frustrated, as the events could have been foreseen and provided for.

The courts, however, have recognised the following events as being sufficient to render performance impossible:

(*a*) *Subsequent statute*

After a contract has been made, an Act of Parliament makes performance impossible or illegal.

Re Shipton, Anderson & Co. (1915). A contract for delivery of wheat was frustrated when, before delivery took place, an Act of Parliament was passed requisitioning all wheat for the government.

(*b*) *Destruction of a thing necessary for performance*

Taylor v. *Caldwell* (1863). A contract for the hire of a music hall was frustrated when the hall was destroyed by fire before the time of performance.

(c) Personal incapacity in contracts for personal services

Robinson v. *Davison* (1871). A piano player was ill on the day of a concert and the artist could not play as had been contracted. The court held that the contract was frustrated, as it was not the artist's fault that he was unable to perform.

(d) Failure of some event which is the basis of the contract

If a contract is based on the happening of a specific event, the contract is frustrated if this event does not take place. The postponed coronation of Edward VII provided several interesting cases.

In *Krell* v. *Henry* (1903), the defendant hired a room which overlooked the route of the procession of King Edward VII's coronation. The King was ill and the coronation was cancelled. It was held that the contract was frustrated because the procession was the basis of the contract.

This case must be contrasted with *Herne Bay Steamboat Co.* v. *Hutton* (1903). After the coronation the King was to travel to Spithead to review the fleet, which was assembled there. Hutton hired a boat to follow the royal barge, but because the King's illness prevented the royal review Hutton did not use the boat. It was held that the contract was not frustrated because the purpose of the contract was to review the fleet, and as it was still assembled at Spithead, the contract was possible. Hutton was liable to pay damages.

Effect of consequence of frustration

When a contract has been frustrated by an event, such as above, it is automatically discharged. Difficulty is sometimes experienced when money or property has been transferred beforehand, or where one party has worked on the contract before the frustrating event. The Law Reform (Frustrated Contract) Act 1943 provides that:

(i) Money or property (other than specific goods which have perished) paid or passed over beforehand may be recovered.

(ii) A party who has incurred expenses on the contract may claim out of the money paid beforehand or the amount payable.

(iii) Money due to be paid before frustration is no longer payable.

(iv) Where one party has gained a benefit from work done before frustration (*e.g.* a half built house) the other party may be awarded an amount which the court considers fair and just.

The Act does not apply to (i) charter parties, (ii) carriage of goods by sea, (iii) insurance contracts.

REMEDIES FOR BREACH OF CONTRACT

When there has been a breach of contract, the injured party, in addition to treating the contract as discharged, may claim certain remedies, the most common of which are damages, specific performance, injunction and rescission.

Damages

Damages are the common law remedy and are awarded to place the injured party in the same financial position as if the contract had been completed. If a contract was made for the sale of a car for £800, and the seller refused to transfer the car, and another similar car was purchased at the market price of £1,000, the purchaser would claim £200 damages. If this sum is deducted from the £1,000 paid for the second car, the purchaser would have paid £800, the price agreed in the original contract.

An injured party will not always receive damages for financial loss suffered as a result of a breach of contract if the court considers the damages too remote from the consequences of the breach.

The plaintiff in *Hadley* v. *Baxendale* (1854) owned a mill and ordered a crankshaft to be delivered by a certain date. The carrier (Baxendale) delayed delivery and Hadley sued for loss of profits for the period during which the crankshaft was not working. The court held that the damages were too remote and the carrier was not liable, because he was unaware that his delay caused the mill to be idle. Baron Alderson considered that damages should be awarded where:

(i) they arise naturally from the contract, or
(ii) the damages were reasonably in the contemplation of both parties at the time they entered into the contract, as the probable result of the breach.

An excellent example of how these principles are followed came in *Victoria Laundry* v. *Newman Industries Ltd.* (1948). A boiler was ordered for the laundry to be delivered by a certain date. The boiler was delivered five months after the agreed date and the plaintiffs sued for:
(i) loss of normal profits;
(ii) loss of profits from special dyeing contracts.

The court held (i) that the defendants were liable for normal profits, because they knew the laundry needed the boiler for ordinary production, (ii) the defendants were not liable for the special profits because they were unaware of the dyeing contracts and, therefore, had not contemplated the loss at the time of making the contract.

Liquidated Damages and Penalties

Damages may be either liquidated or unliquidated. The latter is not decided beforehand but left to the courts to determine. Liquidated damages are decided at the time of making the contract and are a genuine pre-estimation of the damage. The amount agreed as liquidated damages is payable, whether the actual loss caused by a breach is more or less than agreed.

Liquidated damages must be contrasted with penalties. Penalty clauses in a contract are not a pre-estimation of the likely damage, but are usually included to ensure the contract is performed properly. A penalty is void, and unliquidated damages will be awarded by the court to cover the actual financial loss. A penalty will exist:
(i) If the amount stipulated is extravagantly greater than could be reasonably expected.
(ii) When the breach occurs because a sum of money has to be paid and the damages are greater than this amount.
(iii) When the same amount of damages are payable on several occurrences, which would vary with regard to their affect on the financial loss.

Specific Performance

This is an equitable remedy, granted at the discretion of the court. Its effect is that the court orders one party to perform the contract as agreed. It is never awarded in the following cases:

(i) Where damages are an adequate remedy.
(ii) Where either party is an infant (or minor).
(iii) In money lending contracts.
(iv) Where the court would have to supervise the contract.
(v) In contracts for personal services.
(vi) In contracts for sale of goods, unless the goods are unique.

It is usually awarded in contracts for sale of land or interests in land. (See the doctrine of part performance, p. 151.)

Injunction

This is an equitable remedy, granted at the discretion of the court. Its effect in contract is to stop a party from causing a breach of contract. It will not be awarded if damages are an adequate remedy, but will be awarded to restrain a breach of contract for personal services. It will, therefore, be used to stop a party under an exclusive contract, from contracting with another third party. For example, a footballer under a two-year contract cannot join another football club until after the two years have elapsed, unless his club agrees to the move. In *Warner Bros.* v. *Nelson* (1937), the defendant, a film actress better known as Bette Davies, agreed to make a film for another company although she had an exclusive contract with the plaintiffs. The court granted the injunction to the plaintiff and restrained the defendant from carrying out the contract with the third party.

Rescission

This is an equitable remedy, which endeavours to place the parties in the pre-contractual position by returning goods or money to the original owners (see p. 138).

THE FORM OF A CONTRACT

There are two classes of contract:

(i) Specialty (or contracts made by deed).

(ii) Simple contracts.

The important difference is that a simple contract may be formed orally, in writing or by conduct, and must be supported by consideration. (See p. 125.) Specialty contracts must be written, "signed, sealed and delivered," and do not need consideration.

While the majority of contracts may be made informally by word of mouth or by implication, the following contracts need to be made formally to be effective:

CONTRACTS WHICH MUST BE IN WRITING

Certain Acts of Parliament have laid down that the following contracts must be in writing:

Contracts of Marine Insurance.
Transfer of shares in a registered company.
Bills of Exchange, cheques and promissory notes.
Hire-purchase contracts, and other regulated consumer credit agreements.

FOOTBALL LEAGUE CONTRACT

AN AGREEMENT made the . . . . day of . . . . 19 . . . .

between (name) . . . .

of (address) . . . .

. . . .

the Secretary/Manager/Chairman of and acting pursuant to Resolution and Authority for and on behalf of

. . . .

Football Club Limited (hereinafter referred to as "the Club") of the one part and

(name) . . . .

of (address) . . . .

. . . .

a Registered Association Football Player (hereinafter referred to as "the Player")

WHEREBY it is agreed as follows:—

1. This Agreement shall remain in force until the 30th day of June 19. . . . . unless it shall have previously been terminated by substitution of a revised agreement or as hereinafter provided.

2. The Player agrees to play to the best of his ability in all football matches in which he is selected to play for the Club and to attend at any reasonable place for the purpose of training in accordance with instructions given by any duly authorised official of the Club.

3. The Player agrees to attend all matches in which the Club is engaged when directed by any duly authorised official of the Club.

4. The Player shall play football solely for the Club or as authorised by the Club or as required under the Rules and Regulations of the Football Association and the Football League. The Player undertakes to adhere to the Laws of the Game of Association Football in all matches in which he participates.

5. The Player agrees to observe the Rules of the Club at all times. The Club and the Player shall observe and be subject to the Rules and Regulations of the Football Association and the Football League. In the case of conflict such Rules and Regulations shall take precedence over this Agreement and over the Rules of the Club.

6. The Club undertakes to provide the Player at the earliest opportunity with copies of all relevant Football Association Rules, Football League Regulations, the Club Rules for players and any relevant insurance policy applicable to the Player and to provide him with any subsequent amendments to all the above.

7. The Player shall not without the written consent of the Club participate professionally in any other sporting or athletic activity. The Player shall at all times have due regard for the necessity of his maintaining a high standard of physical fitness and agrees not to indulge in any sport, activity or practice that might endanger such fitness. The Player shall not infringe any provision in this regard in any policy of insurance taken out for his benefit or for the benefit of the Club.

8. Any incapacity or sickness shall be reported by the Player to the Club immediately and the Club shall keep a record of any incapacity. The Player shall submit promptly to such medical and dental examinations as the Club may reasonably require and shall undergo, at no expense to himself, such treatment as may be prescribed by the medical or dental advisers of the Club in order to restore the Player to fitness. The Club shall arrange promptly such prescribed treatment and shall ensure that such treatment is undertaken and completed without expense to the Player notwithstanding that this Agreement expires after such treatment has been prescribed.

9. Subject to the provisions of clause 10, in the event that the Player shall become incapacitated by reason of sickness or injury the Club shall, unless provision for the continuation of bonus payments be set out in the schedule to this agreement during the period of incapacity, pay to the Player for the first eight weeks of incapacity his basic wage as specified in the Schedule plus a sum equivalent to the amount of sickness benefit which the Club is able to recoup. After eight weeks of incapacity the Club shall, unless provision for the continuation of bonus payments be set out in the Schedule to this Agreement, pay to the Player his basic wage as specified in the Schedule without reduction for any state sickness or injury benefit that he may receive. The provisions of this Clause apply only to the playing season.
The Player agrees to notify the Club of any sickness benefit received after the end of the playing season in order for the Club to deduct the amount from the Player's gross wage.

10. In the event that the Player shall suffer permanent incapacity the Club shall be entitled to serve a notice upon the Player terminating the Agreement. The Player's minimum entitlement shall be to receive 6 months' notice where the Agreement has not more than 3 years to run with an extra month's notice for each year or part year in excess of the said 3 years, provided that the parties shall be able to negotiate a longer period of notice if they so wish.

The notice may be served at any time after:—

(a) the date on which the Player is declared permanently totally disabled in a case where the Player suffers incapacity within the terms of the Football League Personal Accident Insurance Scheme; or
(b) in any other case, the date on which the incapacity is established by independent medical examination.

11. (a) The Player shall not reside at any place which the Club deems unsuitable for the performance of his duties under this Agreement.
(b) The Player shall not without the previous consent of the Club be engaged either directly or indirectly in any trade, business or occupation other than his employment hereunder.

12. The Player shall be given every opportunity compatible with his obligations under this Agreement to follow courses of further education or vocational training if he so desires. The Club agrees to give the Footballers' Further Education and Vocational Training Society particulars of any such courses undertaken by the Player.

13. The Player shall permit the Club to photograph him as a member of the squad of players and staff of the Club provided that such photographs are for use only as the official photographs of the Club. The Player may, save as otherwise mutually agreed and subject to the overriding obligation contained in the Rules of the Football Association not to bring the game of Association Football into disrepute, contribute to the public media in a responsible manner. The Player shall, whenever circumstances permit, give to the Club reasonable notice of his intention to make such contributions to the public media in order to allow representations to be made to him on behalf of the Club if it so desires.

14. (a) The Player shall not induce or attempt to induce any other Player employed by or registered by the Club, or by any other Football League Club, to leave that employment or cease to be so registered for any reason whatsoever.
(b) The Club and the Player shall arrange all contracts of service and transfers of registration to any other Football Club between themselves and shall make no payment to any other person or agent in this respect.

15. No payment shall be made or received by either the Player or the Club to or from any person or organisation whatsoever as an inducement to win, lose or draw a match except for such payments to be made by the Club to the Player as are specifically provided for in the Schedule to this Agreement.

16. If the Player shall be guilty of serious or persistent misconduct or serious or persistent breach of the Rules of the Club or of the terms and conditions of this Agreement the Club may on giving fourteen days' written notice to the Player terminate this Agreement in accordance with the Rules of the Football Association and the Regulations of the Football League and the Club shall notify the Player in writing of the full reasons for the action taken. Such action shall be subject to the Player's right of appeal (exercisable within seven days of the receipt by the Player of such notice and notification of reasons from the Club) as follows:—

(a) he may appeal to the Management Committee who shall hear the appeal within fourteen days of receipt of the notice of appeal.
(b) either the Club or the Player may appeal against the decision of the Management Committee to the Football League Appeals Committee and such further appeal shall be made within seven days of the receipt of the Management Committee's decision and shall be heard within fourteen days of receipt of the notice of the further appeal.

Any such termination shall be subject to the rights of the parties provided for in the Regulations of the Football League. The Club may at its discretion waive its rights under this Clause and take action under the provisions of Clause 18.

17. If the Club is guilty of serious or persistent breach of the terms and conditions of this Agreement the Player may on giving fourteen days' written notice to the Club terminate this Agreement. The Player shall forward a copy of such notice to the Football League and to the Football Association. The Club shall have a right of appeal as set out in Clause 16(a) mutatis mutandis (exercisable within seven days of the receipt by the Club of such notice from the Player) and the Club or the Player as the case may be shall have a further right of appeal as set out in Clause 16(b).

18. If the Player is guilty of misconduct or a breach of any of the training or disciplinary rules or lawful instructions of the Club or any of the provisions of this Agreement the Club may either impose a fine not exceeding two weeks' basic wages or order the Player not to attend at the Club for a period not exceeding fourteen days. The Club shall inform the Player in writing of the action taken and the full reasons for it and this information shall be recorded in a register held at the Club. The Player shall have a right of appeal as set out in Clause 16(a) (exercisable within seven days of the receipt by the Player of such written notification from the Club) and the Club or the Player as the case may be shall have a further right of appeal as set out in Clause 16(b) of this Agreement. Any penalty imposed by the Club upon the Player shall not become operative until the appeals procedures have been exhausted.

19. In the event of any grievance in connection with his employment under this Agreement the following procedures shall be available to the Player in the order set out:—

(a) the grievance shall be brought informally to the notice of the Manager of the Club in the first instance,
(b) formal notice of the grievance may be given in writing to the Manager of the Club,
(c) if the grievance is not settled to the Player's satisfaction within fourteen days thereafter formal notice of the grievance may be given in writing to the Secretary of the Club so that it may be considered by the Board of Directors or Committee of the Club or by any duly authorised committee or sub-committee thereof. The matter shall thereupon be dealt with by the Board or Committee at its next convenient meeting and in any event within four weeks of receipt of the notice,
(d) if the grievance is not settled by the Club to the Player's satisfaction the Player shall have a right of appeal as set out in Clause 16(a) (exercisable within seven days of the Club notifying the Player of the decision of the Board or Committee) and the Club or the Player as the case may be shall have a further right of appeal as set out in Clause 16(b) of this Agreement.

20. The Player may if he so desires be represented at any personal hearing of an appeal under this Agreement by an official or member of the Professional Footballers' Association.

21. Upon the execution of this Agreement the Club shall effect the Registration of the Player with the Football Association and the Football League in accordance with their Rules and Regulations. Such Registration may be transferred by mutual consent of the Club and the Player during the currency of this Agreement and this Agreement will be deemed to be terminated (but not so as to affect accrued rights) on the Registration by the Football League of such transfer.

22. The Regulations of the Football League as to the re-engagement and transfer of a registration shall apply to the Club and Player both during the currency and after the expiration of this Agreement.

23. The remuneration of the Player shall be set out in a Schedule attached to this Agreement and signed by the parties. The Schedule shall include all remuneration to which the Player is or may be entitled. In the event of any dispute the remuneration set out in the Schedule shall be conclusively deemed to be the full entitlement of the Player.

24. The Player shall be entitled to a minimum of four weeks' paid holiday per year, such holiday to be taken at a time which the Club shall determine. The Player shall not participate in professional football during his holiday.

25. Reference herein to Rules, Regulations or Bye-laws of the Football League, the Football Association, the Club and any other body shall be treated as a reference to those Rules, Regulations or Bye-laws as from time to time amended.

26. All previous agreements between the Club and Player are hereby cancelled.

SCHEDULE

a) The Player's employment with the Club began on the .... 19.......

b) No employment with a previous employer shall count as part of the Player's continous period of employment hereunder.

c) The Player shall become or continue to be and during the continuance of his employment hereunder shall remain a member of The Football League Players' Benefit Scheme (and a member of the .... Pension Scheme) and as such (in the latter case shall be liable to make such contributions and in each case) shall be entitled to such benefits and subject to such conditions as are set out in the definitive Trust Deed or Rules of the Scheme.

d) A contracting out certificate is not in force in respect of the Player's employment under this Agreement.

e) **Basic Wage.**

£.................. per week from .... to ....

£.................. per week from .... to ....

£.................. per week from .... to ....

£.................. per week from .... to ....

f) Any other provisions:—

Signed by the said ....

(Player)

and ....

....

in the presence of (Secretary/Manager/Chairman)

(Signature) ....

(Occupation) ....

(Address) ....

....

CONTRACTS WHICH MUST BE EVIDENCED IN WRITING

The following contracts must be in writing if they are to be enforced in the courts. Technically, without writing they are good contracts but the courts will not enforce them unless the plaintiff has a memorandum in writing signed by the defendant.

1. Contracts of guarantee (Statute of Frauds 1677)

This is a promise to answer for the debt, default or miscarriage of another person. For example, a person may obtain an overdraft (a loan) from a bank on condition that his or her employer or parents may give the bank a guarantee (a promise) to repay the loan if the borrower fails to do so.

2. Contracts for the sale of land (Law of Property Act 1925)

This Act covers any contract for the sale or other disposition of land or any interest in land. The note or memorandum must contain the following information:

(i) the parties (their names and description),
(ii) the property (the subject matter of the contract),
(iii) the price (the consideration),
(iv) any particular or special terms.

There is an exception to this section, in that the equitable doctrine of part performance permits a party who has partly performed the contract to obtain from the court an order of specific performance (see p. 145) to enforce the contract, even though there is no evidence in writing.

Part Performance

Although a contract for sale of land must be evidenced in writing, the doctrine of part performance allows the courts to enforce an oral contract. This doctrine will only be allowed when one party has performed an act which is expressly related to a contract.

Rawlinson v. *Ames* (1925). There was an oral contract for a lease, provided the landlord made certain alterations to the flat.

The tenant later refused to take up the lease after the work was completed, and the court held that a contract was in existence and granted an order of specific performance.

Wakeham v. *MacKenzie* (1968). A widow of 67 agreed orally to look after a man of 72 on the condition that when he died she would have his house and its contents. She gave up her own council flat and moved into the widower's house, paying, as had been agreed, for her own board and heating. When the widower died, it was discovered that there had been no provision in his will for the housekeeper. The plaintiff claimed specific performance for her acts of part performance, and the court held that her acts proved that a contract was in existence and made an order of specific performance.

CONTRACTS WHICH MUST BE MADE BY DEED

A deed is a document which has to have the following formalities:

(i) it must be signed:
(ii) it must be sealed, and
(iii) it must be delivered.

Contracts made by deed are said to be made under seal. In the past the seal was made by melting sealing wax, but now a thin red wafer is usually affixed to the document.

The principal contract which requires the formality of a deed is a lease of land for more than three years. Conveyances of land are made by deed, and the promise of a gift unsupported by consideration (see p. 125) would have to be made under seal to be enforceable.

CONSUMER LAW

Many statutes have been passed to give the consumer certain rights when buying goods or hiring services. In addition, many institutions and bodies have been set up to protect and inform the consumer. The aims of these bodies and statutes are to help the consumer obtain value for money and place the consumer on a more equal standing when bargaining with the more professional and experienced businessman. Previously, English law has tended to follow the doctrine of "*caveat emptor*" (let the buyer beware) and left the buyer to take the goods as he found them. Once the goods had been bought the buyer had no recourse to the courts if they proved unsuitable. To some extent *caveat emptor* still applies, but the Sale of Goods Act and other legislation has eroded this harsh doctrine. One of the reasons for protecting the consumer is that due to the technical development of consumer goods, the ordinary consumer cannot be expected to know if the goods are fit for the purpose for which they were bought, or if they are of good or bad quality. Most companies and firms do give value for money and wish to give to a consumer goods which are serviceable and well made, but there are others who lack such fine intentions. It is to protect the consumer from the latter that the following legislation has been passed:

SALE OF GOODS ACT 1979

This Act consolidates the law relating to the sale of goods, and it repeals the Sale of Goods Act 1893, and certain sections and Schedules of other consumer legislation such as the Misrepresentation Act 1967 and the Supply of Goods (Implied Terms) Act 1973. A contract for sale of goods is a contract whereby the seller transfers or agrees to transfer the ownership of the goods to the buyer for a money consideration (the price) (Section 2).

As the name suggests this Act only deals with contracts for sale of goods and has no effect on other contracts. Goods, within the meaning of the Act may be defined as tangible things which can be physically possessed (cars, hot water bottles, furniture, food, etc.). Things not within the meaning of the Act include land, barter (which is the exchange of goods for goods) and legal rights such as debts, copyrights, patents or trade marks. (The latter group is sometimes referred to as intellectual property.)

Implied Terms

The Act provides that unless the parties agree otherwise there are certain implied conditions and warranties which apply in every contract for sale of goods.

Conditions

A condition is a term of a contract which goes to the root of the contract. In a contract for the sale of a Rolls Royce car, the buyer would expect a car of that make to be delivered; a farmer would expect cattlefood to be delivered which would not poison his cows. If this was not so, a buyer could order, say, a red Liverpool F.C. shirt, but have to accept a white Leeds United shirt. Therefore, if there is a breach of a condition there is no contract and the buyer may treat the contract as ended and return the goods. If it is impossible to return the goods (for example, if only after the cows had eaten the cattlefood, was it discovered the food was poisonous) the buyer may sue for damages.

Warranties

A warranty is not a vital term of the contract and therefore a breach of warranty does not end the contract, but it gives the buyer the right to sue for damages. An example of a breach of warranty would be if the Rolls Royce car was delivered but the cigar lighter was not working properly. This term should not be confused with a guarantee (or warranty) given by manufacturers to repair their goods, if faulty, within a fixed period.

The implied conditions and warranties provided by the Sale of Goods Act 1979 are as follows:

Conditions

1. Implied undertakings as to title
Section 12

(1) An implied condition on the part of the seller that he has the right to sell the goods, and in the case of an agreement to

sell, he will have the right to sell at the time the property (ownership) is to pass.

2. Sales by description

Section 13

(1) Where there is a sale by description, the goods must correspond with the description.

(2) Where sale is by sample as well as by description, the goods must correspond with both.

In *Nichol* v. *Godts* (1854). Nichol agreed to sell "foreign refined rape oil" as per sample. He delivered oil of similar quality, but it was not as described. It was held that Godts could refuse delivery.

(3) A sale of goods shall not be prevented from being a sale by description by reason only that, being exposed for sale or hire, the buyer selects the goods.

This subsection was originally introduced by the Supply of Goods (Implied Terms) Act 1973 to resolve the doubt as to whether or not self-service sales could be sales by description.

3. Undertakings as to quality or fitness

Section 14

(2) Where the seller sells goods in the course of a business, there is an implied condition that goods shall be of merchantable quality, except:

(a) where the defects are specifically drawn to the buyer's attention before the contract is made, or

(b) where the buyer examined the goods before the contract is made, then as regards defects which the examination ought to have revealed, the condition does not apply.

Subsection (6) defines goods as being of merchantable quality if they are fit for the purpose for which goods of that kind are commonly bought, as is reasonable to expect having regard to the description, price and other relevant circumstances.

(3) Where the seller sells goods in the course of a business and the buyer, expressly or by implication makes known to the seller any particular purpose for which the goods are being bought, there is an implied condition that the goods supplied are reasonably fit for that purpose, except:

(i) where circumstances show that the buyer did not rely, or
(ii) that it would have been unreasonable to rely, on the seller's skill or judgment.

In *Grant* v. *Australian Knitting Mills Ltd.* (1936) a doctor bought a pair of woollen underpants and contracted dermatitis when they were worn. The wool contained a chemical which should have been removed before the sale. It was held that the sellers were liable because the buyer had made known the purpose for which the goods were required and they were neither fit for this purpose, nor of merchantable quality.

4. Sale by sample

Section 15

(2) Where sale is by sample, there is an implied condition that:

(i) The bulk shall correspond with the sample in quality.
(ii) The buyer shall have reasonable opportunity of comparing bulk with sample.
(iii) The goods shall be free from defects rendering them unmerchantable, which would not be apparent on reasonable inspection.

Godley v. *Perry* (1960) is an interesting case in that it involved sections 14 and 15. The plaintiff, aged six, bought a catapult which broke when used and injured his eye. The rubber of the catapult had a defect which was not apparent upon reasonable examination. The shopkeeper was held liable in breach of section 14 because the catapult was not of merchantable quality (it was bought by description) and, as a boy aged six relied on the seller's skill and judgment, it was not fit for the purpose for which it was required.

The shopkeeper claimed an indemnity from the wholesaler, who supplied the goods and the court held that as the goods had been bought in bulk by sample the suppliers were in breach of section 15 and liable to indemnify the shopkeeper.

5. Implied warranties

Section 12

(2) The goods shall be free from any charge or encumbrance not disclosed or known by the buyer. The buyer will enjoy

quiet possession of the goods except to a person disclosed or known at the time of making the contract.

Exclusion clause

Section 6 of the Unfair Contract Terms Act 1977 provides that when a person deals as a consumer the seller may not exclude any of the implied terms. "Consumer sales" means a sale of goods bought for private use or consumption, where the buyer does not buy them in the ordinary course of business. With sales in the course of business (*e.g.* a sale by a manufacturer to a retailer, where the goods will be resold), sections 13, 14 and 15 may be excluded, but the exclusion clause may not be enforced, if it could be shown that it would not be fair or reasonable to rely on such a clause.

The implied condition in section 12 may not be excluded or varied in any contract.

Passing the Ownership of the Goods

It is important to know when ownership passes, because between the time of making the contract and the time fixed for delivery, the goods may be destroyed and one party will have to suffer the loss.

Unless it is agreed otherwise, ownership and responsibility for the goods (the risk) pass at the same time. If the buyer and seller do not clearly state the time they intended passing the ownership, the Act provides rules to help find the parties' intention. The rules depend on whether the goods are specific or unascertained.

Specific Goods

Specific goods are identified and agreed upon at the time of making the contract. For example, a seller offers to sell a Ford car, registration number D123 BC, which the buyer accepts.

Ownership of specific goods passes as follows:

Section 18

Rule 1. When goods are in a deliverable state, the ownership passes at the time of making the contract. It is immaterial if time of payment and/or delivery be at a later date.

Rule 2. When goods are not in a deliverable state and the seller is bound to do something to put the goods into a deliverable state the ownership does not pass until this thing has been done and the buyer has been informed.

Rule 3. When goods in a deliverable state have to be weighed, measured, tested or other such things by the seller to ascertain the price, the ownership does not pass until this has been done and the buyer has been informed.

Rule 4. When goods have been delivered on approval, or on a sale or return or other similar terms, the goods do not pass until:

(i) The buyer signifies his approval or keeps the goods beyond the agreed time, or beyond a reasonable time if no limit was agreed, or

(ii) The buyer, by his conduct, adopts the goods (*e.g*. sells or pawns the goods, thereby acting as the owner).

Unascertained Goods

Unascertained goods or future goods are sold by description and at the time of sale have not been identified. For example, a contract for the sale of 10 gallons of oil from a lorry with 500 gallons in the tank.

Rule 5. The ownership of unascertained goods passes when goods of that description and in a deliverable state are unconditionally appropriated to the contract by the seller with the assent of the buyer, or vice versa. The assent may be expressed or implied.

In the above example, when 10 gallons of oil have been poured and separated from the bulk, it has been ascertained and appropriated to the contract.

Supply of Goods and Services Act 1982

The definition of a contract for sale of goods (p. 153) explains the need for a consideration of money, the price. It points out that the Sale of Goods Act 1979 does not cover transactions where money does not pass in the contract, and gives barter as an example (goods for goods).

The Supply of Goods and Services Act 1982, gives protection for contracts which relate to the supply of goods and services but were not covered by the 1979 Act. The Act gives protection, similar to the implied terms in sections 12-15 of the Sale of Goods Act.

The 1982 Act relates to the following contracts:

1. Contracts for the transfer of goods

Contracts under this heading would include barter, offer of goods for tokens or packets (*e.g.* "Send 10 chocolate wrappers for a free record") and offers of free goods in respect of a service ("anyone who introduces a new customer will receive a free kettle").

Goods received as a result of similar contracts would be covered by the implied terms.

2. Contracts of Hire

Such contracts do not include hire purchase contracts (where the goods will eventually become the property of the hirer). Contracts of hire occur when a person has the temporary possession of another's goods. For example, cars, tools, tents, etc. A fee is paid for the loan and the goods are later returned to the owner. While the goods are in his possession the hirer has the benefit of the rights similar to the implied terms of the 1973 Act.

3. Contracts for services

A contract for services (with or without the supply of goods) is subject to the following implied terms where the supplier of a service is acting in the course of a business:

(i) The service will be carried out with reasonable care and skill.

(ii) Where a time for the service to be carried out is not agreed beforehand, the service will be carried out within a reasonable time.

(iii) Where the consideration for the service has not been decided beforehand the supplier will receive a reasonable charge.

In these matters what is reasonable is a question of fact.

An example of how the above Act may work would be an electrician installing a new socket. The supplying of the socket would be subject to the implied terms of the Sale of Goods Act 1979, but supplying the service of installation would be covered by the Supply of Goods and Services Act 1982.

The Act does not cover the services of an advocate in court or tribunal, or the services of a director to the company for which he acts in that capacity. The Secretary of State has power to make other exceptions.

Nemo Dat Quod Non Habet

The rule of law that "no one can give what he has not got" when applied to sale of goods means that a seller cannot give to the purchaser a better title than he has himself. If Tom owns a pen and sells it to Dick, Dick obtains a good title of ownership. But if the pen is then stolen and the thief sells it to Harry, Harry would not own the pen because the thief did not have a good title. The pen would still be owned by Dick and he could claim it back from Harry.

Exceptions to "Nemo Dat" Rule

It can be seen from the above example that with such a sale, one innocent party will suffer; either the real owner or the purchaser. The Sale of Goods Act and other statutes provide exceptions to the general rule. In all the following cases the buyers receive a good title:

1. Estoppel (Section 21)

An owner who is aware that his goods are being sold by a person without a good title and does not inform the buyer, will later be estopped from denying the seller's right to sell.

2. Market overt (section 22)

This rule affects transactions in open markets, and only relates to shops in the City of London, and markets which have been established by custom, statute or Charter. A buyer in market overt will obtain a good title if he purchased for value and without notice of the seller's defect in title. The sale must take place in a public part of a shop which usually deals with the type of goods being sold, and within the usual times of business. Therefore a sale of a diamond ring at the back of a fish stall at midnight, would not be a sale in market overt and the buyer would not get a good title.

3. Sales by persons with voidable titles (section 23)

A sale by a person with a voidable title, will give the buyer a good title provided (a) the seller's title had not been avoided at the time of sale, and (b) the buyer had no knowledge of the seller's defect of title and acted in good faith (see p. 136).

4. Seller or buyer in possession after sale (sections 24 and 25)

If a seller allows the buyer to obtain possession of the goods or documents of title before payment, a sale by the original buyer gives the new purchaser a good title. Similarly, if the seller retains possession of the goods to another purchaser, the second purchaser gets a good title in preference to the original buyer. Obviously, the moral to be derived from this exception is do not part with goods until you have been paid or if you have paid for goods, take possession as soon as possible.

5. Factors (Factors Act (1889), s.2)

A factor is a mercantile agent, whose ordinary business is to sell goods in his possession. A sale by a factor, even if he has no authority to sell, gives the buyer a good title, provided the owner deposited the goods with the factor and the buyer acted in good faith.

6. Motor vehicles subject to hire-purchase agreement

A private purchaser (not a person in the motor trade) will obtain a good title to a motor vehicle which is subject to a hire-purchase agreement or conditional sale agreement provided the buyer had no knowledge of the agreement and acted in good faith.

Rights of Action by the Seller and Buyer

A seller and buyer have the usual remedies for breach of contract (see p. 143). The Sale of Goods Act lays down the following rights of action:

1. The seller

(i) For the price.
When the ownership in the goods has passed to a buyer who refuses to pay for the goods, the seller has a right of action for the price of the goods (s.49).

(ii) Damages for non-acceptance.
When the buyer wrongly refuses to accept and pay for the goods, the seller has a right of action for damages for non-acceptance (s.50).

2. The buyer

(i) When the seller does not deliver the goods, there is a right of action against the seller for:
   (a) recovery of the price if paid beforehand,
   (b) damages for non-delivery of goods. (s.51)
   (c) a decree of specific performance. (s.52)
   The goods would have to be unique or for a special or specific purpose (see p. 145).

(ii) When there is a breach of warranty by the seller, there is a right of action for damages. (s.53).

(iii) When there is a breach of condition by the seller, there is a right of action for rescission and/or damages.

THE UNFAIR CONTRACT TERMS ACT 1977

This Act, which became effective on February 1, 1978, affects many of the terms and exclusion clauses used in contracts between businesses and consumers, and improves (a) a consumer's protection when buying goods or services, and (b) the legal position of the consumer when entering or using business premises.

The Act provides the following protection to consumers:

(i) Generally, a business cannot exclude by contract or by notice, liability for negligence resulting in a consumer's death or personal injury.

(ii) A contract may not exclude or restrict a business' liability for breach of contract or claim that it may perform the contract in a way substantially different from what was agreed. As a result of this Act for example, a holidaymaker is entitled to be booked into the hotel and resort stipulated in the contract, and the travel company may not unreasonably exclude this right.

(iii) A manufacturer's guarantee may not exclude or restrict liability for negligence to a consumer which results in loss or damage.

(iv) The implied conditions in the Sale of Goods Act 1979 (with the exception of condition of title) are similarly available to consumers of goods obtained under hire, rental, and similar contracts, and under contracts for work and materials. Clauses excluding these conditions are subject to a test of reasonableness.

(v) A business may exclude or restrict liability for negligence (other than death or personal injury), but the clause must be reasonable as between the parties.

The effect of this Act is that it protects consumers, when buying goods or services, from unreasonable contractual exclusion clauses or terms, and it protects consumers from injury to their person or property by the unreasonable negligence of businessmen or their employees. For example, a garage would be liable if its employees were unreasonably negligent and damaged your car. The garage may no longer exclude such liability.

THE CONSUMER CREDIT ACT 1974

This Act, which covers most aspects of buying and hiring on

credit, was passed on July 31, 1974, but came into being in stages, with different provisions in the Act being introduced by statutory instrument, the final stage was introduced in May 1985.

Many other Acts are replaced, such as the Hire-Purchase Acts, the Money Lenders Act and the Pawnbrokers Act, while other statutes which affect consumer credit are amended. Any provider of credit who does not comply with the Act will not be able to enforce the debt.

The Act concerns itself with "regulated agreements," and therefore it is necessary to know what this term means, and any exemptions that are not covered by the Act. A regulated consumer credit agreement exists when credit not exceeding £15,000 is provided for an individual, and it is not an exempt agreement. The meaning of "credit" under the Act is very wide, and covers cash advances or loans, hire-purchase, credit sales, conditional sales, credit cards and trading cheques.

There are five exemptions to consumer credit agreements: (i) traders who grant normal trade credit are exempt. It is normal in trade for trade customers to pay all the credit transactions of the period (usually a month) by one payment; (ii) agreements involving low cost credit are exempt, provided that no supplier is involved and the agreement is solely between a debtor and a creditor. The charge for credit must not exceed 13 per cent., or the Bank of England Minimum Lending Rate plus 1 per cent., if this is higher than 13 per cent. An example of a debtor and creditor agreement would be between a bank and a customer, where the customer may spend the loan anywhere or anyway he chooses; (iii) finance for foreign trade; (iv) loans for land transactions which are settled in four instalments or less; (v) mortgages.

The Act requires traders to show the true cost of credit, and all advertisements, whether in shopwindows or in the mass media, must show the A.P.R. This means the Annual Percentage Rate of the total charge for credit. Consumers can easily see which traders are giving the lowest terms of credit, as it includes all costs that the consumer will have to pay.

The Agreement

The debtor must be made aware of all the regulations as required by the Act. An agreement would be unenforceable without this requirement, or if it was not made in the following way:

(i) in writing,
(ii) containing all the express terms in legible form with no small print,
(iii) complying with the provisions of the Act as to form and content,
(iv) signed by the debtor and creditor, or their representatives.

A copy of the agreement must be given to the customer immediately if signed by the creditor, or, if not signed, it must be sent within seven days of the date of the agreement.

Default Notice

If a debtor is in breach of the agreement, the creditor cannot exercise his rights unless a default notice has been given to the debtor. The notice gives details of the breach, the action the creditor intends to take and the time limit, which must not be less than seven days. Should the debtor not comply with the provisions of the notice, the creditor has the right to:

(i) end the agreement,
(ii) demand earlier payment,
(iii) consider that any right of the debtor is terminated,
(iv) recover the property,
(v) enforce any security.

Regardless of the creditor's rights as above, a court order is needed if the goods are "protected." Protected goods are concerned with a regulated hire-purchase or conditional sale agreement, and the debtor has paid more than one-third of the price and has not terminated the agreement.

Credit card holders are liable for a charge of £50 if their cards are lost or stolen and used fraudulently. This liability ends once the credit company has been informed of the loss.

Termination

Section 99 provides that a debtor under a regulated hire-purchase or conditional sale agreement may terminate the agreement if he has paid:

(i) all sums due (including arrears), and
(ii) one-half of the price, or less if the court so orders,
(iii) compensation, if the debtor has not taken reasonable care of the property.

The debtor may pay off the whole debt before the date agreed, and will be entitled to a rebate of the interest or charges due to be paid.

Section 37 provides that a debtor may cancel a regulated agreement, if notice of the cancellation is given before the end of the fifth day following the day on which he received the copy of the agreement provided that:

(i) the agreement was signed at any place other than the place of business of the creditor or his associates.
(ii) in negotiations before the agreement was signed, oral representations were made to the debtor by a person acting as a negotiator.

The Consumer Credit Act 1974 is a very complex piece of legislation, made more difficult to understand by the way in which it has been introduced, step-by-step. It has a great effect on most people as consumer credit is very much a part of modern life. The foregoing paragraphs are only an introduction to the Act, and it is suggested that before making a credit agreement (or taking an examination) advice is sought from a Citizens Advice Bureau or Consumer Advice Centre, on the current situation regarding introduction of this Act. There are excellent booklets and leaflets on all aspects of the Act, available at the offices mentioned above.

CONTRACTS OF EMPLOYMENT

A contract of employment is created when an employee starts to work for an employer. The same essentials of a contract apply to a contract of employment as to a contract for sale of goods. The usual employer/employee relationship is known as a contract of service by which a person called the employee or servant, works for another called the employer or master. This form of employment should not be confused with a contract for services, which is the employment of an independent contractor. If a painter is hired to paint your house, you may say what has to be done but not how. This is because there is a contract for his services, not a contract of employment. The painter does not work for you; he either works for himself or is employed by a firm of painters. The difference between the two contracts may best be summed up to the effect that, in a contract of service, the employee is part of the employer's business, and certain duties are owed by each party to the other. In contracts for services however, the independent contractor is outside the employer's business.

The Nature of the Contract

With the majority of contracts there is freedom by both parties to negotiate or bargain for terms and conditions. With contracts of employment, however, there is often less freedom than would be expected.

An employer, particularly in times of high unemployment, may stipulate the wages and conditions of work, and employees have no opportunity to bargain because it may be a matter of "take it or leave it." If the terms offered are not accepted, they will not be employed.

On the other side, trade unions may have agreed conditions with employers' organisations which have to be followed by both employer and employee, and in such cases neither may be able to bargain for different conditions and wages.

A third agent has, in comparatively recent years, intervened to erode the principle of freedom of contract. There have been successive Acts of Parliament regulating contracts of employment. The Acts, in the main, aimed to protect the employee, giving new rights and greater job security and encouraging collective bargaining.

The main legislation is the Employment Protection (Consolidation) Act 1978, as amended by the Employment Act 1982.

It is probable that the lack of freedom of contract in regard to contracts of employment now works to the benefit of the employee, in that the employer is not able to dictate conditions and terms, but has in many cases, to accept what has previously been collectively agreed.

Form of Contract

As with other contracts, contracts of employment may be by word of mouth, but the Act lays a duty on an employer to give a written statement to an employee within 13 weeks of starting work on matters such as pay, hours, holidays, pensions, sick pay, notice and disciplinary rules and procedures which apply to the employee. The aim of this section is to give employees particulars of their rights and conditions of employment which can be used as evidence of the terms and conditions of an unwritten contract.

Duties of Employer

The duties owed by an employer to his employees are governed by common law and statute.

The most usual duties are:

(*a*) *To pay wages as agreed*

If the rate of pay was not agreed beforehand, the parties may look at external conditions to reach an agreed wage, such as union rates of pay, or the usual rate for the particular type of work.

Most manual workers are entitled to receive wages in cash but the Payment of Wages Act 1960 permits employees to request payment by cheque or by transfer to a bank account.

The Employment Protection (Consolidation) Act 1978 provides that all employees, whether manual or non-manual workers and regardless of the method of payment, are entitled to receive from their employers an itemised pay statement, in writing. The statement must show:

(i) the gross amount of wages or salary,

(ii) any fixed deductions (trade union subscriptions, savings, etc.),
(iii) variable deductions (taxes, pensions),
(iv) the net payment and the method of payment (cash, cheque or paid into bank account).

(*b*) *To indemnify against liability and loss*

An employee, properly performing the duties of employment, is entitled to be indemnified by the employer for any loss or liability incurred (see vicarious liability p. 201).

(*c*) *To provide a safe system of work*

The common law and many statutes place a duty on an employer to provide a safe place to work and safe appliances to work with.

The Health and Safety at Work, etc., Act 1974, for example, places a duty on every employer to ensure, so far as is reasonably practicable, the health, safety and welfare of all his employees. This Act, which became effective from October 1, 1975, will eventually replace or amend the Factories Acts and other such legislation. It is a comprehensive Act, covering all places of work and protects not only most workers, but also the public against risks arising out of the activities of people at work.

There is a Health and Safety Commission and an Executive, which are responsible for the administration and implementation of the Act. Inspectors visit places of work and give advice on the requirements of the Act; failure to comply with the provisions may lead to severe penalties, including imprisonment.

(*d*) *References*

There is no legal duty for an employer to give a reference to an ex-employee, but if one is given, the employer is subject to the law of defamation. Therefore, a false statement may be actionable, but a statement of opinion which is critical of the employee's ability would not be actionable if made without malice. This is because the employer has a duty to other employers, and provided he does not act in spite or with an improper motive (malice) the employer has qualified privilege and would not be liable. The practice of giving references "To whom it may concern" is now declining, and being replaced by confidential references from the current employer to the prospective employer.

Duties of Employee

(*a*) *Obedience*

It is the employee's duty to obey a lawful order, and refusal to do so may justify immediate dismissal without notice. Generally, a single act of disobedience would not warrant dismissal without notice. However, the facts of particular cases need to be examined, so that when a gardener refused to plant flowers, which died as a result, it was held to be grounds for instant dismissal.

(*b*) *To show good faith*

An employee has a duty to work in the best interests of the employer, and the employee's interests should not conflict with those of the employer. For example, a company's buyer should purchase goods on the best terms for his employer, and any secret profit or bribe received from a salesman to persuade the buyer to purchase goods on less favourable terms is legally the property of the employer, and failure to disclose the bribe gives the employer the right to dismiss the employee.

It is also a duty of an employee not to disclose confidential information gained from the employment, which is likely to cause the employer to suffer. If, however, an employee discloses the employer's illegal activities, the courts would consider the duty to the public interest to be more important than the duty to the employer.

It is generally considered that an employee has no duty to disclose his own misconduct or breach of contract, but in *Sybron Corporation* v. *Rochem Ltd.* (1983), the Court of Appeal held that an employee, with certain standing and authority, may have a duty to disclose misconduct of other employees, whether they be of higher or lower positions in the company's staffing hierarchy.

Termination of Employment

(*a*) *With notice*

If a contract of employment has provided for employment to be for a particular period, the contract is terminated at the end of that period. Contracts of professional footballers are usually for a fixed period, but often give either party the option of renewing the contract for a further period.

The usual contract of employment is terminated by either party giving notice. The length of time varies, and may be stated at the commencement of employment. For example, teachers agree to give two or three months' notice on specified dates so that replacements may be appointed in time for the start of the next term. If the period is not agreed beforehand, a reasonable period of notice has to be given, taking into consideration the nature of employment. In the past, the courts have considered that reasonable notice for a newspaper editor was one year, and for a theatrical manager, six months.

The 1978 Act as amended by the Employment Act 1982, provides that most employees are entitled to minimum periods of notice as follows:

(i) after four weeks' continuous service - one week,
(ii) after two years' continuous service - two weeks, and
(iii) for every additional year's service - one week, up to a maximum of 12 weeks.

An employee is required to give at least one week's notice if employed continuously for one month or more. This notice is unaffected by longer service.

(*b*) *Without notice*

Termination by either party without notice ends the contract of employment, and gives the injured party the right to bring an action for damages. It should be noted that this applies to employee and employer. If an employee leaves without notice, the employer may sue if it can be shown that he suffered damages as a result of the employee's illegal termination of the contract of employment. In practice this rarely happens and it is usually the employee who brings an action for dismissal without notice.

Summary dismissal without notice may be considered lawful

if the employee breaks the terms of the contract of employment. The terms may be implied in respect of acts of disobedience, dishonesty, incompetence or misbehaviour.

A dismissed employee who has been continuously employed for 26 weeks or more, has the right to request from the employer a written statement giving particulars of the reasons for dismissal.

(c) Unfair dismissal and employees' rights

Comprehensive procedures to enable employees who have been unfairly dismissed to complain to an industrial tribunal are provided by the Acts. The Acts apply to most employees who work full-time or part-time and who have worked for more than 52 weeks continuously and for not less than 16 hours per week.

The main provisions are as follows:

(i) The right to complain applies to dismissals with or without notice, and where the employee is forced to resign, because of the employer's conduct.

(ii) The employee must make a complaint of unfair dismissal within three months of the effective date of termination.

(iii) The employee has the opportunity of choosing, should the complaint be successful, to continue working for the employer or receiving financial compensation.

Financial compensation, when unfair dismissal is proved, usually consists of a basic award of a number of weeks' pay, plus a compensatory award, which the tribunal considers just and equitable. There are limits to amounts awarded.

(iv) The following may be considered fair reasons for dismissal:

  (a) the lack of capacity of qualification of the employee to carry on working,
  (b) redundancy,
  (c) the employee's conduct,
  (d) where the continued employment of the employee would be illegal, or in breach of a statutory duty or requirement,
  (e) some other substantial reason justifying dismissal.

(v) The following are considered unfair reasons for dismissal:
   (a) trade union membership or activity,
   (b) pregnancy,
   (c) industrial dispute, when other employees involved are not dismissed.

Sex and Race Discrimination

The Equal Pay Act 1970 provided that women should receive the same pay and benefits as men for like work or for work which is rated as similar or equivalent to work done by men. A woman has a right of action to sue for breach of contract if an employer is in default of this requirement.

The Sex Discrimination Act 1975 makes it illegal, with certain exceptions, for employers to discriminate on the grounds of sex. The Act, which applies to most forms of employers, professions, training and employment agencies, covers such things as recruitment, promotion, training and social and fringe benefits. The Act also covers sex discrimination in education, housing and the like.

It should be noted that sex discrimination does not only apply to women, but is available to men who have been discriminated against on the grounds of sex.

The Act does not apply in employment:

(a) in private homes,
(b) when the number of employees in an establishment is less than six,
(c) where a particular sex is necessary for the job (a man would be required to play Superman in films and conversely a woman to play Wonderwoman).

Racial Discrimination

The Race Relations Act 1976 makes it illegal for employers to discriminate on grounds of race, colour or nationality. This Act covers most forms of discrimination as shown above in sex discrimination, and relates to housing, education, training, membership of professions, trade unions and the right to public services and facilities. With relation to employment it does not apply:

(a) in private homes,
(b) when the discrimination can be shown to be a genuine occupation qualification.

Complaints against racial discrimination in employment are brought before certain county courts, or the industrial tribunal.

Revision Test

1. Name six essentials of a contract.

2. Name five ways by which an offer may be terminated.

3. Which two types of contracts are binding on a minor?

4. Which contracts made by a minor are void?

5. Name four ways by which a contract is discharged.

6. Name four remedies for breach of contract.

7. Name four implied conditions provided by the Sale of Goods Act 1979.

Specimen Questions

1. What are the essentials of a contract?

2. Explain the elements which are necessary to distinguish a binding contract from an agreement.

3. Discuss the legal position of the parties in the following situations;
   (a) David offers to sell his cricket bat to Nick for £50. Nick says he will buy for £45. David refuses to sell and Nick then agrees to accept David's original offer.
   (b) Smith Motors Ltd. have a car in their window with a £500 price ticket on the windscreen which should have read £1500. Peter enters the garage and accepts the offer at £500. Smith Motors refuse to sell the car at this amount.

4. Explain the different ways by which an offer may be terminated.

5. What is meant by valuable consideration? Explain the importance of consideration in the law of contract.

6. Jim was rescued from the sea by Linda and he promised to pay her £50. He later refused to pay. Explain to Linda her legal rights to claim the £50.

7. Michael aged 17, went to work away from home:
   (a) he took a one year lease on a flat at an annual rent of £1000 p.a., and moved in, paying one quarter's rent in advance;
   (b) he bought five suits on credit at £60 each; and
   (c) borrowed £2000 after representing that he was 21 years old.

   Explain the legal consequences, if
   (i) after six months he wishes to terminate the lease;
   (ii) refused to pay for the suits; and
   (iii) spent all the £2000 on a holiday.

8. Explain the ways by which a contract may be discharged.

9. Give examples of contracts that are illegal because (i) they are against the law; (ii) they are against public policy.

10. (a) Explain the nature of a contract of hire purchase.
    (b) Debbie enters a hire-purchase agreement for a video set but found she could not afford the instalments. What remedies are available to the company who financed the transaction?

11. Explain the duties owed by an employee to an employer and by an employer to an employee.

12. Explain the implied condition in contracts for sale of goods. May these conditions be excluded?

13. When an employee is dismissed, what are considered to be:
    (a) fair reasons for dismissal and
    (b) unfair reasons for dismissal.

Chapter 7

THE LAW OF TORTS

Tort is a french word meaning a wrong. It is a civil wrong, as opposed to a crime, because it is committed by a private person against another private person. A tort has been defined as a "civil wrong, other than a breach of contract or a breach of trust." The terms of a contract or trust are agreed beforehand by the parties, and a breach of the terms by one party gives the other a right of action. A tort, however, is a duty fixed by law which affects all persons. For example, all road users have a duty not to act negligently. They do not agree beforehand not to injure each other; the duty or liability not to be negligent is fixed by law. A pedestrian who jay-walks and causes injury to a motor-cyclist will be liable to compensate the motor-cyclist for the injury suffered, in the same way as a car driver who negligently damages another car will be liable for the cost of the damage.

The usual remedy for tort is damages, but with certain torts other remedies such as injunctions are necessary because damages would not be an adequate compensation.

It is possible for one event to be a breach of contract, a crime and a tort. For example, David hires Michael to drive Peter to the station, and Michael exceeds the speed limit, crashes and injures Peter. Michael could be liable for:

(a) an action by David for breach of contract,
(b) an action by Peter for the tort of negligence and
(c) a criminal prosecution for dangerous driving.

Malice

The intention or motive with which an act is committed is generally unimportant when deciding whether or not the act is tortious. A wrong intention will not make a lawful act into an unlawful one. In *Bradford Corporation* v. *Pickles* (1895), the Corporation obtained water from springs fed by undefined channels through Pickles' land. In order to coerce the Corporation to buy the land at a high price, Pickles sank a shaft which interfered with the flow of water. The plaintiffs sought an injunction to restrain Pickles from collecting the underground water, but the court held that the defendant had the right to draw water from his own land. The motive behind his act was irrelevant.

Malice, however, in the sense of improper motive, is an essential requirement or an important factor in the following torts:

(*a*) *Malicious prosecution*. This tort is committed when one party, out of spite, brings an unjust criminal prosecution against the other party.

(*b*) *Injurious falsehood*. This tort occurs when a party makes a deliberate false statement with the intention that the other shall suffer loss or damage.

(*c*) *Conspiracy*. When two or more persons conspire together to injure another person.

(*d*) *Defamation*. Malice can defeat certain defences (see p. 200).

(*e*) *Nuisance*. Malice may turn a reasonable use of one's own property into an illegal use (see p. 194).

STRICT LIABILITY

A person is generally liable in tort when an act is done (i) intentionally (*e.g.* trespass) or (ii) negligently. In some cases, however, a person may be liable when he acts neither intentionally nor negligently. In these instances the law has imposed a strict limit on a person's activities, and if this limit is exceeded the defendant is strictly or absolutely liable. The most common example of such liability is known as the Rule in *Rylands* v. *Fletcher* (1868). The rule applies when:

(i) a person brings on to his land for his own purpose some dangerous thing, which is not naturally there (water, wild animals, gas, fire),
(ii) the dangerous thing escapes from the land, (strict liability does not apply if the injury occurs on your own land), and
(iii) causes damage.

If these three events occur the occupier of land is liable for the damage caused, but the following defences may be used:

(i) The untoward event was caused by the act of a stranger.
(ii) It was the plaintiff's own fault.
(iii) It was an act of God.
(iv) There was statutory authority.

NEGLIGENCE

A plaintiff must prove three things to succeed in an action for negligence. 1. The defendant owed the plaintiff a legal duty; 2. There was a breach of that duty; 3. The plaintiff suffered damage.

1. Duty owed to the plaintiff

In *Donoghue* v. *Stevenson* (1932), the plaintiff drank ginger beer from an opaque (dark glass) bottle, in which there was a decomposed snail which caused the plaintiff to be ill. The House of Lords held that a manufacturer of goods is liable if the goods are used by a consumer without an intermediate examination, because the manufacturer owes the consumer a duty of care.

Probably the most important principle to emerge from the judgment came in the definition of Lord Atkin, of who is owed a duty of care. "You must take reasonable care to avoid acts or omissions which you can reasonably foresee would be likely to injure your neighbour." My neighbours are " . . . persons who are so directly affected by my act that I ought reasonably to have them in contemplation . . . "

The neighbour principle has been used in many different situations, for example to show that a duty of care was owed to (i) a lady locked in a public lavatory, (ii) wearers of underpants who caught dermatitis from a chemical in the material, (iii) persons living in the neighbourhood of an open borstal, (iv) the users of a defective hair-dye.

To succeed in an action for negligence a plaintiff must show that a duty of care was owed by the defendant.

In *Bourhill* v. *Young* (1943), a motor-cyclist crashed and was fatally injured. A pregnant fishwife, who was 15 yards away, later looked at the scene of the accident and the sight of the blood caused shock and, subsequently, a miscarriage. The House of Lords held that the lady was not owed a duty of care because it could not reasonably be foreseen that the accident would cause her to suffer such injuries.

In *King* v. *Phillips* (1953) the Court of Appeal held that a mother was not owed a duty of care, when, after hearing her child scream and seeing the child's tricycle under a taxi, she suffered shock. In fact the child was not hurt.

The defendant might be liable if aware that the plaintiff was nearby. In *Boardman* v. *Sanderson* (1964) the defendant negligently backed his car and injured the plaintiff's son. The plaintiff, who was nearby, heard his son's screams and suffered shock. It was held that the plaintiff could recover damages because the defendant was aware the plaintiff was nearby and the consequence of the accident was reasonably foreseeable.

The decision in *McLoughlin* v. *O'Brian* (1983) should be considered carefully. A mother visited a hospital to see her husband and daughters, injured in a serious road accident, and as a result of what she saw and the account she heard from witnesses, she suffered severe nervous shock. The House of Lords held that although distance and time were factors to be considered they were not legal restrictions. The plaintiff was entitled to damages for nervous shock, even though she was not present at the accident, because it was a reasonably foreseeable consequence of the defendant's negligence.

2. A breach of duty

Defendants will be in breach of duty if they have not acted reasonably. The standard of care varies with each situation, but as a general rule, the standard of care is that of a reasonable person who uses ordinary care and skill.

The courts will consider the risk involved. In *Paris* v. *Stepney Borough Council* (1951), the plaintiff had only one eye and the defendants employed him on work that involved a certain risk to the eyes, although not sufficient to warrant ordinary workers to wear goggles. Paris was blinded as a result of his work and the court held that the defendants were in breach of their duty to that particular worker.

A professional person must use the skill expected of the profession, therefore in *Carmarthenshire C.C.* v. *Lewis* (1955) a teacher was dressing young children before taking them out, when a four-year-old under her control left the school premises and ran into the road. A lorry driver was killed when swerving to avoid the child. The court held that the teacher was not negligent, but the county council had been negligent in allowing a situation to arise in which the child could leave the school.

A duty of care is not owed as a matter of public policy by a participant to a crime, to a partner in the crime. In *Ashton* v. *Turner and Another* (1980) the plaintiff and defendants had been drinking together and the second defendant allowed Turner to drive his car without insurance. Ashton and Turner later committed burglary and when driving away from the crime had an accident which injured Ashton (the passenger). Turner pleaded guilty to dangerous driving and driving while drunk. Ashton claimed damages against both defendants and the court held that as a matter of public policy the plaintiff was not owed a duty of care when injured during the commission of a crime. The court also held that Turner could successfully plead the defence of *volenti non fit injuria* (see p. 203).

3. Damage has been suffered

Although a plaintiff must prove damage, not all damage is actionable if it is too remote. The general rule is that a defendant is only liable for damages that a reasonable man should foresee.

In *The Wagon Mound Case* (1961), oil was negligently spilt from a ship and floated across Sydney Harbour to a ship repairers, where sparks ignited the oil and caused damage to the wharf and to a ship. At that time it was not foreseeable that the oil would be set alight and cause the damage, and the Judicial Committee of the Privy Council held that there was no liability.

This decision was followed in *Doughty* v. *Turner Manufacturing Co.* (1964). The plaintiff was injured when a fellow worker dropped an asbestos cement cover into molten liquid. An explosion followed and the plaintiff was injured. It was discovered later that a chemical reaction would be caused by the cement and molten liquid. The Court of Appeal held that the accident was unforeseeable and the defendants were not liable.

It must be stressed that the plaintiff must suffer damage. A person cannot be sued in negligence just because he acted negligently. The negligent act must injure the plaintiff.

Res ipsa loquitur (*the facts speak for themselves*)

It is a general rule of law that a plaintiff must prove that the defendant has been negligent. In cases, however, where the act or omission obviously indicates negligence, the burden of proof moves to the defendant who must shown that, in fact, he was not negligent. This rule has been applied where:

(i) Bags of sugar fell on the plaintiff from an upper floor of a warehouse. *Scott* v. *London & St. Katherine's Dock Co.* (1865).

(ii) Swabs were left in a patient after an operation. *Mahon* v. *Osborne* (1939).

(iii) A customer slipped on yoghurt which had spilled on to the floor of a supermarket. *Ward* v. *Tesco Stores Ltd.* (1976).

The application of the rule does not automatically mean that the defendant was negligent, but it is presumed that the act or omission was negligent, unless it can be shown otherwise. In *Pearson* v. *N.W. Gas Board* (1968), a gas explosion killed the plaintiff's husband and destroyed her home. The court applied the rule, but the defendants were able to show that severe frost caused the gas leak and, as there was no reasonable way in which the explosion could have been prevented, they were not negligent.

Contributory Negligence

The Law Reform (Contributory Negligence) Act 1945 provides that where a person suffers damage which is partly his own fault and partly the fault of another, the injured party will be able to claim damages, but the amount recoverable shall be reduced to the extent that the court considers just and equitable, having regard to the claimant's responsibility for the damage.

In practice the court usually awards damages and then reduces the award by the percentage the plaintiff is deemed to be responsible.

For example, suppose a motor-cyclist suffered injuries caused by the negligence of a motorist and was awarded £5,000 damages. This amount would be reduced if it could be shown that the plaintiff contributed to the damage suffered to the extent of 20 per cent. of the blame, by not wearing a crash helmet. The damages received by the motor-cyclist would be £4,000 (*i.e.* £5,000 less 20 per cent.).

In *Sayers* v. *Harlow U.D.C.* (1958), the plaintiff entered a public toilet and, because of a faulty lock, could not open the door to get out. She was due to catch a bus, so in order to climb over the door she stepped on to the toilet-roll, slipped, and injured herself. The court held the defendants to be negligent, and although the plaintiff had acted reasonably in attempting to release herself, she had contributed to the injury by stepping on a revolving toilet-roll. The damages were reduced by 25 per cent.

The plaintiff in *Meah* v. *McCreamer* (1985) was a passenger in a car and was injured as a result of the defendant's negligent driving. Both driver and passenger had drunk a large amount of alcohol. Before the accident the plaintiff had a criminal record, but was not particularly violent. Afterwards he developed an aggressive personality and was convicted of sexual assault and rape, and received a life sentence. His claim for damages included compensation for the personality change and its consequences, including the prison sentence. The court held that as the injuries from the accident caused the personality change the defendant was liable for the plaintiff's pain and suffering, his injury and the consequences of the personality change. The judge awarded £60000, but reduced the damages by 25 per cent. because of the plaintiff's contributory negligence in accepting a lift, when he knew the defendant's ability to drive had been affected by alcohol.

As a point of interest, in a later case a victim of his act successfully sued for damages for the assault. It was the first occasion in English law that a rape victim recovered damages from her attacker.

It is generally considered that a young child is never guilty of contributory negligence.

Occupiers' Liability for Dangerous Premises

The Occupiers' Liability Act 1957, provides that the occupier of premises, or the landlord if responsible for repairs to the premises, has a common duty of care to see that all lawful visitors will be reasonably safe when using the premises.

Lawful visitors include persons invited expressly or impliedly (milkman, postman, paper-boy), or people who enter the premises under a contract (spectators at a football match). (See below for the 1984 Act which deals with the liability for visitors outside the scope of this Act).

The standard of care varies according to the visitor. Obviously the care shown for a child must be greater than for an adult. A notice "danger" would be of little use to a young child who could not read. Some dangers on premises may actually allure or attract children. In the case of allurements the occupier must take greater care to protect children. Occupiers have been held responsible for injuries to children caused by a railway turntable, red berries on trees, building sites, railway trucks, and threshing machines.

An occupier may not be liable for injuries to a very young child if it could be expected that the child would be accompanied by parents or other responsible persons.

In addition to the general defences (see p. 203), the occupier may show that:

(i) adequate notices or warnings of the danger were given (*e.g.* a "wet paint" sign).

(ii) with visitors under contract, liability was excluded. For example it is usual for exclusion notices to be displayed at most sporting events, but it should be noted that the Unfair Contract Terms Act 1977 may limit exclusion clauses to a test of reasonableness (see p. 163).

(iii) the injury was caused by the negligence of a competent independent contractor. For example, the occupier would escape liability if electrical fittings, erected by a qualified electrician, fell on a visitor. The occupier would be liable, however, if the fittings had been erected by a gardener. Independent contractors may be liable if they leave premises in a dangerous state and lawful visitors are injured as a result.

A. C. Billings & Sons Ltd. v. *Riden* (1958). Building contractors had to remove a ramp from the front of a house. Mrs. Riden left the house after dark and fell into a sunken area and suffered injury. It was held that the contractors were negligent as they had not taken reasonable care to ensure that visitors were not exposed to dangerous premises.

(iv) the person injured was a trespasser and not a lawful visitor. The occupier is liable for trespassers for intentional dangers such as man-traps, and for injuries caused when all that a humane person should have done for the safety of a trespasser had not been done.

British Railways Board v. *Herrington* (1972). A child trespasser was electrocuted and severely injured on the defendant's land. The fence guarding the line was broken. The House of Lords considered that there was a high degree of danger and as the defendants were aware of the possibility of such a trespass, and could easily have repaired the fence, they had not acted humanely and were liable.

The Occupiers' Liability Act 1984 is concerned with civil liability of an occupier to persons on his land who are outside the scope of the 1957 Act, namely trespassers. The aim of section 1 is to resolve points of doubt following *British Railways Board* v. *Herrington* (see above.)

An occupier has a duty to persons other than lawful visitors in respect of any risk receiving injury on his premises by reason of any danger due to the state of the premises, or to things done or omitted to be done on them.

The duty is owed by the occupier if:

(a) he is aware of the danger or has reasonable grounds to believe that it exists,

(b) he knows or has reasonable grounds to believe that there are others in the vicinity of the danger, or may come into the vicinity, and

(c) the risk is such that he may reasonably be expected to offer the other persons some protection.

The duty is to take such care as is reasonable to see that the others do not suffer injury by reason of the danger on the premises. The duty may be discharged by giving warning of the danger or discouraging persons from taking the risk. No duty is owed by the occupier if the other persons willingly accept the risk. There is no liability in respect of loss or damage to the other person's property, only personal injury.

Section 2 of the Act deals with visitors using premises for recreational or educational purposes. Occupiers of business premises may exempt themselves from provisions of the Unfair Contract Terms Act 1977, where access is granted for purposes not connected with the business. For example, a farmer allowing a football team to play on a field normally used for pasture.

TRESPASS

Trespass is probably the oldest tort, and many other torts owe their origin to the writ of trespass, which has been described as the "mother of actions." There are three forms of trespass:

1. trespass to the person,
2. trespass to chattels (goods), and

3. trespass to land.

All trespasses are actionable *per se* (by itself); that is, the plaintiff does not have to prove that the defendant caused any damage.

1. Trespass to the person

This tort consists of three separate actions:

(*a*) *Assault*. This tort is actionable when a person threatens or attempts to physically injure another, and the other person has reasonable fear that the threat will be carried out. Words are not sufficient by themselves, they must be accompanied by actions. If a person 100 yards away shouted an abusive threat it would probably not be assault, because there would be no fear of immediate danger and no action to indicate an attack. However, if a knife or fist was raised in close proximity to a face, this would be assault as there would be good reason to be in fear of a physical attack.

It is possible for words to remove the fear of an attack. For example, if a person lifted a fist to strike another, but said "I won't hit you because it's your birthday."

(*b*) *Battery*. This occurs when an act goes beyond a threat and a person is actually touched. The attacker does not have to physically touch the other person, the injury could be caused indirectly by such as throwing a stone.

It should be noted that the mere touching is actionable, regardless of the motive. A kiss given with love and affection, is assault and battery if the receiver does not authorise the act, even if it takes place under the mistletoe at Christmas time. It is intentional bodily contact and a woman or man may claim damages if they did not voluntarily stand under the mistletoe and accept the kiss.

Assault and battery are usually joined in one action, and both are criminal offences. Conviction in a criminal court may be used as evidence when claiming a remedy in a civil action.

(*c*) *False imprisonment*. This tort is committed when a person's liberty is totally restrained by the intentional, but unjust, act of another. The imprisonment must be for an unreasonable length of time, and be total so that if a person has reasonable means of leaving the premises it is not actionable.

In *Bird* v. *Jones* (1845) the public footpath over Hammersmith Bridge was closed. The plaintiff climbed over a fence and was stopped by the defendant from proceeding further along the footpath. The court held that it was not false imprisonment as the plaintiff could have left the bridge by the way he entered. In *John Lewis & Co. Ltd.* v. *Tims* (1952) Mrs Tims and her daughter were suspected of stealing and were kept in an office, against their will, until the store manager was informed. The House of Lords held that, as the detention had not been for an unreasonable period of time, there had not been false imprisonment.

A person may have a right of action even though he did not know at the time that he had been locked in a room while he slept. *Meering* v. *Grahame-White Aviation Co.* (1919).

Specific defences to trespass to the person

(*a*) *Parental or quasi-parental authority.* Parents or guardians may use reasonable force to chastise or imprison children. A similar authority may be given to others who take the place of parents (*quasi* means "as if"). A teacher, therefore, would not be liable for keeping pupils in school after lessons provided good reason could be shown.

(*b*) *Self defence.* The force used must be reasonable, regarding the facts of the case. It may not be a good defence to shoot an attacker dead if the person was unarmed. In *Lane* v. *Holloway* (1968), the plaintiff aged 64 hit a 24 year-old man on the shoulder, and in return received a blow to the eye which necessitated 19 stitches and a month in hospital. It was held that the blow received by the older man was out of all proportion to the provocation. (The defendant had also been found guilty in the criminal courts.)

(*c*) *Statutory or judicial authority.* For example, lawful arrest by a police officer.

2. Trespass to chattels (goods)

Chattels are items of tangible moveable property, such as personal possessions (pens, books, desks, cars, records, etc., and money and cheques, etc.).

This tort is committed when a person intentionally interferes with goods in the possession of another, or carries out an unjustifiable act which denies a person of the legal right to possess the goods. The merest touch of the goods without causing damage is sufficient, and it is not necessary for the defendant to dispossess the goods.

Kirk v. *Gregory* (1876). In order to place another person's jewellery in a safe place, the defendant removed the goods from one room to another. The jewellery was later stolen by an unknown party and the defendant was held liable in trespass.

The tort may also be committed without touching the goods, *e.g.* opening a farm gate and driving cows or horses out of a field.

Possession is the basis of this tort, as it is the lawful possessor of the goods, not necessarily the owner, who may bring an action. For example, a hirer of a car, not the owner, would sue for damages from the defendant who had taken possession of the car.

Most actions under this tort are brought for the intentional dispossession of the possessor's rights to the goods.

(i) Conversion arises when the defendant intentionally interferes with goods in a way that may be regarded as denying the plaintiff's rights of possession or use. If, for example, a car subject to a hire-purchase agreement is sold to a private person, the seller has given the buyer a good title (see p. 161) and denied the hire-purchase company the right of ownership of the car. The hire purchase company could sue the seller for conversion. The usual remedies for conversion are damages and injunction.

(ii) Detinue arose when goods were wrongfully detained by another party. This tort was abolished in 1977 (see below).

Torts (Interference with Goods) Act 1977

The Act abolished detinue, and section 1 defined "wrongful interference with goods" to mean:

(i) conversion of goods,
(ii) trespass to goods,
(iii) negligence and other torts in so far as they result to damage to goods or interests in goods.

In proceedings against a person, section 3 provides that the following relief may be given by the court when appropriate:

(i) an order for delivery of the goods, and payment of any consequential damage, or

(ii) an order for delivery of the goods, but the defendant has the alternative of paying damages to the value of the goods, and in either case with payment of any consequential damage, or

(iii) damages.

Under section 3, the claimant can choose his remedy, although (i) is at the discretion of the court.

Any person may apply to the High Court for an order providing for the delivery of any goods which are, or will be, the subject-matter of proceedings under this tort. The goods may be delivered to the claimant or to any person appointed by the court, on such terms or conditions as are specified in the order (s.4).

In proceedings for wrongful interference, a person who has improved the goods may have an allowance of the value of the improvement taken into consideration when the value of the goods is being assessed, provided that it is shown that the improver acted in a mistaken but honest belief that he had a good title to the goods. The allowance would also be granted to a person who purchased the goods from the improver in good faith.

A co-owner may not destroy or dispose of goods or their title. He would be liable to the other co-owner.

Uncollected goods

If you take goods to a shop to be mended, you are the bailor and the shopkeeper is the bailee. After the goods have been mended, you have a duty to pay for, and collect your goods. The shopkeeper has a duty to return the goods. The situation often arises when you (the bailer) do not collect your goods.

This Act sets down the rights of the shopkeeper (the bailee) and the procedure to follow. In cases where the bailor has not collected the goods, the bailee has a right in certain circumstances to write to the bailor in a prescribed manner, giving notice of an intention to sell, and if the goods have not been collected within the period stated in the notice, the bailee may sell the goods (s.12).

3. Trespass to land

This tort may be defined as the intentional entering on to another person's land without lawful permission or remaining on the land after permission has been withdrawn.

The entering or interference with the land must be direct. Rubbish dumped on to another's land would be trespass, but if the rubbish was blown on to the land by gales, it would not be trespass because it was not the direct action of the defendant which caused the interference.

An invasion of air space may be a trespass of land, even though the land is not touched. The courts have held in *Kelson* v. *Imperial Tobacco Co.* (1957) that a sign erected on a building, but which protruded over another person's land was trespass, as it was in *Woolerton and Wilson* v. *Costain* (1969), where a crane swung over another person's land. In *Lord Bernstein of Leigh* v. *Skyviews and General Ltd.* (1978) it was held that an aircraft which took an aerial photograph would not be trespassing if it was at a height which did not affect the use of land.

Trespass is a civil wrong and a mere trespasser, as a general rule, is not liable for criminal prosecution, and therefore the familiar sign, "Trespassers Will Be Prosecuted," has no legal effect, except in relation to certain government undertakings where an Act of Parliament has provided a fine for trespassing.

Specific defences to trespass to land

It is a defence to claim that entry on to land was justifiable. The following reasons may be used as a defence to show that entry was made:

(i) by leave or licence granted by the occupier of the land,
(ii) by authority of law (such as a bailiff),
(iii) involuntarily (such as landing in a parachute),
(iv) where the highway was impassable, and
(v) to retake and retain possession of one's own property.

The remedies available to the plaintiff:

(i) Damages. If no real injury has been incurred the damages awarded may be nominal (*i.e.* 1p).
(ii) Injunction. This may be used to stop the defendant from repeating the trespass.
(iii) Forcible ejection. The occupier may only use reasonable force to move the trespasser after first requesting him to leave and giving him reasonable time to do so.

NUISANCE

There are two forms of nuisance which have quite different meanings and little in common. They are public nuisance and private nuisance.

Public Nuisance

This wrong arises when acts or omissions have caused annoyance, inconvenience or danger to a class or part of the general public. Public nuisance includes such things as obstructing the public highway, throwing fireworks in the road, smoke from chimneys causing damage to cars parked on the highway and quarry blasting which projects stones and dust on to the surrounding neighbourhood.

Public nuisance is a crime and the offender is prosecuted, usually by the Attorney-General. A private person who has suffered special damage of a different kind from that of the general public may sue in tort. An example would be where, in the case of blasting, an entire neighbourhood was covered in dust, but one individual was hit by falling stones.

Private Nuisance

This tort covers the interference with the plaintiff's enjoyment or use of his land or the disturbance of some legal interest over the land. An example of interference with the enjoyment of land would be playing music very loudly in the middle of the night so that your neighbour's sleep is disturbed. To block your neighbour's access from the road to his house would be to disturb his legal right of way.

Nuisance and trespass

Nuisance differs from trespass to land in that,

(i) the interference must be indirect. Therefore the smell of a garden compost heap would be a nuisance to your neighbour, the throwing of the garden rubbish on to the neighbour's garden would be trespass. *Esso Petroleum* v. *Southport Corporation* (1956). A tanker ran aground and had to discharge oil at sea, which was carried by the tide and wind on to the foreshore. The Court of Appeal held the Corporation's action could not succeed in trespass as the damage was not caused by the direct act of the defendants, but by the indirect act of the wind and tide.

(ii) Nuisance is only actionable by proof of special damage.

The following factors have to be considered when establishing whether or not a nuisance exists.

(*a*) *Reasonableness*

It is a good defence to claim the act was a reasonable use of one's own property. The courts take an attitude of "live and let live." What is reasonable is based on the conduct of the ordinary man.

(*b*) *Sensitiveness*

An act which would not disturb a normal person will not be a nuisance just because the plaintiff, or his property, is unduly sensitive. In *Robinson* v. *Kilvert* (1889) the plaintiff stored brown paper in the defendant's premises. The heat from the defendant's boiler damaged the paper, which was extremely sensitive to heat. The court held the defendant was not liable in nuisance.

(*c*) *Locality*

"What would be a nuisance in Belgrave Square would not necessarily be so in Bermondsey" said a judge in 1879. He was pointing out that different standards are necessary for different areas, so it is possible that noise from a club in the city centre may be reasonable, but would be unreasonable in a residential area and would be a nuisance.

(*d*) *Continuity*

The general rule is that a single event is not a nuisance and the plaintiff must show that there was some degree of repetition of the offending act. In *Stone* v. *Bolton* (1950), a ball was hit out of a cricket ground and injured a lady. It was shown that a ball had been hit out of the ground only six times in 35 years. The court held that this was not often enough to be a nuisance.

(*e*) *Malice*

The intention behind an act may be relevant in deciding whether a person's act was reasonable or not.

To shout, shriek, whistle and bang trays may be a reasonable use of your own property, but if it is done with the express purpose of spoiling your neighbour's musical evening, it may be a nuisance, because the acts would not be reasonable. *Christie* v. *Davey* (1893).

The parties to an action

The occupier of property has the right to bring an action but any other person injured on the property has no claim in nuisance. The person liable in an action for nuisance is likewise the occupier of the property from which the nuisance emanated.

In *Malone* v. *Laskey* (1907), the plaintiff, the wife of a tenant was injured when a bracket on a lavatory cistern fell on her. The defendants who leased the property owned a generator which vibrated and caused the bracket to fall. The plaintiff sued in nuisance but the court held that, as she was only the wife of the tenant and not the tenant, she had no interest in the land.

Remedies

The usual remedies are damages and an injunction, which are obtained from the courts. In *Kennaway* v. *Thompson* (1981), the plaintiff lived near a lake used for motor boat racing. She was awarded damages by the High Court for nuisance already suffered and damages for future nuisance. The Court of Appeal varied the award and in the place of damages for future suffering, substituted an injunction which restricted the number of races that the defendants could hold.

With regard to the remedy of injunction, it must be stressed that it is awarded at the discretion of the court.

In *Miller* v. *Jackson* (1977), the defendants, a cricket club, had played on a village ground since 1905. The plaintiffs in 1972 moved into a house that adjoined the ground. A ball was hit into their house causing damage, and while a game was in progress there was always the danger of personal injury. The plaintiffs sought an injunction to restrain the club from playing cricket on the ground as it interfered with their enjoyment of the land. It was held by the Court of Appeal that the interests of the public should prevail over the plaintiffs' individual suffering. The public had watched cricket for 70 years and their interest had to be guarded. The injunction was not granted.

There is an extra-judicial remedy of abatement which is available when the nuisance can be terminated without entering another person's land. It could be applied to overhanging trees or roots, but it must be noted that the branches which are cut away still belong to the owner of the tree. If the nuisance cannot be abated without entering the other's land, permission must first be obtained, unless there is immediate danger to person or property.

Defences

1. Statutory authority

It is a complete defence that a nuisance was expressly authorised by an Act of Parliament.

2. Prescription

When a nuisance has been in continuous existence for not less than 20 years, the right to carry on the act may be acquired.

3. Reasonable use of one's own property

4. That the damage caused was minute or minimal

It should be noted that it is no defence that the plaintiff came to the nuisance. *Sturges* v. *Bridgman* (1879).

LIABILITY OF PARENTS FOR THE TORT OF CHILDREN

It is a general rule that parents are not liable for the torts of their children. A parent will be liable, however, if he is negligent in allowing his child to be in a position to commit a tort.

In *Bebee* v. *Sales* (1916), a father gave his 15-year-old son a shotgun, and the father was held to be liable when the son injured another boy.

However, the parent is not negligent if he has taken steps to lessen the risk of injury, as was the case in *Donaldson* v. *McNiven* (1952). A father showed his son how to use an air-rifle, warned him of the dangers and told him not to use it outside the house. The father was held not to be liable when his son injured another child.

It should be noted that, under the Firearms Act 1968, it is an offence for any person to make a gift of an air weapon or ammunition to a person under 14 years of age.

DEFAMATION

Defamation is a false published statement, either made orally, in writing or by gestures, which attacks a person's reputation. It has been defined as a statement which tends to lower a person in the estimation of right-thinking members of society generally. Although there is the public interest of freedom of speech, the tort of defamation protects an individual's private interest in his reputation. Two points from the definition must be noted:

(i) The statement must be published to a third party. It is not defamation if the statement is published only to the plaintiff. It would be defamation if a third party heard the defamatory words, even by accident. Each time a defamatory statement is repeated, it is actionable even if the maker does not know the statement is defamatory. So, if Peter made a statement to Jim about David, Jim would be liable (as would Peter) if he repeated the statement to any other person.

Post cards and telegrams are deemed to be published, even if the postal authorities have not actually read them.

(ii) The statement must lower the plaintiff's reputation in the minds of right-thinking members of society. A bank robber would not be liable for defamation if he informed other thieves that one of the gang had served a prison sentence for theft. This is because the gang would not disapprove, and they are not held to be right-thinking members of society.

In *Byrne* v. *Dean* (1937) a golf club had some illegal gaming machines which the police removed. A verse was placed on the notice board, which inferred that Byrne had informed the police. ("May he Byrne in hell and rue the day.") Byrne sued, but it was held that he had not been defamed, because right-thinking members of society would have approved of a person informing the police of an illegal practice.

In addition to showing that the statement was defamatory and published to a third party, a plaintiff must prove that the third party understood that the statement referred to the plaintiff. It is for the judge to decide if the statement is likely to be understood as referring to the plaintiff and for the jury (if there is one) to decide if the third party actually did so.

Not all defamatory statements are actionable. Consider the following statements and decide whether or not they are defamatory.

"All students in class 1A cheated in their examination."

(There were six students in the class.)

"Half of the Maths 'A' level class (four students) cheated in the examination."

"One or two of the law students (60 students) cheated in the examination."

The first statement would be defamatory because the class is small enough for all students to consider that they have been individually defamed.

The second statement would also be defamatory because, although it referred to only half of the class, it is small enough for any of the class to bring an action.

The last statement would not give a law student a right to sue because the class is too large for any one person to claim that it referred to him.

Innuendo

A statement may be defamatory by implication, even though the words are not defamatory in their ordinary sense, if it can be shown that another person's reputation has been affected.

In *Cassidy* v. *Daily Mirror Papers Ltd.* (1929), the newspaper published a photograph of the plaintiff's husband and another lady, and the caption announced the engagement of the couple. The plaintiff alleged that the words inferred that she had lived with the man without being married, and the court held that the picture and caption would lead a reasonable person to that conclusion.

It should be noted, however, that only a person defamed by innuendo may bring an action. If, for example, a student magazine wrongly stated a brother and sister to be illegitimate children (or words to that effect), the named persons would not be able to sue the editor, because they have not been defamed. Their parents would be able to sue, because the statement implies and infers that they are not married.

Libel and Slander

Defamation is either:

1. Libel

This is defamation in a permanent form, such as writing, or

broadcasting on radio or television. It could be in a painting or cartoon, or on record, cassette or tape recorder. Libel is actionable *per se*, that is, the plaintiff does not have to show special damage. Libel may also be a crime.

2. Slander

This is defamation in a non-permanent form, such as by words and gestures. Slander is not actionable *per se*, and a plaintiff must prove special damage, except with regard to statements which:

(i) Impute that a person has committed a crime punishable by imprisonment.
(ii) Impute that a person has an existing infectious disease (for example, leprosy or venereal disease).
(iii) Impute unchastity of a woman.
(iv) Impute against the plaintiff in respect of his office, profession, calling, trade or business.

Defences

1. Justification

It is a defence to show that the statement was completely or substantially true. Defamation must be a false statement, and a true statement which damaged a person's reputation would not be actionable.

2. Fair comment on a matter of public interest

People in public life, such as politicians, T.V. stars, footballers, etc., receive praise, and must by the same token accept criticism. Provided the comments concern their public activities, and are not made with malice or spite, they are not actionable.

3. Absolute privilege

The following carry complete protection from actions for defamation, regardless of the truth or motive behind the statement.

(*a*) *Parliamentary proceedings*

This means any statement made by a Member of Parliament in either House, and officially authorised reports on parliamentary proceedings.

(*b*) *Judicial proceedings*

This includes all statements made in court by judge, jury, counsel, witnesses, etc.

(*c*) *Statements between solicitor or counsel and client*

(*d*) *State communications*

(*e*) *Statements between husband and wife*

4. Qualified privilege

The following carry similar protection to absolute privilege, unless it can be shown that the maker of the statement acted from malice, such as an improper motive or out of spite.

(*a*) *Reports on parliamentary and judicial proceedings*

This covers newspaper and broadcasting reports and would also include reports on the proceedings of other public and international organisations (*e.g.* the United Nations).

(*b*) *Statements made in performance of a duty*

An employer has a duty to give a truthful reference concerning an employee who has applied for a position with another employer, although it should be noted that an employer is not legally bound to give a reference.

(*c*) *Statements made to protect an interest*

The interest may be to the benefit of the maker of the statement, the recipient or both, but the maker of the statement must have a duty, legal, moral or social, to protect the interest. An example would be a company director reporting to the chairman of the company about the misbehaviour of an employee.

5. Apology

A newspaper or periodical may offer this defence if it can show that the libel was published without malice or gross negligence. In addition to publishing an apology, a payment of money must be paid into court before the commencement of the case.

The Defamation Act 1952 provides that, as regards unintentional defamation, apology and amends will be a good defence.

While apology and amends is only a defence for defamatory statements in newspapers, it may serve to reduce damages if offered by a private person.

VICARIOUS LIABILITY

This expression is used when a person is liable for the torts of another, and mainly arises in employer/employee relationships.

The reasoning behind such liability is:

(i) To stop an employer hiring an employee to commit a tort.

(ii) To encourage the employer to install and maintain a safe system of operation.

(iii) That, as a general rule, the employer is in a better financial position to compensate the injured.

The employer is only liable for torts committed by employees during the course of their employment.

In *Lloyd* v. *Grace, Smith & Co.* (1912), L asked the defendants, a firm of solicitors, for advice. All the negotiations were with a managing clerk and he persuaded L to sign documents which conveyed property to him. The property was sold by the clerk and he kept the money. It was held that the firm was liable because the clerk was employed to give advice and convey property although in this case he did it for his own benefit.

An employer is liable if the employee commits a tort in the course of his employment, even though the latter performs his duty in a manner expressly forbidden by the employer.

In *Limpus* v. *London General Omnibus Co.* (1862) the

defendants had expressly warned their drivers not to race against buses of another company. One of their drivers injured a third party while racing his bus and the court held that he was was acting within the course of his employment.

An employer is not liable, however, if the employee goes on a "frolic of his own," and leaves his duties to follow a personal pursuit. For example, a driver who decides to watch a football match while on his delivery round, and damages another vehicle when parking. If an employee performs a function for which he has no authority, the employer will not be liable. In *Beard* v. *London General Omnibus* (1900) the conductor drove a bus and injured the plaintiff. The court held that the employer was not liable because the conductor was not acting within the scope of his employment.

An employer will be liable, however, when the employee carries out an authorised task in an incorrect way, as in *Bayley* v. *Manchester Sheffield and Lincolnshire Ry.* (1873). A porter thought a passenger was on the wrong train and pulled the person off the train, causing him injuries. The company was liable because the porter acted within the scope of his employment.

In *Harrison* v. *Michelin Tyre Co. Ltd.* (1985) S, an employee, whose duties included pushing a truck within a passage marked by chalk lines, deliberately moved the truck outside the lines as a practical joke and the plaintiff was injured. The plaintiff sued the company, arguing that S's negligence was within the course of his employment. The company contended that S was "on a frolic of his own." The court held that S's act could reasonably be regarded as incidental to the performance of his employment, regardless that the company had not authorised or condoned it. The company, therefore, was vicariously liable.

An employer is not generally liable for the torts of independent contractors, unless:

(i) They were expressly hired to commit a tort.
(ii) The work must create a dangerous situation.
(iii) The work obstructs the highway, thereby creating a public nuisance.
(iv) The employer delegates a duty imposed by statute or common law.

Independent contractors are employed to do specific tasks

but can choose the method of carrying out the work. An employee, on the other hand, is under the control of his employer as to what to do, and how to do it.

GENERAL DEFENCES IN TORT

There are specific defences to specific torts. Absolute privilege applies to defamation only. Often the defence may be a straight denial of the alleged facts. There are, however, the following defences which may be raised in most actions for tort.

1. Statutory authority

If a statute grants indemnity for a particular act, damages cannot be claimed unless the statute provides for compensation to be paid.

2. Consent (volenti non fit injuria)

Where there is consent, there is no injury. Consent may be given expressly or by implication. Most sporting activities involve a certain element of risk and it is common practice for organisers to make it a condition that spectators enter at their own risk. Next time you go to a football or cricket match, look for the notice as you enter the stadium. It is usually implied that participants in sport have consented to the risk of injury. If a hockey player misses the ball and hits an opponent on the shin, no action would arise, because the players accept "trespasses" as part of the game.

Knowledge of the existence of risk does not necessarily imply consent. If a worker knows that a crane passes dangerously overhead, he has not consented to the danger, and, if injured by a falling stone, may sue for damages. *Smith* v. *Baker & Sons* (1891).

In *Dann* v. *Hamilton* (1939), a young lady accepted a lift from a driver whom she knew had been drinking, and, as a result of his negligence, she was injured. The court held that, although she knew of the risk, she had not consented to the driver's negligence. In *Ashton* v. *Turner* (1980) the court considered that the defence could be accepted when both parties had been drinking together (see p. 181).

It is considered that, if a person has an alternative to riding with the drunk, the defence of *volenti* would be accepted, because the plaintiff has agreed to take the risk, rather than accept the alternative.

Rescue cases

A person who is hurt when attempting to rescue another person or to save property from damage may wish to sue the person who created the dangerous situation. The defence of consent may be invoked if there was no immediate danger to others, as the courts may consider the injured party volunteered to take the risk. In *Cutler* v. *United Dairies Ltd.* (1933), C was injured when he tried to stop a runaway horse on a quiet country road. It was held he had consented to the risk.

The plaintiff will not be a volunteer, however, if there was danger to others or if the plaintiff acted under a moral or legal duty, as in *Haynes* v. *Harwood* (1935). A police officer was injured when he tried to stop a horse that had bolted in a town and was an immediate danger to women and children. It was held that, although the plaintiff knew of the danger, he had acted under a duty and had not consented to the risk.

In *Baker* v. *T. E. Hopkins & Son Ltd.* (1959), a similar decision was made, when a doctor went down a well to help men overcome by fumes. The doctor died as a result of the fumes and the court held that the defendants who created the dangerous situation were liable.

3. Inevitable accident

It is a good defence to show that the injury was caused by an accident which could not have been prevented through forethought or by taking ordinary precautions. In *Stanley* v. *Powell* (1891) the plaintiff was injured during a shooting party when a pellet glanced off a tree. It was held that the defendant was not liable as his act was neither intentional nor negligent.

4. Necessity

It may be a defence to show that the damage was caused in trying to prevent a greater evil.

In *Cope* v. *Sharpe* (1912), fire broke out on the plaintiff's land and the defendant, who was a gamekeeper, set fire to other parts of the plaintiff's land with the intention of preventing the fire from spreading to his employer's land, where there were pheasants. The fire was extinguished by other means and the plaintiff sued for damages. The court held that the defendant had carried out a reasonably necessary act and was not liable.

5. Act of God

This is an act of nature which could not have reasonably been foreseen.

In *Nichols* v. *Marsland* (1876), the defendant owned an artificial lake which overflowed as a result of a thunderstorm and caused damage to the plaintiff's land. The court held the defendant was not liable as the damage was caused by an act of God.

Revision Test

1. What three things must a plaintiff prove to succeed in the tort of negligence?

2. What is the latin phrase to show that the defendant must prove he was not negligent?

3. Name the three forms of trespass.

4. Who may sue in the tort of nuisance?

5. Name three remedies for nuisance.

6. What is the name given to a permanent form of defamation?

7. Name the five categories of defences for defamation.

8. Name five general defences in tort.

9. What does "actionable *per se*" mean?

Specimen Questions

1. Explain the general defences available in tort.

2. Explain the nature of the defence of "*volenti non fit injuria.*"

3. Distinguish the torts of nuisance and trespass to land.

4. (a) What factor must a plaintiff prove in order to succeed in the tort of negligence?
   (b) Steve, by negligent driving, injured Paul and his son Mark, aged five. Paul's wife was immediately informed of her family's accident and suffered shock and a consequent nervous breakdown. What are Steve's legal liabilities to the wife?

5. Frances invited Lance to her house for tea. Lance hurt his knee as he tripped on a loose carpet. Ben entered her garden to take a short cut to the shops and fell into a ditch. Explain to Frances whether she will be liable to pay damages to Lance and Ben.

6. (a) Explain the effect of *res ipsa loquitur* in the law of tort.
   (b) Terry slipped on fruit juice which had spilled on to the floor of Debbie's shop by Gareth, a customer. Will Terry be able to sue Debbie for his injuries?

7. Distinguish public nuisance from private nuisance.

8. Smith was driving his employer's van to deliver goods to a customer when he negligently crashed into Jones' car. Inform Jones as to whom he may sue. Would the information be different if Smith was using the van to attend a football match?

9. Explain the differences between libel and slander in the tort of defamation.

10. Describe the defences available for the tort of defamation.

11. The Daily Echo correctly reported that "Jack Jones of Richmond was yesterday convicted of theft and fined £50." Another Jack Jones also lived in Richmond and he wished to sue the newspaper. Discuss Jack's chances of obtaining an award of damages for defamation.

12. Describe the different aspects of the tort of trespass, and explain how trespass to goods has been affected by the Torts (Interference with Goods) Act 1977.

Chapter 8

CRIMINAL LAW

DEFINITION

There are as many definitions of a crime as there are text-books on criminal law. This is because it is difficult to attach an exact definition to something which has many aspects; from motoring offences to murder; from theft to treason; from bigamy to blackmail and so on. From these examples it is possible to see the great variety and difference in gravity of the offences, although they are all crimes.

Earlier in the book, criminal law was classified as public law, because it is an offence against the State and is punished by the State. It would appear, therefore, first that a definition of a crime must show that an offence is against the public, although it might affect only one person, and, secondly, that the person who committed an offence either by a positive act or by omitting to do something which was a legal duty will be punished in some manner prescribed by the State. A definition which contains these points arose in the House of Lords when Lord Tucker, in *Board of Trade* v. *Owen* (1957) considered that the correct definition of a crime in the criminal law was the following passage from Halsbury's Laws of England. "A crime is an unlawful act or default which is an offence against the public and renders the person guilty of the act or default liable to legal punishment."

CLASSIFICATION OF OFFENCES

Crimes may be classified in several ways as follows:

1. Method of trial

In order to establish the method of trial, offences are classed as:

(*a*) *Indictable offences*

These are serious offences, triable by judge and jury, for which a Bill of Indictment sets out the charges alleged to have been committed by the person(s) sent to the Crown Court for the trial.

(*b*) *Summary offences*

These are offences which are subject to trial by magistrates' courts. The cases are decided in these courts.

(*c*) *"Hybrid" offences*

These are offences created by statute and may be tried either summarily or on indictment.

2. Power to arrest

A new classification of offences was introduced by the Criminal Law Act 1967, which is important with respect to the power to arrest without a warrant (see p. 224).

(*a*) *Arrestable offences*

These are offences established by The Criminal Law Act 1967, " . . . for which the sentence is fixed by law or for which a person (not previously convicted) may . . . be sentenced to imprisonment for a term of five years." The Police and Criminal Evidence Act 1984 extended the list by including certain offences under Customs and Excise law, Official Secrets Act, Sexual Offences Act, Theft Acts and offences of corruption in office. For a more detailed summary see p. 225. This classification is important in that arrestable offences are subject to the power to arrest without a warrant.

(*b*) *Non-arrestable offences*

Although this class is not defined by the Act, it relates to all other offences which are not arrestable offences.

ELEMENTS OF A CRIME

The rule of *mens rea* is an established tenet of criminal law by which an act does not make a person guilty unless it is done with a guilty intention. A person is generally guilty of a crime (but not always) if two elements are present. First, there must be a wrongful act which would be a crime and, secondly, there must be the intention to do the wrongful act, knowing it to be a crime.

Therefore, in most crimes there must be the physical element; a wrong act (the *actus reus*) and the mental element; a guilty mind (*mens rea*), and if both elements are not present there is no crime. It should be noted that there are some crimes for which both elements are not necessary. These crimes are committed by the act, and the intention is not necessary (see strict liability below).

Mens Rea

Mens Rea means the guilty mind or wrongful intention and, obviously it differs from crime to crime. The wrongful intention of a person committing a theft is completely different from that of a person committing treason. To be criminally liable, a person must have intended to do wrong or have acted in such a reckless and negligent manner that a reasonable person must have realised that a crime would be committed. If a terrorist leaves a bomb in a train and kills a passenger, it would not be a defence to claim that there was no intention to kill anyone. Such an act is so reckless, and the likelihood of death so foreseeable, that the wrong or criminal intention is present.

In *Hyam* v. *D.P.P.* (1975), Hyam, who had been the mistress of J. set fire to the home of B, J.'s new mistress, and B's two daughters were killed. H claimed she intended no physical harm to anyone, but merely wished to frighten B. The House of Lords upheld the conviction of murder and considered that no distinction is to be made between the state of mind of one who does an act designed to produce a particular illegal consequence, and the state of mind of one who does the act knowing that it is likely to produce that consequence, although it was not the object of the act. What is common to both states of mind is the willingness to produce the particular illegal consequence. The *mens rea* is to have acted with intent to produce a particular illegal consequence.

The House of Lords have since ruled that intent to kill or inflict serious harm is necessary to establish malice aforethought.

In *R.* v. *Moloney* (1985) the accused received a friendly challenge by his step-father to see who was "quicker on the draw" with shotguns. Both men were drunk, but good friends. Moloney shot and killed his step-father, although he claimed he had no intention to do so and did not appreciate that the gun was aimed at the victim. The House of Lords held that Moloney was not guilty of murder as a person only intends the result of an act if his purpose is to bring about that result. As Moloney did not intend to kill his step-father he was not guilty of murder. He was, however, guilty of manslaughter.

Certain offences have strict or absolute liability, and *mens rea* is not essential. For example, the Health and Safety at Work, etc., Act provides that certain machines must have safety covers, and if these covers are not fixed, the employers are strictly liable. In one case, the employers asked an outside contractor to supervise the safety regulations but the employers were still liable when the contractors did not comply with the statutory requirements. Strict liability arises when the crime consists of performing a forbidden act or not performing a statutory duty (the *actus reus*); the wrongful intention (the *mens rea*) is irrelevant here. In *Meah* v. *Roberts* (1977) two children were served with glasses of caustic soda instead of lemonade. Meah was found guilty of selling food unfit for human consumption, contrary to the Food and Drug Act 1955, even though another person was responsible for the cleaning fluid being in the lemonade bottle.

When interpreting statutes, there is a general presumption

that *mens rea* is necessary in all crimes. This rule can only be replaced if an Act of Parliament expressly or impliedly excludes the necessity of *mens rea* (*Sweet* v. *Parsley* (1970)).

Actus Reus

This element includes all circumstances relating to a crime other than the mens rea. It is the wrongful act or omission which leads to a crime. For example, burglary is committed when a person enters a building as a trespasser with intent to steal, or to inflict grievous bodily harm on any person, or to rape a woman, or to do unlawful damage to the building.

The *actus reus* of burglary is the entering into a building without right to do so. The *mens rea* is the intention of committing certain crimes when in the building. It is not burglary to enter a building without this intention, but merely the tort of trespass. The crime is committed when both elements are present. The *actus reus* of entering the building and the *mens rea* of intending to commit the other crimes, even though the other crimes were not actually committed. The above is only a part of the definition of burglary, see page 218 for the complete definition.

SPECIFIC CRIMES

OFFENCES AGAINST THE PERSON

1. Unlawful homicide

Homicide is the killing of a human being by another human being and it is not necessarily a crime. To kill as a means of lawful self-defence is not unlawful homicide and is not a crime. The following are examples of unlawful homicide, and are crimes.

(*a*) *Murder*

Murder is unlawful homicide, and it is defined as unlawful killing with malice aforethought, with the death taking place within a year and a day of the attack or event that caused the death.

Malice aforethought may be defined as the intention to kill or cause grievous bodily harm to the other person. It could be murder if the killer intended to murder one person, but killed another instead.

When a person kills whilst committing a crime or avoiding arrest, it would not be murder unless there was an intention to kill or inflict serious bodily harm (*R.* v. *Maloney* (1985) see p. 211).

The punishment for murder is imprisonment for life, and, when sentencing, the judge may recommend a minimum term to be served.

The defences to a murder charge are:

(i) Diminished responsibility. The defence is that the killer was suffering from an abnormality of the mind, that impaired the mental responsibility for committing the act or omission. If this defence is accepted the charge would be manslaughter. In the "Yorkshire Ripper" case the jury did not accept this defence, and found Peter Sutcliffe guilty of murder.

(ii) Provocation. The act by the dead person was such that would have made any reasonable person lose control of the mind. If the defence is accepted the charge would be manslaughter.

(*b*) *Manslaughter*

Manslaughter is unlawful homicide without malice aforethought. Manslaughter occurs when:

(i) A person acts with gross negligence and kills another person.
(ii) A person kills another person whilst carrying out an unlawful act which would not normally kill or seriously hurt that other person.
(iii) A person is directly the cause of another's death, although the actual killing was the act of a third party. For example, where a person involved in a shooting incident with police uses the victim as a shield as protection against the police bullets.
(iv) The defences of provocation, suicide pact or diminished responsibility are pleaded successfully.

Examples (i) (ii) and (iii) above are classed as involuntary manslaughter because of the absence of malice aforethought. The last example is classed as voluntary manslaughter because the crime would have been murder but for the specific defences. The maximum punishment for manslaughter is imprisonment for life.

(*c*) *Suicide*

Suicide and attempted suicide are not crimes, but it is a criminal offence to aid, abet, counsel or procure the suicide of another. (Suicide Act 1961 s.2.) A suicide pact occurs when two or more persons agree that they shall be killed by some means. Survivors of such a pact are charged with manslaughter, whether they killed another or whether the dead person killed himself.

(*d*) *Infanticide*

Infanticide is committed when a child under the age of 12 months is killed:

(i) by its mother, and
(ii) at the time of the killing, the mother was mentally disturbed as a result of not fully recovering from the effects of the child's birth.

The maximum punishment is the same as for manslaughter.

(*e*) *Causing death by reckless driving*

This offence is committed when a motorist does not drive with due care and attention and causes the death of another. It is punishable by imprisonment of up to five years and/or a fine.

2. Assault and battery

It is common to hear these two charges joined as one. They are, however, separate offences.

(*a*) *Assault*

This is an act which causes another person to be in immediate fear of an unlawful physical attack. It is generally considered that mere words are not sufficient but that they must be accompanied by some positive action. An action which arouses fear, although there was no intention to harm, would still be an assault.

(*b*) *Battery*

This is the actual unlawful force on another person, without lawful reason or just cause. The force may be the merest touch which caused no physical harm or injury.

It is usual for both offences to occur at the same time, but assault is not committed if the person is unaware that the battery is to take place. For example, if an attack takes place behind a person's back. Defences include lawful consent, parental or quasi-parental authority and reasonable self-defence.

3. Wounding with intent

This offence is committed when a person, with intent, unlawfully and maliciously wounds or causes grievous bodily harm to another person. (Offences Against the Person Act 1861, s.18.) It is only possible to make this charge if there has been serious bodily harm or wounding by a breaking of the skin.

A bruise, burn or scratching of the skin is not wounding in this sense, nor would the breaking of a bone be so if the skin was not broken. It would appear, therefore, that bleeding from the wound is necessary for this offence. In *C.* v. *Eisenhower* (1983) a pellet from an airgun did not break the skin, but caused internal bleeding. The court held the defendant to be not guilty of unlawful wounding as there had not been a breaking of the skin.

4. Rape

This offence occurs when a man has unlawful sexual intercourse with a woman without her free consent. It would still be rape if consent was given by a trick, such as a man pretending to be the woman's husband.

A husband cannot rape his wife unless they are legally separated but a husband may be charged with assault or causing bodily harm if he uses violence to force his wife to have intercourse.

Boys under 14 may not be charged with rape. A woman who

forces a male to have unlawful sexual intercourse would be liable to the charge of indecent assault.

OFFENCES AGAINST PROPERTY

The Theft Acts 1968 and 1978 provide many offences against property. The main crimes are as follows:

1. Theft

"A person is guilty of theft if he dishonestly appropriates property belonging to another with the intention of permanently depriving the other of it."

The punishment for theft is a maximum of 10 years' imprisonment. The definition of theft, set out above, which is found in section 1(1) of the 1968 Act contains certain words or phrases which need to be explained.

(*a*) *"Dishonestly appropriates"*

This could be considered the "*mens rea*" of stealing, so that if a person did not intend to be dishonest, there would be no theft. For example, if I took another person's coat from a rack, thinking it was my own, there would be no theft, but if I took it knowing it was not my coat, it would be dishonest. If I took the coat thinking it was mine, but later discovered it belonged to another person, it would be theft if I decided to keep it.

The Act does not define "dishonestly" but gives examples of when the appropriation of another's property would not be dishonest.

(i) If a person believes in law that he has the right to deprive the other person of the property.
(ii) If a person believes he would have the owner's consent. For example, borrowing £5 from a friend's locker.
(iii) If a person (other than a trustee) believes that, after taking reasonable steps, the owner of the property which he holds cannot be found. This example would apply to the finding of lost property.

Appropriation takes place when a person assumes or takes over the rights of an owner. In *R.* v. *Morris* (1983) the defendant took articles from shelves in a supermarket and substituted the price labels with labels from lower priced goods. The House of Lords held that there had been a dishonest appropriation.

(*b*) *"Property"*

The term includes all things which can be owned, money, goods, rights of action and, in certain circumstances, land. As a general rule, it is not theft to pick mushrooms, flowers, fruit or foliage from a plant or trees growing wild, provided that the picking is not done for sale or other commercial purposes. It would not be stealing to pick flowers growing wild and give them to a friend, but it would be stealing to sell them for gain.

(*c*) *"The intention of permanently depriving"*

This phrase is essential to the definition of theft. If I take a book intending to return it to the owner, I have not committed theft. It is, however, possible to "steal" the book while it is still in my possession if, after borrowing it, I later decide to keep it. Theft takes place at the time I decide to keep the book permanently. Section 6(1) provides that in certain cases, although there was no intention to permanently deprive the owner of the property, borrowing goods would be theft. It would be theft in the following cases:

(i) to take a train ticket from British Rail with the intention of returning it to them when arriving at the station of destination;
(ii) to take a football club season ticket and return it to the owner at the end of the football season;
(iii) to take a sack of potatoes from a farmer and sell it back to him by pretending to be the owner of the potatoes.

In these cases the true owners were not permanently deprived, but they were cases of theft, because there was an intention by the borrowers to treat the property as their own, and to deprive the owners of their rights to the property. It is the period of time that is important in (i) and (ii) above, because it amounts to an outright taking of the goods.

2. Robbery

Section 8 (1) provides that: "A person is guilty of robbery if he steals and immediately before or at the time of doing so, and in order to do so, he uses force on any person or puts or seeks to put any person in fear of being then and there subjected to force." The maximum punishment is imprisonment for life.

The principal elements of this offence are:

(i) Stealing.
(ii) Using force; or
(iii) Fear, on the victim's part, of force being used.

A person does not commit robbery if there is no theft. The force used must be more than a gentle push, or more than is needed to take the property from a passive victim. It has been considered that merely snatching a handbag from a woman who did not resist would not be using force as required by the Act.

3. Burglary

Section 9 of the Theft Act 1968 provides that this offence occurs when a person:

(i) enters any building or part of a building as a trespasser and with intent to commit an offence of theft, inflicting grievous bodily harm, rape or unlawful damage, or
(ii) having entered a building as a trespasser, steals or attempts to steal anything in the building or inflicts or attempts to inflict grievous bodily harm upon any person therein.

The maximum punishment is 14 years' imprisonment.

The main elements of this offence are: (a) entering as a trespasser; (b) the intention of entering the building to commit one of the offences mentioned in (i) above; or (c) having entered without intention to commit any offence, the commission or attempted commission of one of the offences mentioned in (ii) above.

Section 10 provides that a person is guilty of an aggravated burglary if he commits burglary while he has a firearm or imitation firearm, any offensive weapon or explosive. The maximum penalty for aggravated burglary is imprisonment for life.

The Theft Act 1968 sets out many more offences against property, of which the following will be of interest:

(i) Section 12. This makes it an offence to *take a conveyance*, other than a pedal cycle, without the consent of the owner, or to drive or travel in the conveyance knowing it has been taken without the owner's consent. When the conveyance is a pedal cycle, it is far less serious, but still an offence. It is not an offence if the person believed he had the owner's consent, or would have had it if the owner had known he was taking the conveyance. It is not an offence if permission to use the conveyance is obtained by fraud. In *Whittaker* v. *Campbell* (1983), W, who did not have a driving licence, hired a van by showing a licence belonging to another person. The court held he was not guilty of this offence because he took the van with the owner's consent, although he obtained this consent by fraud. The "conveyance" includes anything constituted to carry persons on land, sea or air.

The offences carry a maximum punishment of three years' imprisonment. The penalty for the offence when the conveyance is a pedal cycle is a maximum fine of £50.

(ii) Section 13. This provides for the *dishonest use of electricity*. It is theft to dishonestly use, divert or waste electricity.

(iii) Section 15. This provides that it is an offence to dishonestly obtain *property* belonging to another by deception. It carries a maximum of 10 years' imprisonment. For example, it would be an offence to obtain a T.V. set on rental by showing the owner a means of identity which belonged to another person.

(iv) Section 16. This provides that it is an offence for a person to dishonestly obtain a pecuniary *financial advantage* by deception. The maximum penalty is five years' imprisonment. Examples of pecuniary advantages would be obtaining an overdraft, or insurance policy, or obtaining employment or advancement at work, or winning money by betting. The deception may be by words or conduct. This offence would be committed, for example, if a person applying for a job falsely claimed to have a certain qualification (say two "A" levels) and was employed as a result of the deception.

(v) Section 21. This provides that it is the offence of *blackmail* when a person with a view to profit, makes an unwarranted demand with menaces. Menaces may be expressed threats of violence, or threats of action that would be detrimental or unpleasant to the person addressed, or the conduct of the accused may justify the opinion that a demand with menaces has been made. The maximum punishment for blackmail is imprisonment for 14 years.

(vi) Section 22. This makes it an offence to *handle stolen* goods, if a person knows or believes them to be stolen and dishonestly receives the goods, or helps or arranges for the goods to be removed or sold. This offence has a maximum sentence of 14 years' imprisonment.

(vii) Section 25. This provides that it is an offence for a person, when not at his place of abode, to have any article for use in the course of, or in connection with, any burglary, theft or threat. Any person may arrest without warrant a person whom he reasonably suspects to be committing this offence. It is sometimes referred to as "going equipped for stealing." The maximum penalty is three years' imprisonment.

In the following case, the court had to decide if the car of the accused was a "place of abode."

R. v. *Bundy* (1977). The police stopped the appellant's car and found articles for use in the course of theft. Bundy claimed that his car was his place of abode and therefore he had not committed a crime under section 25 of the Theft Act. The Court of Appeal held that "a place of abode" meant a place in which the occupier intended to stay, and, as a car was a means of transport, it was not a place of abode within the meaning of the Act.

The Theft Act 1978

The Theft Act 1978 introduced three offences.

Section 1 makes it an offence to dishonestly *obtain services* by *deception*, and it applies when services are obtained where the other person is induced to confer a benefit on the understanding that the benefit has been or will be paid for.

This section would apply when a person paid for a service by cheque knowing that the cheque was worthless.

Section 2 provides for the offences of *evasion of liability* by deception. It applies where a person by any deception:

(a) dishonestly secures the remission of the whole or part of any existing liability to make a payment, whether his own liability or another's; or

(b) with intent to make permanent default in whole or in part on any existing liability to make a payment, or with intent to let another do so, dishonestly induces the creditor or any person claiming payment on behalf of the creditor to wait for payment (whether or not the due date for payment is deferred) or to forgo payment; or

(c) dishonestly obtains any exemption from or abatement or liability to make a payment.

Examples of the above offences are:

(a) Jones owed the butcher £100 and falsely informed him that he was out of work and, as a result, the butcher reduced the debt.

(b) Smith had a car on hire and owed the rental for one month. Robinson, the owner of the car, demanded payment of the arrears or the immediate return of the car. If Smith needed the car for another day and gave Robinson a cheque for the overdue rental, knowing that she was leaving the country in two days and had closed her bank account, it would be an offence under this section because she had intended to permanently default the payment of an existing liability by deceiving Robinson into thinking the cheque was good.

(c) Barclay had a period contract on the railways and his friend Lloyd borrowed the contract and used it to obtain a free journey, although the contract was not transferable.

Section 3. creates an offence of *making off without payment*. It applies where a person knows that payment on the spot is required for any goods supplied or services done, and dishonestly makes off without paying with the intent to avoid payment.

This offence would apply in cases such as leaving a café, or a petrol station or bus or train without paying.

The section does not apply when the payment cannot be legally enforced.

CRIMINAL DAMAGE

(1) The Criminal Damage Act 1971, s.1 provides that it shall be an offence to unlawfully destroy or damage any property belonging to another, either intentionally or recklessly.

Section 1(2) provides that it is an aggravated offence to unlawfully destroy or damage property with the intention of endangering the life of another, whether the property belongs to the offence, or to another. Section 1(3) provides that if the damage or destruction to property in the above offences is by fire, the charge shall be arson.

The maximum penalty for offences under sections 1(2) and (3) is life imprisonment.

"Property," for the purposes of this Act, means real and personal tangible objects, including money and wild animals.

MISLEADING TRADE DESCRIPTIONS

The Trade Descriptions Act of 1968 and 1972 provide that it shall be an offence carrying criminal sanctions for a person to make a false or misleading trade description. Under the 1968 Act the offence is committed when, in the course of business, a person makes a false description of goods with regard to such matters as price, size or quantity and method or place of manufacture.

In *Wings Ltd.* v. *Ellis* (1984), a holiday brochure was published with false information. The brochure was later amended but a customer booked a holiday relying on the original brochure. The House of Lords held that it is no defence that the defendant did not know at the time of publication that the statement was false.

Section 24 provides that it would be a defence to show that:

(i) The misleading description was caused by information supplied by a third party, or through some fault of a third party, over which the defendant had no control.

(ii) The defendant did not and could not know, after reasonable inquiry, that the goods did not correspond with the description, or that the goods had been so described, and

(iii) The defendant took all reasonable precautions to ensure that the offence was not committed by himself or by persons under his control.

The 1972 Act makes it an offence not to indicate the origin of goods which bear certain United Kingdom names and trade marks and have been produced or manufactured outside the United Kingdom.

There have been many prosecutions under the 1968 Act. A typical example would be selling a motor car with the mileage meter showing a mileage far less than the car has actually travelled. It should be noted, however, that, as a result of this Act many garages now sell cars expressly stating that they do not guarantee the mileage shown to be correct.

It should be noted that the provisions of the Acts do not give buyers a right to enforce a contract as, unfortunately, the Acts only carry criminal sanctions.

THE POWERS OF ARREST

In an earlier chapter, the functions of the criminal courts were discussed and in this chapter some specific crimes have also been covered. It is now necessary to see how persons accused of a criminal offence are called or brought before a particular criminal court. There are three ways by which a person suspected or accused of committing a crime may be brought to court.

1. By summons,
2. By warrant for arrest,
3. By arrest without a warrant.

The first two methods are known as "process."

1. Summons

A summons is a document which orders the accused to attend court. It is issued and signed by a magistrate and states the nature of the offence and the time and place at which the accused should attend court. The summons is served or sent to the accused, who remains at liberty until the court hearing. A summons must be issued unless the offence is indictable or subject to punishment by imprisonment.

2. Warrant

This document is an order for the arrest of a particular person and is addressed to police officers in the area concerned. The accused person must be named or described in sufficient detail to be recognised as that person. It is unlawful to issue warrants that do not state the name or description of a person.

A warrant has a statement of the offence and is signed by a magistrate and it empowers the police to arrest the accused in order to bring him before the court. It is not necessary for a police officer to possess the warrant at the time of arrest but, if the accused demands, it must be shown as soon as is practicable.

A person arrested by warrant is not automatically at liberty until the time of trial, as he would be under a summons. However, the magistrate may endorse the warrant at the time of issue so that the person named may be released on bail on an undertaking that he will appear in court at the specified time and place. This is referred to as "backed for bail," and the accused is released as soon as he has complied with the conditions of the undertaking.

Basically, a warrant may only be issued for offences which are indictable or punishable by imprisonment. In addition, however, warrants may be issued if a person does not appear in court to answer a summons, or if the address of the accused is not sufficiently established or known to enable a summons to be served.

3. Arrest without a warrant

The Police and Criminal Evidence Act 1984 which became law on January 1, 1986 provides new powers of arrest by the police and lessens the powers of arrest by a private citizen as follows:

A. Police officers may arrest without a warrant, when they have reasonable grounds for suspicion, any person who:

(i) (a) has committed an arrestable offence,
(b) is committing an arrestable offence, or
(c) is about to commit an arrestable offence

If there are no reasonable grounds for the above suspicion, the arrest is unlawful.

(ii) has committed or is committing any offence which is not an arrestable offence and the police officer has reasonable grounds for suspecting that (1) the service of a summons is impracticable or (2) inappropriate because:
(a) the person arrested is unknown to the police or
(b) is likely to cause injury or damage to other persons or property, or
(c) a child or other vulnerable person needs protection from the person arrested.

B. Private citizens may arrest a person when an arrestable offence has been committed and the private citizen suspects that other person of committing the offence. An arrestable offence is:

(i) an offence which carries a penalty fixed by law, (an example would be murder for which the penalty has to be a sentence of life imprisonment.),
(ii) an offence for which a person aged 21 or more, not previously convicted, may be sentenced to imprisonment for five years or more,
(iii) an offence under certain Customs and Excise legislation, Official Secrets Act, Sexual Offences Act, Theft Acts and corruption in office and,
(iv) to attempt, or to conspire, incite or procure the commission of, the offences listed in (iii) above.

A new classification was introduced, of "serious arrestable offence" which gives the police extended powers of investigation, with regard to offences such as murder, rape, causing an explosion and other arrestable offences which might become "serious" depending on the circumstances.

Stop and Search

Section 1 of the 1984 Act provides that the police may search anything which is in or on a vehicle for stolen or prohibited articles (burglary tools, offensive weapons and the like), and detain a person or vehicle to carry out the search, if there are reasonable grounds for suspecting that such articles will be found. The search must take place in a public place. A person may also be searched, although the police may only request the removal of a coat or jacket. Before making a search the police officers must identify themselves or, if in plain clothes, show a warrant card. As soon as practical after the search the police officer must make a written report of the time, date, place of the search and any information regarding articles found, injuries to persons or damage to property as a result of the search.

Entry and Search

Police officers may enter private premises to search for evidence and seize items connected with an arrestable offence. The Code of Practice provides that the search should be at a reasonable hour and with due consideration for property and the occupants' privacy. A police officer may enter and search, with the occupiers' written permission, to:

(i) execute a warrant,

(ii) arrest for an arrestable offence (without a warrant),

(iii) arrest a person unlawfully at large.

In addition, when a person has been arrested for an arrestable offence, a police officer may search that person's premises provided the officer has reasonable grounds for suspecting that evidence of that, or some other, offence will be discovered.

Seizure

In addition to all the powers mentioned above, a police officer, lawfully on premises, may seize any article or items which is reasonably believed to be evidence of an offence and, if not seized, would be lost, destroyed, concealed or damaged.

Complaints against the police

The Act set up the Police Complaints Authority which has

the power to investigate complaints against the police. Complaints may be made by anyone in writing or in person.

Bail

In the previous section, it was shown that a magistrate may endorse a warrant that the accused may be released on bail, which means that he is at liberty and not in custody. On other occasions the decision to grant bail is made in court or by the police. Bail is a security given by other persons that the accused will attend court on the appointed day and time. If bail is granted, the accused may carry out the normal functions of a free person and will not be in custody for the period between the arrest and the magistrates' hearing, and between trial in the magistrates' court and the Crown Court.

The sureties (the persons who give the security) usually promise to pay a sum of money into court if the accused does not attend for the hearing. In addition, the court may require the accused to surrender his passport. If the court or police are satisfied that the sureties are able to meet their promised commitment, the accused is handed into their custody. The Bail Act 1976 abolished the accused's own recognisance but introduced a new offence of absconding whilst on bail. The sureties have the right of arrest if they consider that the accused will not attend court on the appointed day and the police also have power to arrest the accused if he is not following the conditions of his release on bail.

When an accused has been committed by the magistrates for trial to the Crown Court, he may apply for bail for a period up to the trial. The Bail Act 1976 provided that there is a presumption that bail will be granted and, therefore, the accused is entitled to bail unless a good reason can be shown why it should not be granted.

The magistrates will ask the police if they oppose the application, and if there is no objection, they will grant bail. The value of the security will depend on the seriousness of the offence but if the terms of bail are unreasonable, the accused may appeal to a High Court judge. Bail is very rarely granted for murder and may not be granted for other offences if the accused:

(i) cannot obtain the necessary sureties;
(ii) has previously been granted bail and did not attend court as ordered;
(iii) is likely to commit other offences;
(iv) does not have an established address;
(v) is suspected of committing a violent offence or was in possession of firearms or other offensive weapons;
(vi) is likely to leave the country and avoid the trial.

GENERAL DEFENCES

There will be specific defences to all crimes, even if it is simply "I didn't do it," or "I was in another place at the time of the offence." Sometimes a specific defence may be more technical, and with a charge of theft, the defence may be that there was no intention to permanently deprive the owner but merely to borrow for a short period of time.

There are certain defences, applying generally to criminal charges, under which the accused will not deny performing the offence but will claim one of the following as a reason why he or she is not guilty:

1. Insanity

The defence of insanity in criminal cases is based on the M'Naghten Rules. In 1843, Daniel M'Naghten, motivated by an insane delusion of persecution by Sir Robert Peel, killed Edward Drummond who was Peel's secretary. M'Naghten was acquitted on the grounds of insanity, and the House of Lords, in its Parliamentary role, produced the following rules which still apply today.

(a) Every person is presumed sane until the contrary is proved.

(b) The defence must show that the accused was labouring under a defect of reason caused by a disease of the mind, and that he did not know the nature and quality of his act, or, if he did know it, he did not know that he was doing wrong.

(c) Where a person commits a crime under an insane delusion, he is considered to have the responsibility that he would have had if the facts as he imagined were real.

If a man had insane delusions that another man was about to kill him, and in self-defence he killed the other man, there would be no criminal liability. If, however, his delusions were that the man was making friendly advances to his girl friend, and he killed him, he would be liable for punishment, because his delusion did not warrant the action he took.

It should be noted, (i) that the defence has to prove insanity, (ii) the verdict is "not guilty by reason of insanity."

Diminished responsibility is not a general defence, as it specifically applies to charges of murder.

2. Automatism

This is an act done by the muscles of the body without any control of the mind. It could be a reflex action, a blackout, an act done when sleepwalking, or any other involuntary movement, provided the person's physical and mental state was not caused by his own negligence.

The defence is based on a general rule that an offence is not punishable if the action of the defendant was involuntary.

3. Mistake

A mistake of law is no defence, but a person may claim that, had he known the true facts, the crime would not have been committed. In *R.* v. *Tolson* (1889) a woman remarried during the lifetime of her husband. It was shown that she honestly believed her husband to be dead, and the court upheld her defence to the charge of bigamy.

Mistake when pleaded must be reasonable. In Tolson's case, the plea was accepted because the husband had been reported drowned at sea and had been missing for five years.

4. Intoxication (by drugs or alcohol)

Although it is not a defence in itself, and in some cases it is an offence, the plea may be used to show that the *mens rea* required for the offence was not present.

In *R.* v. *Hardie* (1985) the defendant was under the influence of valium, which had not been prescribed for him, and he set fire to a friend's flat, endangering lives. The Court of Appeal held that he did not have the *mens rea*, and considered that while intoxication cannot usually be pleaded as a defence to offences of recklessness, the rule will not generally apply to drugs which are merely sedative. Obviously, this defence could not be used in cases such as reckless driving.

It may also be a defence to show that intoxication produced insanity and that the M'Naghten Rules are relevant.

A person who forms the intention of committing a crime whilst sober and becomes drunk to acquire "Dutch courage" will not be able to use this defence. In *Att. Gen. for Northern Ireland* v. *Gallagher* (1963) a man planned to kill his wife and drank a bottle of whisky before committing the crime. His defence of drunkenness was refused by the House of Lords.

5. Necessity

There is no general defence of necessity, except in cases of self-defence or prevention of violent crimes. It would appear that the defence cannot be used for the murder of an innocent person. In *R.* v. *Dudley & Stephens* (1884) two seamen who had been shipwrecked for nearly three weeks killed and ate the cabin boy, who was the only other survivor. The defence of necessity was rejected and they were found guilty of murder, even though the jury considered that they would have died from starvation had they not killed the boy.

Revision Test

1. Name the class of offence which is decided in the magistrates' court.

2. Name four crimes of unlawful homicide.

3. Name the two elements usually required for a person to be guilty of crime.

4. What is the name given to offences which only require one of these elements to be present?

5. Name five general defences to criminal charges.

6. What are the three ways by which a person suspected or accused of committing a crime may be brought to court?

Specimen Questions

1. (a) Explain the terms *actus reus* and *mens rea.*
   (b) Explain the crime of strict liability and give examples.

2. Define "murder" and "manslaughter," and discuss the defences to murder which, if successful, result in conviction of manslaughter.

3. Wilson and Betty entered a bar and ordered drinks. When they have finished they decide to leave without paying, Keple the barman, tried to stop them but Wilson pushed him and he banged his head on the bar counter, which caused a swelling above the eye. Explain the crimes which Wilson and Betty may have committed.

4. When does a policeman without a warrant have the power to arrest a person? Do other persons have the power to arrest?

5. As Ben left a cafe he took a coat which was hanging next to his own. Explain Ben's criminal liability.

6. Anne has been charged by the police with taking a car without the owner's consent.
   (a) What crime has Anne committed?
   (b) What specific defences could she plead?
   (c) Would it be the same offence if she had taken a pedal cycle instead of a car?

7. Explain the general defences to a criminal charge.

Chapter 9

FAMILY LAW

MARRIAGE

The standard definition of marriage is "The voluntary union for life of one man and one woman to the exclusion of all others." (*Hyde* v. *Hyde* 1866.)

In this country marriage is monogamous, which means, as the definition above indicates, one man and one woman. When a party is allowed to have more than one spouse at the same time, it is polygamy. In certain countries polygamy is allowed.

Before looking further into the definition, with all the obligations and legal duties which marriage brings upon the parties, it is helpful to consider the legal consequences of the preliminaries that may lead to marriage, such as engagement and co-habitation.

1. Engagement

There is now no action for "breach of promise." Until the Law Reform (Miscellaneous Provisions) Act 1970 abolished this right of action, a party (usually the woman) could sue for damages for breach of contract if the other party refused to marry.

Engagements are usually formalised by the man giving the woman an "engagement" ring. The ring remains the property of the woman should the engagement be broken, unless at the time it was given the man made it clear that in the event of the marriage not taking place the ring was to be returned.

2. Cohabitation

The legal status of an unmarried couple living together as man and wife is very complex, as the law does not recognise such a "marriage." Parliament has recognised, however, that in certain matters these partners have similar duties and problems as legally married partners and has provided appropriate legislation.

For example a woman may claim against the estate of her deceased partner as a dependant, and the Supplementary Benefits Act 1976 treats the partners as though they were married.

The Requirements of a Valid Marriage

1. Both parties must be 16 years of age or over

If either is under 18, consent must be given by both parents, if alive. If the parents refuse to give permission, the minor may apply to the magistrates' court where the magistrates will make a decision based on what they consider to be in the best interests of the minor. A marriage which is formally solemnised without this permission will be valid. A marriage where one of the parties is under 16 years is void.

2. The prohibited degrees

The parties must not be closely related, as marriage is not allowed between parties within the prohibited degrees. This means that certain persons who are closely related, either by blood or marriage, may not marry each other. The obvious relations that are not allowed to marry are parents to their children (*e.g.* father and daughter, mother and son) and brothers and sisters. The Marriage Act 1949 as amended by the Marriage (Enabling) Act 1960, provides two complete lists of the prohibited degrees; a list showing the relations a woman may not marry, and a list of relations a man may not marry. Generally, uncles may not marry nieces, nor aunts their nephews, but first cousins may wed, and a woman may marry her husband's brother, uncle or nephew if her marriage has ended by death or divorce. A man has a similar right to marry his former wife's sister, niece or aunt.

The reason for these prohibitions is, first, public policy, and, secondly, the genetic risk which might produce undesirable side-effects or characteristics in a child born of a marriage between blood relatives.

3. Neither party must have an existing marriage

A person who marries for a second time whilst the first marriage is in existence may commit the crime of bigamy, although the following defences may be pleaded:

(i) that in good faith and on reasonable grounds, it was believed the spouse was dead.

(ii) That in good faith and on reasonable grounds, it was believed that the first marriage was annulled or dissolved.

(iii) That the first spouse had been missing continuously for seven years, and there was no reason for supposing that partner to be alive.

4. The formalities required by statute

A marriage ceremony must be performed and solemnised as provided by the Marriage Act 1949 and 1983.

Void and Voidable Marriages

A void marriage means that, as far as the law is concerned, no marriage has existed and the parties are in a single state. On the other hand, a voidable marriage is regarded as legally valid until a court of competent jurisdiction pronounces it a nullity. Marriages are void because of some defect which is so fundamental that it is considered the marriage never existed.

Voidable marriages are valid, but, because of certain circumstances after, or at the time of the wedding, they may be annulled by the courts:

1. Void marriages

The Nullity of Marriage Act 1971, as now consolidated in the Matrimonial Causes Act 1973, provides that marriages shall be void for the reason that a valid marriage had not taken place because:

(i) one or both of the parties -
   (a) were under 16 years old (see p. 234)
   (b) were within the prohibited degrees (see p. 234)
   (c) were already married (see p. 235)
   (d) had entered a polygamous marriage whilst being domiciled in England or Wales (see p. 233)

(ii) there was a basic defect in the marriage ceremony (see p. 237)

(iii) the parties were not respectively male or female (see p. 233)

2. Voidable marriages

Section 2 of the Nullity of Marriage Act 1971, as consolidated in the Matrimonial Causes Act 1973, provides that marriages are voidable for the following reasons:

(i) the marriage had not been consummated, owing to incapacity or the wilful refusal to consummate, by either party. This means that one party was incapable of having sexual intercourse or refused to do so.

(ii) either party did not validly consent to the marriage because of duress, mistake, unsoundness of mind or otherwise. Parties to marriage must give their consent freely. Similarly, an insane person cannot give a valid consent because he does not know the consequences of what he is saying. This situation may also exist if one of the parties is drunk or under the influence of drugs.

(iii) either party was, at the time of the marriage, suffering from a mental disorder within the Mental Health Act 1959, which makes them unfitted for marriage.

(iv) one party was suffering from venereal disease in a communicable form and the other party did not know.

(v) at the time of the marriage, the man did not know that the bride was pregnant by some person other than him.

A petition for nullity of a marriage may be made to the court immediately. There is no need, as with divorce, to wait for a period of time. Petitions for reasons (iii), (iv) and (v) above, must be made within three years but this period may be extended if the petitioner has been suffering from a mental disorder. The court has the discretion to refuse to grant a decree if it considers it would be unjust to do so.

It must be noted that children born of a voidable marriage are legitimate, even if the marriage is later declared void by the court, and children born of a void marriage are legitimate, if, at the time of conception (or the marriage, if later), the parties reasonably believed the marriage to be valid.

The Formalities of a Marriage

A marriage may be solemnised by a Church of England ceremony, by ceremonies of another religion or in a Registrar's Office. The formalities of each ceremony are different.

1. Church of England

(i) Banns have to be published. Banns are a public announcement that the marriage is to take place and they must be published on three Sundays in the churches of either or both of the parties.

(ii) A common licence has to be issued by a Bishop for the marriage to take place within the parish of one of the parties, or the Archbishop of Canterbury has to issue a special licence which permits the parties to marry anywhere.

(iii) A superintendent registrar's certificate has to be issued, which authorises the church to solemnise the marriage.

(iv) The wedding must take place between the hours of 8 a.m. and 6 p.m. within three months of the banns being published, and there must be two or more witnesses.

2. Marriages solemnised by a superintendent registrar's certificate

The certificate authorises a marriage to take place:

(i) in the superintendent registrar's office, or

(ii) in a registered building (usually a church of a non-Anglican religion) except in marriages between two professing Jews or between members of the Society of Friends (Quakers).

(iii) between the hours of 8 a.m. and 6 p.m. before open doors and witnessed by at least two persons (except Jewish or Quaker marriages).

(iv) within three months of the issue of the certificate.
(v) The Marriage Act 1983 enables marriages of housebound and detained persons to be solemnised at the place where they reside.

The Duties of Husband and Wife

The legal consequence of marriage is that certain duties fall upon the parties. Some of the duties are laid down by statute, while others are provided by the common law.

The principal duties are as follows:

(i) The husband has a common law duty to maintain his wife but she loses the right if she commits adultery or deserts him. A wife may be ordered to maintain a husband who, because of illness, is incapable of earning an income. A wife has the right to pledge her husband's credit (buying goods on his account) by the presumed implication that she is his agent. This presumption may be rebutted by the husband informing the trader not to give credit to his wife, or by his showing the court that the wife had a sufficient supply of the goods in question, or that she had a sufficient allowance to pay for them herself.
(ii) Both have a duty to maintain their children and send them to school.
(iii) Both spouses have a duty to cohabit (live together) and this usually means a duty to have sexual relations.

DIVORCE

The Matrimonial and Family Proceedings Act 1984 provides that either spouse may petition for divorce after one year of marriage. The courts have no discretion to shorten this period.

The only reason for petitioning for divorce is that "the marriage has broken down irretrievably." The basis of the law on divorce is the Divorce Reform Act 1969, now consolidated into the Matrimonial Causes Act 1973. A petitioner for divorce must prove to the court any one of five "facts" which can establish that the marriage has irretrievably broken down. Even if one or more of these facts are established, however, the court will not grant a divorce if it remains unconvinced about the breakdown of the marriage. The five facts which can establish the breakdown of the marriage are:

1. Adultery

Adultery is voluntary sexual intercourse between two persons, one or both of whom are married, but not to each other. The petitioner must prove that the other spouse committed adultery and that this act makes it intolerable to continue living with the respondent.

2. Behaviour

The petitioner must show that the respondent's behaviour was such that the petitioner could not reasonably be expected to live with the respondent.

It is a question of fact in each case, but the court would obviously expect to see evidence of very unreasonable behaviour, such as violence, extreme bad temper, drunkenness, obsessive jealousy and so on.

3. Desertion

It must be shown that the respondent deserted the petitioner for a period of two years or more. Generally desertion means living apart, but if the parties live in the same house, not as man and wife but following completely separate lives, this might be considered sufficient to prove desertion. It would be desertion if the respondent acted in such a way that the petitioner had to leave the family home.

4. Living apart for two years

The petitioner must show that the parties have lived apart continuously for more than two years immediately before presentation of the petition and that the respondent consents to the decree being granted.

5. Living apart for five years

It is sufficient under this heading to show that the marriage has broken down and the consent or otherwise of the other party is irrelevant to a spouse's right to petition.

In practice the vast majority of petitions are made on facts one to three.

Divorce Decrees

When a petition is successful the court grants a "decree nisi." The effect of this decree is not to dissolve the marriage immediately but it will be dissolved unless good cause be shown to the court, within six weeks, why the decree should not be made absolute.

After six weeks have elapsed, the party who was granted the decree may apply to the court for a "decree absolute." Until this decree has been granted the parties may not remarry, and would be committing bigamy if they did so.

Undefended Divorces
Well over 90 per cent. of petitions are undefended and procedure for such cases has been simplified and made slightly impersonal because neither party nor their lawyers need attend the hearing. It is commonly known as the "postal divorce."

Throughout the United Kingdom in 1982 there were 387,000 marriages and 159,000 divorces.

JUDICIAL SEPARATION

There are occasions when the parties to a marriage do not wish to live together as man and wife, but do not want to obtain a divorce. The reasons for petitioning for a judicial separation and not for divorce are usually religious or because children are involved. There are less than 1,000 petitions each year for judicial separation.

The petition may be made at any time, based on one of the five grounds for divorce outlined above. Its main effect is to release the parties from their obligation to cohabit.

MAINTENANCE

A wife whose husband neglects to maintain her or the children of the marriage, may apply to the courts for a matrimonial order for maintenance. Maintenance is a financial payment or settlement from a husband to maintain a wife and family. An order for maintenance may be obtained from the magistrates' court, county court or High Court. It is possible for a man to apply for maintenance from his wife, but, because it is more usual, the text that follows refers to wives claiming from husbands, although it would apply to the reverse situation.

Maintenance is usually claimed when the married parties do not live together, because of a breakdown in the marriage. A party may claim as a result of a judicial separation or divorce or when the parties are separated but no legal action has been taken.

1. Maintenance claims made before or after divorce or legal separation

(*A*) *Before the divorce or legal separation,* the courts may award periodical cash payments to be paid by the spouse. The amount payable is what the court considers reasonable in the circumstances; and it is provided to enable the claimant to maintain herself until the court action. Maintenance for children may also be claimed at this time.

(*B*) *After legal proceedings,* the courts may award in addition to a periodical cash payment:

(i) a lump sum for the wife and children, or
(ii) a part of the husband's capital (usually no more than one-third) to be secured for the benefit of the wife and children,
(iii) a transfer of property belonging to the husband or which was owned jointly.

The court has discretion as to the size and nature of an award, but section 25 of the Matrimonial Causes Act 1973 provides that it has a duty to consider all the circumstances of the case, and it must try to place the parties in the same financial position as if the marriage had not broken down. The court must consider:

(i) the income, earning capacity and financial resources of both parties,
(ii) the financial needs and obligations the parties have or are likely to have,
(iii) the standard of living enjoyed by the family before the breakdown of the marriage,
(iv) the age of the parties, and the length of the marriage,
(v) any disability of either of the parties, physical or mental,
(vi) the contribution each party made to the welfare of the family,
(vii) after a divorce or nullity, the value of the loss of some benefit (such as a pension) which cannot be acquired because of the termination of the marriage.

The courts have power to vary the awards on the application of either party. The amounts may be increased or reduced or the method of payment varied or the payment stopped. For example, in *Cann* v. *Cann* (1977) a wife obtained a matrimonial order from the magistrates' court and a year later, in 1961, the couple were divorced. In 1974, the wife successfully applied for a variation and the order was increased to £7 per week. Two years later the husband retired and applied for a reduction. His weekly income was £23 and the wife's income was £13. The court reduced the order to £5 per week, and considered that the one-third rule was inappropriate in this case. The result of the variation was that both the husband and wife had weekly incomes of £18.

2. Maintenance claims when there are no judicial proceedings for divorce or separation

A wife may apply to the courts (magistrates or superior courts) for maintenance on the grounds that her husband has neglected to provide maintenance for her and her children (if any). The claim may also be made on the grounds that, because of the husband's desertion or behaviour, the wife could not reasonably be expected to live with him. This behaviour could include such acts as adultery, cruelty, violence, drunkenness, and the like.

Maintenance paid to claimants is a weekly sum and is loosely based on one third of the gross total income of the parties. For example, if a husband earned £120 and the wife had no income, the wife would receive £40 a week. However, if the husband earned £60 and the wife earned £60 per week, the wife would receive nothing because she earned more than one-third of the total income. A county court or High Court may award a lump sum.

An important factor when assessing maintenance is the payment of supplementary benefit. A woman receiving supplementary benefit will have the payment reduced by the amount of maintenance received. In such circumstances the Supplementary Benefits Commission gains from the award of maintenance.

Revision Test

1. What is the minimum age for marriage?

2. If a minor marries over this age but under 18 is the marriage valid?

3. Name the only reason for petitioning for a divorce.

4. What are the five facts which establish the reason for divorce?

5. What are the decrees granted by the court to a successful petitioner for a divorce?

Specimen Questions

1. Outline the essential requirements of a valid marriage?

2. How may a marriage be legally ended?

3. What is the legal position of minors if they wish to marry?

4. Distinguish between void and voidable marriages.

5. What is judicial separation and how does it differ from divorce?

6. Explain what maintenance is and how it may be claimed.

7. Describe the duties and responsibilities of a man and wife when they marry.

Chapter 10

LAW OF SUCCESSION

Death comes to all and the law of succession deals with the ways by which property of a dead person is transferred to the new owners. The duty of transferring the property falls to personal representatives, called executors and administrators depending on whether or not the dead person left a will. The law allows (with some exceptions as shown later) for a person to decide the destination of his property after death by leaving a will. If, however, a will is not made a dead person's possessions are distributed according to rules laid down by statute.

WILLS

A will is a declaration by a person about the distribution after death of his property, both real and personal. It must be noted that a will has no legal effect, and does not come into operation, until the death of the testator. A person named in the will, therefore, has no claim or right to any property until the testator's death, and until that occurs, the testator may do what he likes with the property. It could be sold, destroyed or given away to someone not named in the will. It is desirable for a person with a large estate to make a will, although for those who have little property the need is not so great. A will is necessary, however, when it is the intention to leave property to persons who are not members of the testator's immediate family, or on the negative side to ensure that a certain near relative does not inherit anything. For example, a wife may not wish a husband who deserted her to inherit her property, so she may make a will leaving the property to someone else.

Anyone aged 18 or over and of sound mind may make a will, provided it complies with the requirements of the Wills Act 1837 and the Administration of Justice Act 1982. There is no need to have it drawn up by a solicitor, although it is not usually expensive if professional services are required. Wills in blank form may be bought from most stationers, and, provided the testator's intentions are straightforward, there should be no difficulty. The "do-it-yourself" variety may give solicitors work, however, because of the possibility that the will may be disputed in court. It is impossible to know how many adults make wills, but it is estimated that is is less than 25 per cent. of those entitled to do so.

Requirement of a Valid Will

1. A will must be in writing, and must be signed by the testator (the person making the will). The writing can be on any type of paper or parchment (a will has been accepted which was written on an egg shell), and the will may refer to several other documents, provided that they are capable of being identified and were in existence at the time of making the will. The testator's signature should normally be at the end of the writing but if it is, say, at the top of a will, it would be effective if it appears that the testator intended his signature to make the will valid. The intention could be shown by evidence, such as independant witnesses. If the testator cannot write, a "mark" (usually a cross), or an ink thumb-print will be sufficient provided the "mark" can be identified as the testator's. Another person may sign if the testator cannot, say for reasons of infirmity, sign himself. The will must be signed in the presence of the testator, who must acknowledge that the other person signs on his behalf.
2. The testator's signature must be witnessed by a least two witnesses who are present at the same time. Witnesses do not have to be present when the signature is made, provided the testator acknowledges the signature as his. If the witnesses are not present together at the time of the signature or acknowledgement the will is generally void. The Administration of Justice Act 1982, provides that if only one witness

is present when the testator signs a will, both the testator and witness may acknowledge their signatures at a later date, when a second witness is present and adds the second signature. This provision would not apply when an attestation clause is used (see p. 256).

A witness must reasonably understand that he is witnessing a signature, but it is not necessary for him to know the nature or contents of the document. A competent witness could be a person under 18 or over 80, or an illiterate, provided that he had sufficient understanding. A blind person would not be a competent witness because he would not be able to observe the signature or acknowledgement.

It is not necessary for the will to have an attestation clause, but it is usual. The witnesses may sign or make their marks immediately below the testator's signature.

Witnesses, or their spouses, generally cannot benefit from a will, but it must be stressed that provided there are other beneficiaries named in the will it would not be invalid, but only the gift to the particular witness or spouse would be void. The Wills Act 1968 provides that, if there are two or more disinterested witnesses, gifts to additional witnesses will be valid. See *Re Bravda* (p. 3).

Soldiers' Wills

It has been recognised that in times of emergencies or war, there may not be the opportunity to comply with the requirements needed to make a valid will. A sailor, for example, could not be expected to have his signature attested while his ship was sinking into the sea. Witnesses may be difficult to find in such circumstances.

The strict rules for making a will as stated above are relaxed for soldiers, sailors and airmen on actual military service, or for any seaman at sea.

An informal or nuncupative will may be made by the above if they are aged 14 or over. If a will is in writing witnesses are not needed, although if made orally there obviously must be witnesses.

In *Rapley* v. *Rapley* (1983) a 15 year old sailor wrote an unwitnessed will while on shore leave. When he died more than 40 years later the court held that as he was not at sea when the will was made, it had no effect and he died intestate (see p. 253).

Whether or not the forces are on actual military service depends on the nature and activities of the force to which they are attached. In *Re Jones* (1981), Jones was a soldier stationed in Northern Ireland. In 1978 he was shot and on the way to the hospital and before two officers said "If I do not make it, make sure Anne gets all my stuff." (Anne was his fiancée.) Jones died on the following day. It was held by the court that this statement be accepted as his last will even though he had previously made a formal will in favour of his mother. The court considered that he was on actual military service at the time of making the statement although there was no state of war and the forces to which he belonged were not engaged against a regular or uniformed enemy. (see p. 24.)

An informal will remains valid even after the hostilities or emergencies have ended.

Revocation of a Will

The absence of the necessary formalities makes a will invalid and this usually means that the intentions of the testator are ignored by law and the property distributed as an intestacy. A testator may change, vary or completely revoke a will. A will may be revoked expressly, or impliedly from the conduct of the testator.

1. By expressly revoking the will

An express revocation has to be made in exactly the same way as making a will, *i.e.* in writing, signed and witnessed.

2. By making a new will or codicil

A new or subsequent will revokes all previous wills which are not inconsistent or different. It is usual to start a new will with a statement revoking all previous wills, thereby making an express revocation. If this statement is not made, any gifts in a previous will would still be effective if not accounted for in the subsequent will. For example, if a will provided, "my money in the bank to Peter, my car to Michael, my dog to Linda," and a subsequent will provided, "my money to David, my car to Nicholas and my boat to James," and there was no clause revoking previous wills, Linda would be entitled to the dog, because the second will made no provision for this property. Without the express exclusion clause it would be necessary to study all previous wills to find the testator's intentions.

Sometimes a will is amended or varied by a codicil, which is inserted in or attached to the will. It is necessary to have a codicil signed and witnessed.

3. By destroying a will

A will is only revoked if it is intentionally destroyed by the testator or by someone else in the testator's presence and as instructed by the testator. It may be destroyed by burning, tearing or any other means, but it must be done with the intention of destroying the will. A will destroyed accidentally would still be valid. In such a case, the personal representative would refer to other material, such as a copy of the will or oral evidence, to find the testator's intentions.

4. By subsequent divorce

A divorce or nullity of marriage revokes any gift to a former spouse and revokes the appointment of a former spouse as executor. If other persons were to benefit from the will the will would be valid, but the gifts to the spouse would be a partial intestacy (see below).

5. By subsequent marriage

A will of a man or woman is revoked by a subsequent marriage, but a will made after 1925 will not be revoked if it is made in contemplation of marriage. It is not sufficient to state in the will that the testator intends to marry, the will would still be revoked by a subsequent marriage unless the name of the intended spouse was also stated and the testator intended that the will would not be revoked by the marriage.

FAMILY PROVISION

Before 1938 a man could leave his property to whomsoever he wished, and there was no requirement to provide for his family. A man could give his entire estates to charity and leave his wife penniless. The Inheritance (Family Provision) Act 1938 gave the court power to make a financial provision out of the husband's estate to a wife and certain other dependants if they had not been provided for in the will. Further and more extensive powers were given to the courts by the Inheritance (Provision for Family and Dependants) Act 1975. This Act provides that the court has a discretion to make an award out of the dead person's estate to dependants who have not received "reasonable financial provision," from a will or intestacy, or from both. The following persons may apply to the court for family provision:

1. The husband or wife of the dead person and former spouses who have not remarried.

2. Children of the deceased, whether they be illegitimate, adopted, or treated as a child of the family. There is no restriction as to age, incapacity, sex or whether married or not.

In Re Callaghan Deceased (1984), a married man, over 40, made a successful claim to be treated as a child of the family and was awarded a lump sum because the deceased, who died intestate, had treated him as a son from the age of 12.

3. Any other persons who immediately before the death of the deceased were being maintained, either wholly or partly, by the deceased. This heading would cover other relatives such as sisters, brothers, mothers and fathers, friends, common law wives and mistresses who were receiving substantial financial support before the deceased's death.

"Reasonable financial provision" means:

(a) In the case of a spouse, financial provision as would be reasonable in all the circumstances, whether or not that provision is needed for maintenance,

(b) In the case of other persons, such financial provision, as would be reasonable in all the circumstances, needed for their maintenance.

The applications must be made within six months of grant of probate or letters of administration being taken out. The court would consider the value of the estate and the provision already made to the applicant. In the case of a spouse, consideration would be given to age, duration of marriage and the contribution made by the applicant to the family and its welfare.

With regard to young children, educational needs would be considered and with older children, the ability to reasonably maintain themselves. The court would also take into consideration statements made by the deceased as to the reason why certain provisions were made or were not made.

The court may award lump sums or periodical payments, transfer certain property, such as the family house, and make settlements of other property.

LEGACIES

The legal terms for the gifts named in a will differ according to the property. A transfer of real property (freehold land) is called a devise, and the transfer of personal property (chattels) are called legacies or bequests.

Types of Legacies

1. General legacy

This is a gift where no specific thing is named, "I leave a car to . . . " or "I give a boat to . . . "

2. Specific legacy

As the name suggests, a specific thing is given. "I leave my Rover car . . . " or "I leave my boat the 'Skylark' to . . . "

3. Residuary legacy

After all the debts have been paid and the general and specific devises and legacies distributed, the residue is what is left.

It should be noted that if a general or specific gift is not in the testator's possession at the time of death, the gift "is adeemed" and there is no inheritance. Should a person named in a will die before the testator, the gift lapses and goes into the residue, unless the person is the child of the testator and he dies leaving an issue (see below), or the will provides for another to receive it. For example, it is quite common to leave property to X, if X dies before the testator, it is left to Y.

4. Children of testator

When a testator leaves property to sons or daughters, the gifts shall not lapse if they die before the testator, provided they die leaving an issue (children). The property passes per stripes, to the issue living at the time of the testator's death. If, for example, a gift was to a son or daughter who died before the testator childless, the gift would lapse and pass to the residuary estate, but if the son or daughter had one or more children alive at the time of the testator's death, the issue would take, in equal shares, the gift intended for their father or mother.

PERSONAL REPRESENTATIVES

Property of a deceased person vests in personal representatives who have a duty to collect all money and property due to the deceased, pay all debts owed by the deceased, including funeral expenses, and sell or convert property as is necessary.

An executor is usually named in the will and has the above duties to perform immediately upon the death of the testator. Before an executor may deal with the estate, it is necessary to apply to the court for a grant of probate. It is normally a formal exercise in presenting the will and giving details of the property and value of the deceased's estate. Provided that there are no complications, probate should be granted in a comparatively short period of time. A beneficiary may be appointed executor, and frequently more than one executor is named in the will. Solicitors and banks often act as executors.

As soon as probate has been granted, an executor may collect and pay off debts, and then distribute the estate according to the terms of the will.

An administrator is appointed if an executor is unwilling or unable to act, or not named in the will, or if there is no will and the deceased died "intestate."

Administrators are appointed by the court (usually the spouse or children of the deceased) and they apply for Letters of Administration in a similar way as an executor applies for probate. They distribute the estate according to the will or if there is no will, according to the rule of intestacy (see below).

INTESTACY

When a person dies without making a will, he is said to die intestate, and property is distributed according to the rules laid down by the Administration of Estates Act 1925, as amended by other Acts. These rules also apply to a partial intestacy which occurs when all the testator's property has not been disposed of by a will. For convenience, the following rules assume that it is a man that has died, but the rules are similarly applied when a woman is deceased.

1. A surviving wife only

There are no children to the marriage and the deceased has no living parents, brothers or sisters, or their issue - the wife receives the whole estate.

2. A surviving wife and children

The wife receives the personal chattels (furniture, etc.) and the first £40,000 of the estate, plus interest at 7 per cent., from the date of death to the time of payment. The balance of the estate is then halved. The wife receives interest on one half for life; the children share the other half immediately, and the mother's half on her death.

The share for children under 18 is kept in trust until they reach that age. The issue of a child of the deceased would receive the share of its parent who had predeceased the intestate (*e.g.* a grandchild would inherit if its parent had died before the grandparent).

An illegitimate child may claim against the estate of both parents.

3. A surviving wife with no children, but a surviving parent, brother or sister, or their issue

The wife would receive the chattels, the first £85,000 with interest at 7 per cent. as above, and the absolute ownership of half of the remaining balance. Surviving parents would equally share the other half, but if there were no surviving parents, brothers or sisters (or their issue if they predeceased the intestate) would share this half of the residue.

4. Surviving children but no wife

The children take absolutely all the estate, but if under 18 the property would be held on trust. They take the estate regardless of all other relatives.

5. Surviving parents, but no wife or children

The parents share absolutely the whole estate.

6. No surviving wife, children or parents

The following relations will be entitled to the estate in the following order:

- (i) brothers and sisters of the whole blood
- (ii) brothers and sisters of the half blood
- (iii) grandparents
- (iv) uncles and aunts of the whole blood
- (v) uncles and aunts of the half blood

If none of these relations survive the intestate, the estate passes to the Crown as Bona Vacantia. The property which comes the way of Bona Vacentia is disposed of and the proceeds paid into the Exchequer. It is possible to recover the proceeds at a later date if an unknown relative makes a belated claim.

Forfeiture Rule

It is a general rule of law that a person who unlawfully kills another is stopped from benefitting as a consequence of the killing. The "forfeiture rule" arises from public policy. Obviously, a person named in a will cannot benefit from the will if he murders the testator.

The Forfeiture Act 1982 was created to enable certain persons found guilty of unlawful killing (other than murder),

(i) to obtain relief from forfeiture of inheritance,
(ii) to enable such persons to claim for financial provision out of the deceased person's estate, and
(iii) to receive certain pensions and social security benefits.

The Act allows persons convicted of unlawful killing (manslaughter, death caused by reckless driving, suicide pacts, infanticide, etc.) to make a claim, within three months of conviction, to the court to modify the "forfeiture rule." The court will only do so if the justice of the case requires it to do so. It must be stressed that convicted murderers do not come within this Act.

In *Re K.* (*Deceased*) 1985 (the first case under this Act) a wife, during a quarrel, killed her husband with a shotgun. She pleaded guilty to manslaughter, and as she had been subject to unprovoked violent attacks by the husband, she received a two year probation order. The court held that although the "forfeiture rule" applied on the facts of the case it would be unjust if she was stopped from receiving benefit under the will, and ordered that the effect of the "rule" should be modified accordingly.

Specimen Form of a Draft Will

This is the Last Will and Testament of James Doe, 4 Somerset Street, Manchester.

1. I Hereby Revoke all former wills made by mc and declare this to be my last will.

2. I Appoint My Son John Doe as the executor of my will.

3. I Bequeath to my son John Doe my car and £5,000.

4. I Devise and Bequeath all the residue of my estate both real and personal whatsoever and wheresoever to my wife Jane Doe.

In Witness Whereof I have hereunto set my hand this thirty-first day of July One Thousand Nine Hundred and Eighty Two.

Signed by the above named James Doe as and for his Last Will and Testament in the presence of us both present at the same time who at his request in his presence and in the presence of each other have hereunto subscribed our names as witnesses.

James Doe
(signature).

Uriah Heap—(signature)
Solicitor,
Manchester.

Ebenezer Scrooge—(signature)
7 South Street,
Manchester,
Secretary.

NOTE. The writing opposite the signature of James Doe is the attestation clause. You will note that the witnesses sign as being "both present at the same time". (See page 247.)

Revision Test

1. What is the minimum age that a person may make a formal will?

2. What is the name of a person who makes a valid will?

3. May a person claim a legacy before the person making the will dies?

4. May a blind person be a witness to a will?

5. Name the five ways by which a will may be revoked.

6. What is the name given to a personal representative
   (a) named in a will,
   (b) where there is no will.

Specimen Questions

1. What are the requirements of a valid will? When are these formalities not required?

2. How may a will be revoked or amended?

3. Discuss the validity of the following wills:
   (a) Joyce signed her will in the presence of Tim (who is blind) and David (aged 17), both of whom signed as witnesses. At a later date Nick also signed the will as a witness.
   (b) By his will Henry left his estate to Fred and Perry. Henry's signature was witnessed by Fred, Perry and their two secretaries.

4. What are the legal titles and duties of personal representatives of a deceased person?

5. Explain how the estate of a dead person is distributed when he dies without leaving a will.

6. Explain the present position of the law with regard to family provision.

Chapter 11

WELFARE LAW

LANDLORD AND TENANT

The Rent Act 1977 as amended by the Housing Act 1980 covers most kinds of tenancies and provides protection for security of tenure and rent control. The 1977 Act consolidated the provisions of the Rent Act 1968 and the Rent Act 1974 and amends the law of certain related statutes, such as the Housing Finance Act 1972, the Housing Rents and Subsidies Act 1975 and the Rent (Agriculture) Act 1976.

The purpose of these enactments is to control the rent that a landlord may charge and to enable people who rent accommodation (*e.g.* houses, flats, rooms) to live without fear of being unreasonably or unjustifiably evicted from their homes. The protection provided by the Acts depends on the type of tenancy. Not all tenancies have the same protection afforded by the Acts, and it is, therefore, necessary to define the different tenancies.

1. Protected tenancies

The Housing Act 1980 abolished controlled tenancies and converted them all into regulated tenancies.

Regulated tenancies exist when the rateable value of the property is less than £1,500 in Greater London or £750 elsewhere, and they can be either contractual tenancies or statutory tenancies.

(a) A contractual tenancy exists when an agreement, in writing or by word of mouth is made between the landlord and tenant. The period of the tenancy may be fixed (*e.g.* two years) or it may be periodic (*e.g.* weekly) with no fixed length of tenancy.

(b) A statutory tenancy exists because of provisions in the Rent Acts. Common examples are when a fixed term tenancy expires and the tenant continues to live in the premises and pay the same rent as before, or in cases when the tenant dies and the tenancy may be passed on to certain members of the family, who become statutory tenants by succession.

It should be noted that the following are not protected tenancies.

(a) When the dwelling-house has a rateable value exceeding £1,500 in Greater London or £750 elsewhere.

(b) When no rent is payable or a "low rent" is payable which is less than two-thirds of the rateable value which does not exceed £400 in Greater London or £200 elsewhere.

(c) A tenancy which includes in the rent, payment for board or attendance. A landlord cannot evade the provisions of the Act by providing a trivial service; the rent attributable to the attendance would have to form a substantial part of the whole rent.

(d) Rooms or lettings to a student following a course at a specified educational institution, such as a university or college.

(e) Houses let for a holiday.

2. Restricted contracts

A "restricted contract" applies when one person grants to another person the right to occupy a dwelling as a residence and,

(i) the rent includes payment for the use of furniture or for services, such as the supply of hot water and heating and lighting.

(ii) the tenant has exclusive occupation of certain accommodation but shares other necessary accommodation (*e.g.* bathroom, kitchen) with the landlord or other persons.

3. Secure tenancies

The Housing Act 1980 provided certain protection for some tenancies that were not previously covered to the same extent by the Rent Acts. They include tenancies granted by:

(a) local authorities (council houses),
(b) housing trusts and charities, and
(c) housing associations.

4. Shorthold tenancies

The 1980 Act created this new form of tenancy for agreements that came into effect after 1980, for a fixed period of more than one year but less than five years.

Rent Control

1. Regulated tenancies

Most rents for regulated tenancies are fixed by the rent officer and recorded in the Rent Register, or they are agreed between the landlord and tenant.

The landlord and/or tenant may apply to the rent officer to fix the rent, although either or both parties must indicate what they consider to be a fair rent for the premises. A registered rent is determined for the particular dwelling, and to ensure uniformity the rent is calculated on the following guidelines:

(i) the age, character, locality and state of repair of the dwelling,
(ii) the quantity, quality and condition of any furniture to be provided under the tenancy,
(iii) the assumption that the number of persons seeking similar dwellings in the locality is not substantially greater than the number of such dwellings available in the locality, and
(iv) the provision or improvement of any amenity provided at the cost of the landlord.

It should be noted that the financial position of either party is not considered before fixing the rent. It is not the rent officer's duty to consider if the tenant can afford the rent, or if the landlord could afford a reduction in the rent. The rent may be changed after it has been registered, but usually only after two years from the date of registration. The Acts provide the following reasons for changing a fixed rent before this time:

(i) when both landlord and tenant jointly apply,

(ii) when either party claims there has been a substantial change in:

(a) the condition of the premises. The landlord, for example, could apply for an increase because of improvements or renovations to the property or the provision of an amenity; while the tenant could apply for a reduction because the condition of the property has deteriorated.

(b) the furniture or services provided,

(c) the terms of the contract, or

(d) any other circumstances which would make the registered rent no longer a reasonable rent.

(iii) when the landlord pays the rates any increase in the rates may be added to the rent. After the two year period of registration has expired, a landlord may apply by a new registration for an increase.

A notice of increase is usually served on the tenant when a landlord wishes to increase the rent for any reason mentioned above. The notice is in prescribed form and is effective from the date of registration. The Acts provide that when a rent officer registers a rent which is higher than the rent payable before registration, the amount of the increase may not be recoverable at once, but should be phased over two years, half in the first year and the other half in the second year. If, for example, the rent was increased by £1 a week, the rent would be increased by 50p in the first year and the final 50p would be added in the second year.

Rent agreements

Landlords and tenants of regulated tenancies may agree the rents in writing between themselves and there is no need to register the rent. Such an agreement does not stop either party going at any time to a rent officer for the rent to be fixed and registered. Should the rent be increased by the rent officer the increase would be subject to phasing as stated above.

2. Restricted contracts

Initially the rent is agreed between the landlord and tenant, but either party under a restricted contract may refer the contract to a rent assessment committee (rent tribunal).

3. Secure tenancies

The fixing of rents for tenants of council houses has not been changed by the Housing Act 1980. The rent is still decided by the council. The Act, however, provided that rents should not be increased because the tenant had lawfully improved the condition of the property.

4. Shorthold tenancies

The rent is registered or a certificate of fair rent is made, by the rent officer, or if subject to appeal, by the rent assessment committee.

Rent Book

Any tenant of furnished or unfurnished premises whose rent is paid weekly is entitled to a rent book provided by the landlord. It is a criminal offence not to provide a rent book. The recordings in the book are evidence of the payment of rent, although either party may question the accuracy of the entries. The rent book is also evidence of the tenant's rights, although the absence of a rent book does not mean that the tenant has no rights and may lose the tenancy. Oral and implied evidence, such as the landlord receiving the rent, may be sufficient to prove that an agreement of tenancy exists.

A rent book does not have to be in a particular form or size, but it must contain the following information:

(i) The landlord's name and address.
(ii) The amount of rent to be paid.
(iii) The tenant's rights under the Rent Acts, together with an up-to-date leaflet giving details of rent allowances.
(iv) The number of persons who may live in the premises.
(v) The law and offences against overcrowding.

The Rent Act 1977 provides that the rent book may be corrected by the court when it shows arrears which the court has determined to be irrecoverable.

Rent Allowances

Any tenant or person hiring rooms or lodgings on low incomes may claim a rent allowance from the local authority. The method of calculating the allowance is based on income, less certain outgoings and allowances for dependants. The net figure will determine whether or not a tenant is entitled to an allowance, and the amount, if the tenant is so entitled. A tenant receiving supplementary benefit or an old aged pensioner whose sole income is the state pension will probably be entitled to a rebate for the whole rent. The right to receive these benefits applies equally to tenants of council and private houses.

Security of Tenure

Protected and statutory tenants are protected from arbitrary eviction for life, unless a court makes an order for possession. A court shall not make such an order unless it considers it reasonable to do so and either the court is satisfied that suitable accommodation is or will be available or the circumstances are as specified in the Act as follows:

(i) Non-payment of rent,
(ii) the tenant has been guilty of causing a nuisance, or has used the dwelling-house for immoral or illegal purposes,
(iii) the condition of the premises has deteriorated owing to the neglect of the tenant,
(iv) the tenant has caused damage to the furniture provided under the tenancy,
(v) the dwelling-house is reasonably required by the landlord as a residence for himself or family.

Tenants under a restricted contract have the right, after receiving notice to quit, to apply to the county court for security of tenure, up to a maximum of three months.

Tenants under *secure tenancies* now receive similar security of tenure as enjoyed by protected tenants.

Shorthold tenancies exist for the length of the fixed term agreement, and only the tenant has the right to end the tenancy before the fixed term expires. Should the tenancy continue after the first fixed term, it becomes a protected tenancy.

Notice to Quit

A landlord who wishes to end a tenancy must give notice to the tenant. The notice must be in writing and provide a minimum period of four weeks' notice. (Protection from Eviction Act 1977.)

The notice must contain certain information as prescribed by regulations made by the Secretary of State by statutory instrument. A notice to quit would contain the following information:

(i) the tenant's rights,
(ii) the necessity for the landlord to obtain a court order before the eviction may take place,
(iii) the grounds for which a landlord may obtain a court order,
(iv) the rent tribunal's power to postpone the effective date of the notice and, with restricted contracts, grant up to six months' security of tenure,
(v) advice as to where a tenant may obtain information concerning his legal rights, such as the Citizens Advice Bureau, the rent tribunal office and the right to legal advice and assistance.

Harassment

It is legal for a landlord to offer an inducement to a tenant in an attempt to obtain an agreement to quit the premises; it is illegal to attempt to force a tenant to leave the premises. An offer of a payment of money which the tenant agreed to accept would be a binding contract, but a threat of force if the premises were not vacated would be harassment. Section 1 of the Protection from Eviction Act 1977 provides that a person shall be guilty of an offence if he unlawfully deprives an occupier of his premises or attempts to do so, or with intent to cause the occupier to give up the occupation of the premises, does acts calculated to interfere with the peace or comfort of the occupier or members of his household, or persistently withdraws or withholds services reasonably required for the occupation of the premises as a residence. A person guilty of this offence is liable to a fine and/or imprisonment for a term not exceeding two years.

Examples of acts which could be considered as harassment are physical bullying, causing a nuisance, terminating the supply of gas or electricity and other such conduct which would make the tenant's life unbearable.

In addition to the criminal punishment mentioned above, a tenant may apply to the civil courts for damages and an injunction to restrain the landlord from continuing the acts.

Ownership

The first part of this chapter dealt with renting property, either from a private landlord or the local council. A large number of people, however, "own" and occupy their own houses or flats and are not affected by the law relating to landlord and tenant. House ownership falls under two headings; either freehold or leasehold.

Freehold land

This form of ownership has the technical name of "fee simple absolute in possesion" and it gives the owner the right to reside in the property or to receive or collect rents from other persons who may reside in the property. "Fee simple," means that the property is an estate of inheritance and may be left in a will to whoever the owner wishes, without any restriction; "absolute" means that it is not subject to any condition of length or period of time; and "in possession," means that the owner has the right of possession, or to receive rents, immediately.

Leasehold land

It is not complete ownership of the land, but gives the holder the right to enjoy the "ownership" of the land for the period of the lease. Its technical name is "term of years absolute," and the term can be for a very small period of time, say one week or one month to say 999 years. Leasehold land may be sold or inherited during the term of years as may freehold, but at the end of the term of the lease, the land reverts back to the freeholder, together with any house or other buildings that have been erected on the land. There is statutory provision for leaseholders to purchase the freehold under certain conditions and within the period of the leasehold.

Means of Purchasing Houses

Mortgage

The vast majority of house buyers do not have the money to buy a house or flat, and they borrow the money from institutions. A loan is made on the security of the house, and a mortgage is created. A mortgage is a conveyance of real property (freehold) or personal property (leasehold) as security for the repayment of the money borrowed. If the owner does not or will not repay the loan, the mortgagee (the lender) may take possession of the property. Building Societies are the most common lenders of money for house purchases. The borrower usually has to provide a proportion of the cost of the house, usually between 10 per cent. and 20 per cent., and the balance is repaid, plus interest, over a given period of time, usually between 20–30 years.

Insurance companies, local councils and banks will also make loans to assist home buyers. An insurance company may make the loan on the security of a life assurance policy. This method means the borrower has to repay the interest, plus the premiums of the life assurance policy, and in some cases, the loan.

It should be noted that home ownership does not give unrestricted rights over the property, as it will be subject to many restrictions contained in covenants, local bye-laws and government statutes.

SOCIAL SECURITY

Social security is a system of State financial assistance to persons aged 16 and over. The aim of social security is to ensure that persons who do not have sufficient income to maintain themselves or their dependants will receive a minimum income.

1. National insurance

Most employed and self-employed persons pay a national insurance contribution, and employers also pay a contribution for every employee. The scheme is administered by the Department of Health and Social Security (D.H.S.S.). The scheme aims to reduce the risk of workers suffering financial loss through occurrences such as:

(i) sickness,
(ii) unemployment,
(iii) maternity.

Most national insurance benefits are subject to contributions being kept up-to-date. A break in payment of contribution could mean a reduction of benefit. With the exception of the self-employed, persons who are sick, unemployed or widowed receive an additional benefit which is related to their previous income, so that a person who earns more receives more. It should be noted that contributions are calculated on income, so a person who earns more also pays higher contributions.

(i) Sickness benefit generally lasts as long as a person is too ill to work, but earnings related payments are ended after six months. Officially sickness benefit ends after six months, but invalidity benefit is then claimed in its stead.
(ii) Unemployment benefit lasts for a year, with related supplement paid for six months.
(iii) There are special regulations which govern the national insurance payments made to expectant mothers, and the payments by employers if the mothers wish to return to work after the baby's birth. Generally the social security benefit is a lump sum grant and a weekly allowance.

2. Supplementary benefit

This benefit is paid to anyone over 16 who is not receiving an income which is considered necessary to maintain that person's particular needs. It is not necessary to pay national insurance, and persons who receive this benefit are usually unemployed. There is provision in the Supplementary Benefits Act 1976 to award benefit to low-paid workers in cases of exceptional need. It is generally accepted practice, however, that persons engaged in full-time employment are not entitled to supplementary payments.

Old-age pensioners may receive benefit to help supplement their pension, in order to pay for rent, heating, etc.

Who may claim?

(i) Any person over 16 who is not in full-time work may qualify for a supplementary benefit, allowance or pension.
(ii) Part-time workers, depending on the amount of income.
(iii) Full-time workers generally do not qualify for benefit, but if there is an urgent need, a person may be able to obtain a grant or loan.

Benefit is calculated on such things as rent, mortgage interest, repairs and house insurance and a living allowance which varies depending on the number of dependants in the family.

3. Family income supplement

Any person in full-time work whose family includes at least one dependant child may qualify for family income supplement if they have a low income. This supplement is available to single persons and couples whether married or unmarried.

The dependant child must be under 16, or attending school if over 16, and live with the family. The head of the family must work 30 hours or more. A man is considered to be the head of a family when a couple claims, so that if the woman works and the man does not, the couple would not qualify. As we saw above, the head of the family who works under 30 hours per week would be able to claim supplementary benefit.

Family income supplement is usually paid for a year, at the end of which a new claim may be made. Payment of F.I.S. means that the receiver is entitled to many more benefits. The payment book is sometimes referred to as a "passport" to benefits such as free prescriptions, dental treatment, free milk and vitamins for children under 16 and expectant mothers, free school meals, a refund of fares for hospital treatment and free legal advice provided disposable capital is not greater than £250. Help may also be given with electricity costs.

The rates for most social security benefits are set for the year and are generally revised each November. The D.H.S.S. produce many pamphlets giving the current rates of benefit.

Specimen Questions

1. What are
   (i) regulated tenancies
   (ii) secure tenancies
   (iii) shorthold tenancies?
   Explain how the rent for these tenancies is controlled.

2. What security of tenure have tenants in regulated, secure and shorthold tenancies?

3. Explain the law with respect to:
   (a) "Notice to quit."
   (b) Harassment.
   (c) Council tenants' rights of security of tenure and rent control.

4. Discuss the different social security benefits and allowances that are available.

5. What is
   (a) supplementary benefit,
   (b) family income supplement?
   Explain which persons are entitled to claim for these allowances and benefits.

6. (a) Explain and distinguish between freehold and leasehold land.
   (b) Discuss the different methods of borrowing money to buy a house or flat.

Chapter 12

EXAMINATION TECHNIQUE

Many candidates do not make the most of their knowledge when answering examination questions. In law examinations, the questions which describe hypothetical situations cause the greatest concern.

An examiner may set a question which asks the candidate to write an essay on a given topic, or the question may be set in the form of a problem. In either case the examiner wishes to ascertain if the candidate knows a particular aspect of law. The question could be: (i) "Distinguish an offer from an invitation to treat," or it could be (ii) "Jane saw a coat in a shop window marked £5. She offered to buy the coat at this price, but was told it should have been £25, but the 2 in the sign had fallen. Can Jane enforce the contract?"

The first answer would contain the definition of an offer and invitation to treat. References would be made to leading cases - Boots Cash Chemists, the "flick knife" in *Fisher* v. *Bell*, *Harvey* v. *Facey's Bumper Hall Pen*, etc. Most well prepared candidates would experience little difficulty.

What should the answer to the second question contain? The examiner is again requiring an explanation of the difference between an offer and an invitation to treat. This time, however, the candidate must reveal knowledge by advising Jane.

As a guide to answering problems or situation questions, follow these rules:

1. Discuss the law to which the situation relates, but forget about the problem at this stage, and write an essay or discussion of the law.

2. Support your discussion with the authority of the law, bringing in statutes and cases which are the source of this particular aspect of law. There is generally no need to give details of cases. The names will usually be sufficient, but if you feel the need to explain the case, confine your answer to the principle involved (the *ratio decidendi*).

3. From what has been written under the other two rules, argue the problem, if possible come to a decision and support your decision with the authorities already stated. If you have stated the law correctly, and argued and discussed the problem fully, it will not matter if you come to the wrong decision. In many examinations for legal qualifications, the problems set have no correct answer because they have not come before the courts in the particular form posited.

General Comments

Always read the paper carefully before attempting any questions and jot down facts or cases which immediately come to mind. When you have decided to answer a question, write down on rough paper all your thoughts in note form and then arrange them into a plan for your answer. By following such a course of action, you should ensure that your answer is complete and you have not forgotten to include any relevant information.

Do not write for too long on any one question as it restricts the time available for the last questions. Remember, it is always considered easier to obtain the first five marks for an answer than it is to earn the last five. Always answer the required number of questions and try to write neatly and legibly. An examiner cannot give marks if there is nothing to mark or if the writing cannot be read.

Never leave the examination room before the end of the examination unless you are completely satisfied that you have answered every question to the best of your ability. Have you noticed the sheepish look on the first candidate to leave the room and how happy he or she is when another candidate also leaves early? If the examination appears hard, stay in the room and give your brain a chance to show its powers of recall. Once a candidate has left the examination, there is no second chance to go back and write down any thoughts that have just come to mind. You have paid your money, so stay and fight for your marks. Good luck.

INDEX

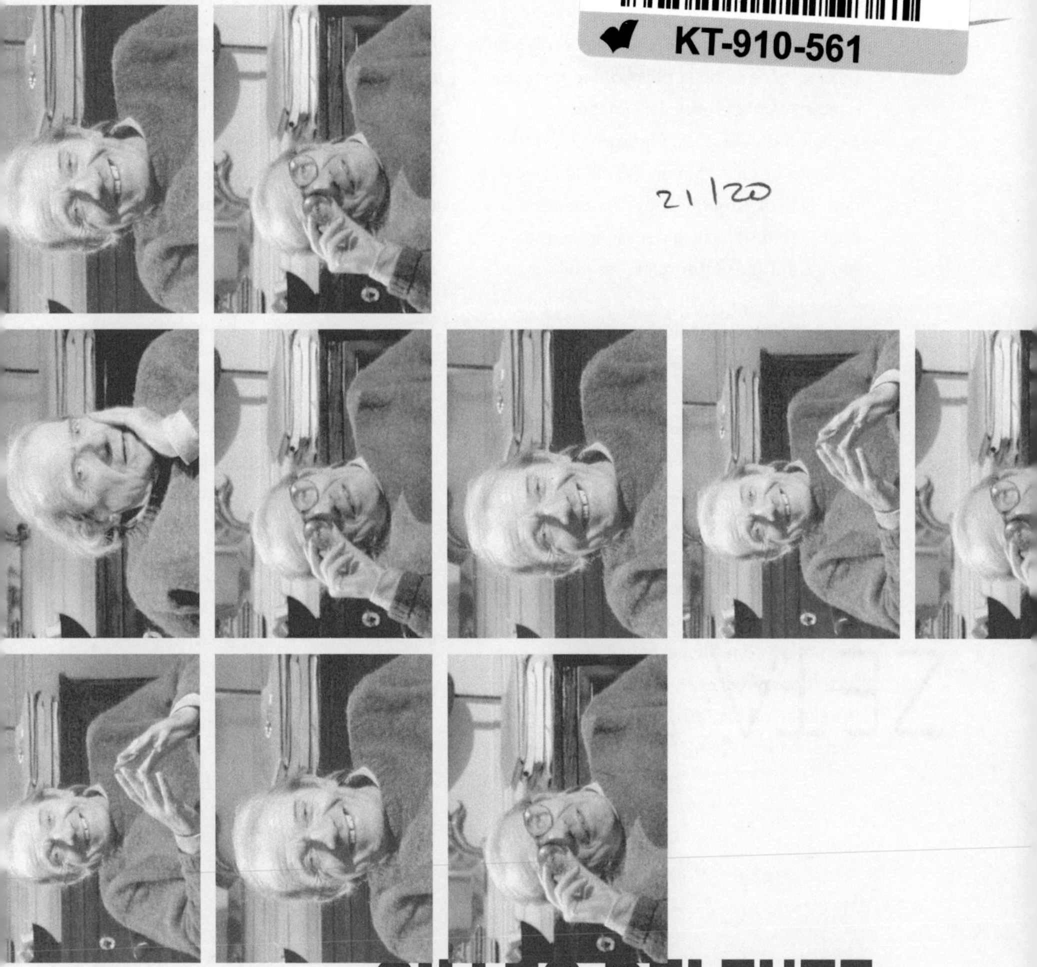

GILLES DELEUZE

Avant-propos

Après avoir ces dernières années dressé un tableau général de la philosophie française depuis 1950* et rendu hommage à Claude Lévi-Strauss, Georges Dumézil, Georges Bataille, Simone Weil, le ministère des Affaires étrangères et l'Association pour la diffusion de la pensée française souhaitent présenter quelques philosophes dont l'œuvre, traduite en plusieurs langues, a acquis une reconnaissance internationale ou au contraire, sur laquelle il est nécessaire d'appeler l'attention des lecteurs, des traducteurs et des éditeurs étrangers.

Seront ainsi publiés livrets, portfolios, expositions documentaires sur Gilles Deleuze, Paul Ricœur, Maurice Merleau-Ponty, Jean Cavaillès, Jean-Paul Sartre (à l'occasion du centenaire de sa naissance) ; Emmanuel Lévinas, Raymond Aron, Michel Foucault, Luce Irigaray, Jacques Derrida, Jean-François Lyotard, Jean-Luc Marion, Jean-Luc Nancy, etc.

Nous ouvrons cette série par Gilles Deleuze dont l'œuvre désormais est traduite, étudiée, commentée dans le monde entier.

Nous remercions vivement David Lapoujade, auteur de ce livret et de l'exposition documentaire.

Nous exprimons aussi notre gratitude à Mesdames Fanny Deleuze et Irène Lindon pour leur cordiale coopération.

Yves Mabin
Chef de la division de l'écrit et des médiathèques

François Neuville
Directeur de l'association pour la diffusion de la pensée française

*
1994 « Philosophie contemporaine en France » livret par MM. E. Alliez, J. Benoist, C. Descamps
1998 « Cinquante ans de philosophie française » livrets et expositions documentaires par B. Sichère et alii.

Isbn 2-914935-13-7

adpf association pour la diffusion de la pensée française •
6 rue Ferrus 75014 Paris + ecrire@adpf.asso.fr + www.adpf.asso.fr

Cet ouvrage accompagne une exposition sur affiches, tirée à 550 exemplaires, intitulée « Gilles Deleuze ».

adpf association pour la diffusion de la pensée française •
Ministère des Affaires étrangères
Direction générale de la coopération internationale et du développement
Direction de la coopération culturelle et du français
Division de l'écrit et des médiathèques

GILLES DELEUZE

P52

“LES NOMS PROPRES DÉSIGNENT DES FORCES, DES ÉVÉNEMENTS, DES MOUVEMENTS ET DES MOBILES, DES VENTS, DES TYPHONS, DES MALADIES, DES LIEUX ET DES MOMENTS, BIEN AVANT DE DÉSIGNER DES PERSONNES.”

"Naissance à Paris, le 18 janvier 1925.
Études secondaires au Lycée Carnot.
1944-1948 **Études de philosophie à la Sorbonne où il connaît François Châtelet, Michel Butor, Claude Lanzmann, Olivier Revault d'Allones, Michel Tournier.**
Professeurs principaux: Ferdinand Alquié, Georges Canguilhem, Maurice de Gandillac, Jean Hippolyte.
Fréquente La Fortelle, un château où Marie-Madeleine Davy organisait des rencontres entre intellectuels et écrivains à la Libération: le père Fessard, Pierre Klossowski, Jacques Lacan, Lanza del Vasto, Jean Paulhan.
1948 **Agrégation de philosophie**
1948-1957 **Professeur de philosophie aux lycées d'Amiens, d'Orléans, Louis-le-Grand.**
1957-1960 **Assistant à la Sorbonne, en histoire de la philosophie.**
1960-1964 **Attaché de recherche Cnrs.**
1962 **Rencontre avec Michel Foucault à Clermont-Ferrand, chez Jules Vuillemin.**
1964-1969 **Chargé d'enseignement à la Faculté de Lyon.**
1969 **Thèse principale,** Différence et répétition **(directeur, Maurice de Gandillac); thèse secondaire,** Spinoza et le problème de l'expression **(directeur, Ferdinand Alquié).**
1969 **Rencontre avec Félix Guattari. Projet de travail en commun.**
1969 **Professeur à Paris VIII-Vincennes dont Michel Foucault vient de partir et où il retrouve François Châtelet.**
Après 1969 **Activités gauchistes ordinaires.**
1987 **Prend sa retraite.**
Signes particuliers: voyage peu, n'a jamais adhéré au parti communiste, n'a jamais été phénoménologue ni heideggerien, n'a pas renoncé à Marx, n'a pas répudié Mai 68."

GILLES DELEUZE

Se donne la mort à Paris le 4 novembre 1995.

CHIENDENT

Comme l'exposition, ce livret est une présentation de la pensée de Deleuze à partir de certains concepts ou notions qui reviennent de manière insistante dans son œuvre. Le choix est nécessairement arbitraire ; il l'est d'autant plus que l'œuvre de Deleuze est d'une richesse considérable. Beaucoup d'autres propositions étaient possibles qui n'auraient en rien ressemblé à celle-ci. L'arbitraire est encore présent d'une autre manière : Deleuze n'a jamais écrit sous forme d'aphorismes ou de fragments ; il n'aimait pas cette forme pour son compte. Or, on ne trouvera ici que des fragments ou des extraits de textes dont on peut juste espérer qu'ils témoignent un peu de la profonde continuité qui traverse son œuvre. Tous sont reliés les uns aux autres, de plusieurs manières. Il n'y a donc aucun ordre défini. On peut lire l'ensemble de ces extraits à la suite ou séparément, de manière suivie ou discontinue, comme on veut.

Ce n'est pas que la pensée de Deleuze manque de rigueur ; c'est plutôt que sa rigueur s'exerce précisément à travers cette circulation ouverte d'un concept à un autre, pour favoriser des parcours variés et des connexions en tous sens, comme dans une taupinière. C'est ce que Deleuze appelle une pensée « rhizomatique » en hommage aux radicelles de certains végétaux qui poussent par le milieu dans plusieurs directions à la fois et prolifèrent sans racine première comme le chiendent.

Dans l'espace de l'exposition et du livret qui l'accompagne, c'est ce qui a été constamment recherché :

non pas les moments essentiels d'un édifice, mais des fragments de «lignes», prélevés dans ce vaste réseau de galeries qu'est la pensée de Gilles Deleuze.

NB Le livret reprend l'ensemble des textes de l'exposition, augmenté de certaines «entrées» et de certains extraits. Je remercie vivement Fanny Deleuze pour son aide et son soutien. Merci également à Jean-Jacques Lebel et Michel Tournier pour leur contribution.

David Lapoujade, maître de conférences à l'université de Paris-I Panthéon-Sorbonne, qui travaille sur la philosophie et la littérature anglo-américaine du XIXe siècle et sur la philosophie française contemporaine, a notamment édité les recueils des textes posthumes de Gilles Deleuze.

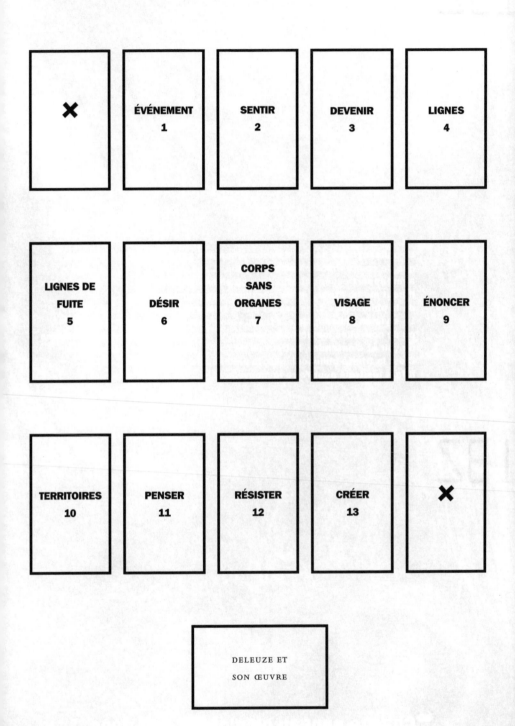

✕	ÉVÉNEMENT 1	SENTIR 2	DEVENIR 3	LIGNES 4
LIGNES DE FUITE 5	DÉSIR 6	CORPS SANS ORGANES 7	VISAGE 8	ÉNONCER 9
TERRITOIRES 10	PENSER 11	RÉSISTER 12	CRÉER 13	✕

DELEUZE ET SON ŒUVRE

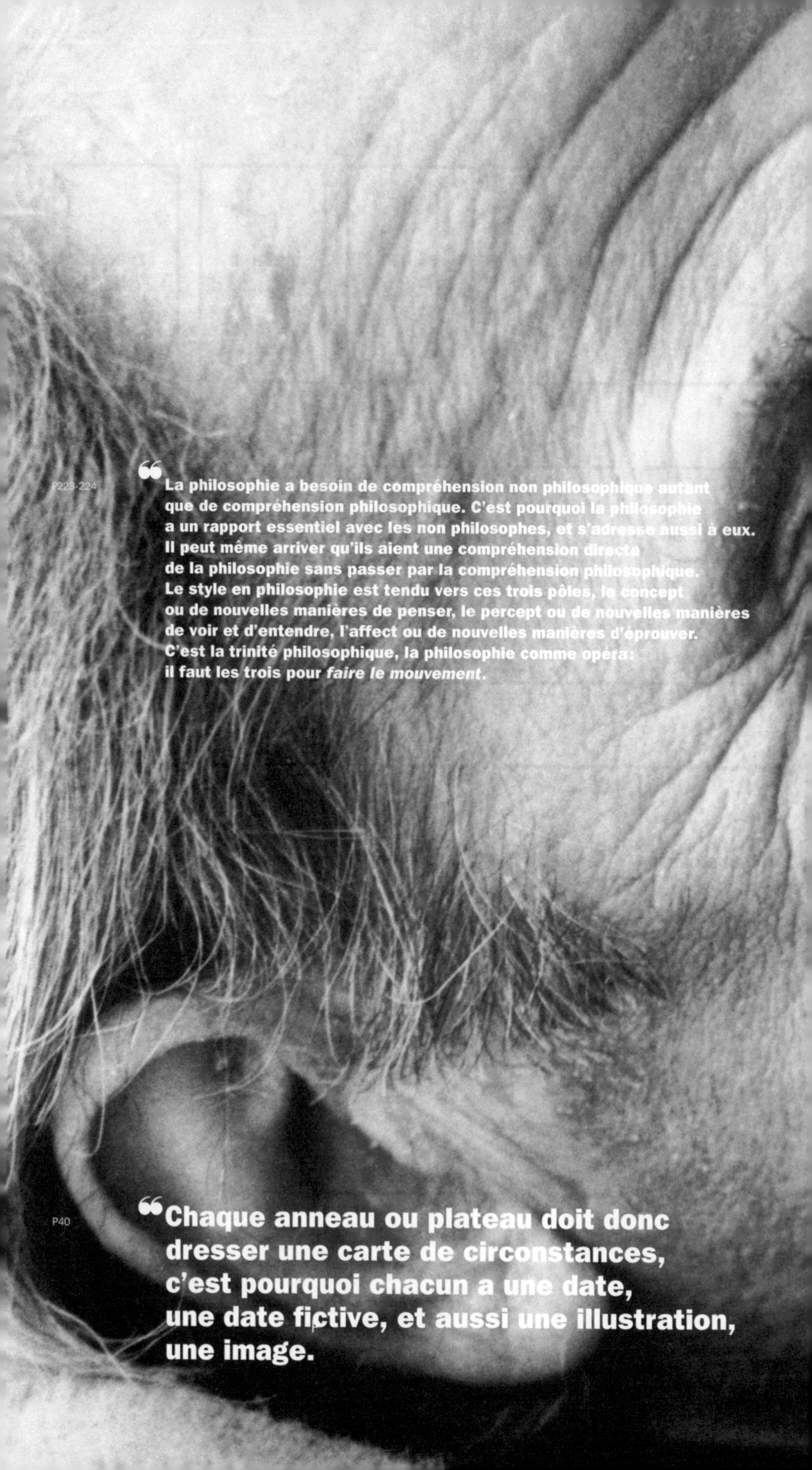

P223-224 “La philosophie a besoin de compréhension non philosophique autant que de compréhension philosophique. C’est pourquoi la philosophie a un rapport essentiel avec les non philosophes, et s’adresse aussi à eux. Il peut même arriver qu’ils aient une compréhension directe de la philosophie sans passer par la compréhension philosophique. Le style en philosophie est tendu vers ces trois pôles, le concept ou de nouvelles manières de penser, le percept ou de nouvelles manières de voir et d’entendre, l’affect ou de nouvelles manières d’éprouver. C’est la trinité philosophique, la philosophie comme opéra: il faut les trois pour *faire le mouvement*.

P40 **“Chaque anneau ou plateau doit donc dresser une carte de circonstances, c’est pourquoi chacun a une date, une date fictive, et aussi une illustration, une image.**

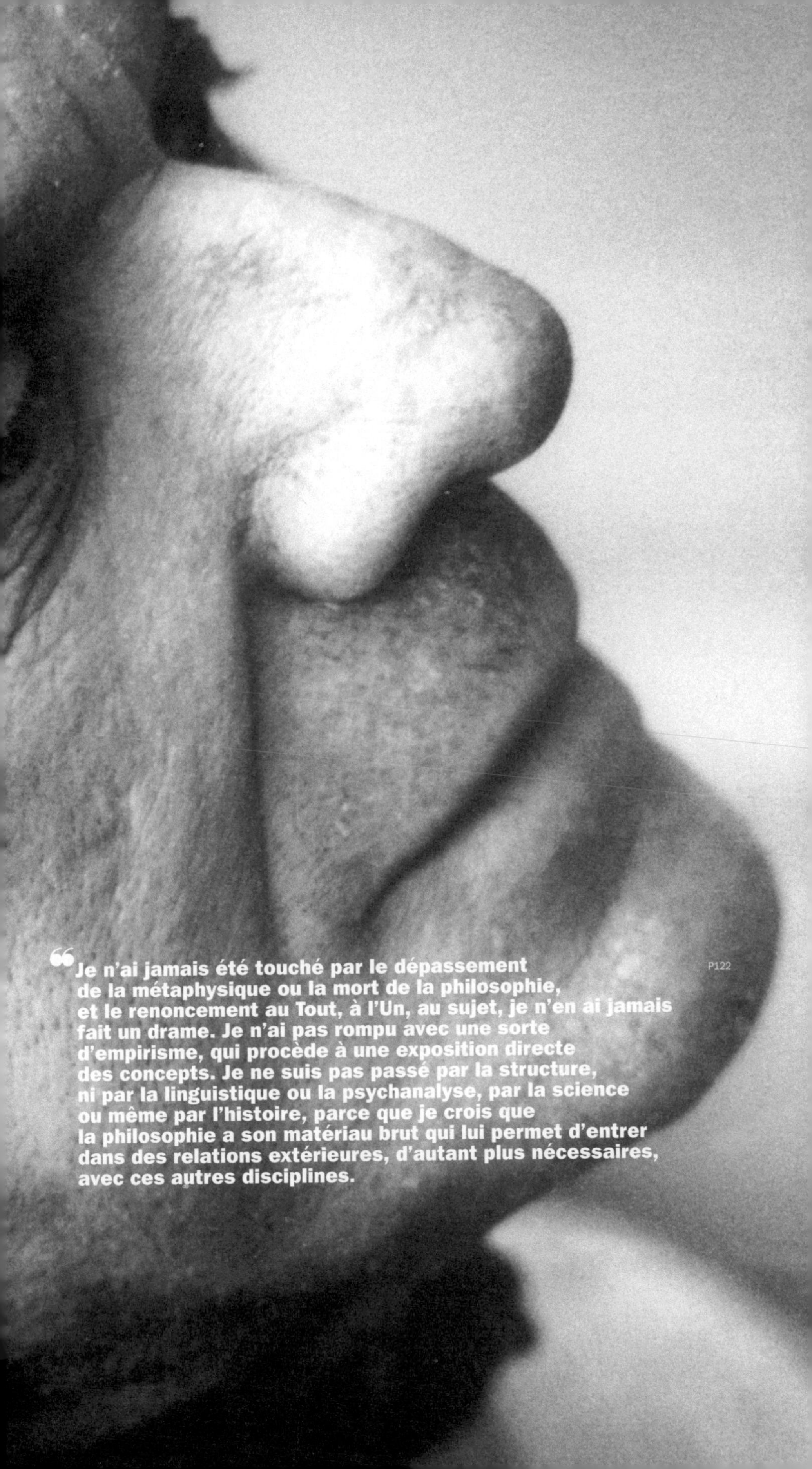

“Je n’ai jamais été touché par le dépassement de la métaphysique ou la mort de la philosophie, et le renoncement au Tout, à l’Un, au sujet, je n’en ai jamais fait un drame. Je n’ai pas rompu avec une sorte d’empirisme, qui procède à une exposition directe des concepts. Je ne suis pas passé par la structure, ni par la linguistique ou la psychanalyse, par la science ou même par l’histoire, parce que je crois que la philosophie a son matériau brut qui lui permet d’entrer dans des relations extérieures, d’autant plus nécessaires, avec ces autres disciplines.

P122

1

ÉVÉNEMENT

P217 “Je ne crois pas que les médias aient beaucoup de ressources ou de vocation pour saisir un événement. D'abord ils montrent souvent le début ou la fin, tandis qu'un événement même bref, même instantané, se continue. Ensuite ils veulent du spectaculaire, tandis que l'événement est inséparable de temps morts. Ce n'est même pas qu'il y ait des temps morts avant et après l'événement, le temps mort est dans l'événement, par exemple l'instant de l'accident le plus brutal se confond avec l'immensité du temps vide où on le voit arriver, spectateur de ce qui n'est pas encore, dans un très long suspens.

P218 “C'est l'art, pas les médias, qui peut saisir l'événement : par exemple, le cinéma saisit l'événement, avec Ozu, avec Antonioni. Mais, justement, le temps mort n'est pas chez eux entre deux événements, il est dans l'événement même, il en fait l'épaisseur.

LS 122 “Si la bataille n'est pas un exemple d'événement parmi d'autres, mais l'Événement dans son essence, c'est sans doute parce qu'elle s'effectue de beaucoup de manières à la fois, et que chaque participant peut la saisir à un niveau d'effectuation dans son présent variable... La bataille *survole* son propre champ, neutre par rapport à toutes ses effectuations temporelles, neutre et impassible par rapport aux vainqueurs et aux vaincus, par rapport aux lâches et aux braves, d'autant plus terrible pour cela, jamais présente, toujours encore à venir et déjà passée... C'est pourquoi le soldat se voit fuir quand il fuit, et bondir quand il bondit, déterminé à considérer chaque effectuation temporelle du haut de la vérité éternelle de l'événement qui s'incarne en elle, et, hélas, dans sa propre chair.

“**Dans tous mes livres, j’ai cherché la nature de l’événement [...].** P194

“**Faire un événement, si petit soit-il, la chose la plus délicate du monde, le contraire de faire un drame, ou de faire une histoire.** D81

“**Non pas vouloir ce qui arrive, avec cette fausse volonté qui se plaint et se défend, et se perd en mimique, mais porter la plainte et la fureur au point où elles se retournent contre ce qui arrive, pour dresser l’événement, le dégager, l’extraire dans le concept vivant. Devenir digne de l’événement, la philosophie n’a pas d’autre but [...].** QLP151

“**Pour nous, le concept doit dire l’événement, et non plus l’essence.** P40

“**L’événement est toujours produit par des corps qui s’entrechoquent, se coupent ou se pénètrent, la chair et l’épée; mais cet effet lui-même n’est pas de l’ordre des corps, bataille impassible, incorporelle, impénétrable, qui surplombe son propre accomplissement et domine son effectuation. On n’a jamais cessé de demander: où est la bataille? Où est l’événement, en quoi consiste un événement: chacun pose cette question en courant, «où est la prise de la Bastille?», tout événement est un brouillard de gouttes. Si les infinitifs «mourir», «aimer», «bouger», «sourire», etc., sont des événements, c’est parce qu’il y a en eux une part que leur accomplissement ne suffit pas à réaliser, un devenir en lui-même qui ne cesse à la fois de nous attendre et de nous précéder comme une troisième personne de l’infinitif, une quatrième personne du singulier.** D79

2

SENTIR

Je suis finie, j'ai peur, quel mystère,
quelle beauté, mon Dieu...

P218 “L’événement le plus ordinaire fait de nous un voyant.

DR186 “Il faut porter chaque faculté au point extrême de son dérèglement… Nous demandons par exemple : qu’est-ce qui force la sensibilité à sentir ? et qu’est-ce qui ne peut être que senti ? et qui est l’insensible en même temps ?

CC14 “La littérature apparaît comme une entreprise de santé : non pas que l’écrivain ait forcément une grande santé, mais il jouit d’une irrésistible petite santé qui vient de ce qu’il a vu et entendu des choses trop grandes pour lui, trop fortes pour lui, irrespirables, dont le passage l’épuise, en lui donnant pourtant des devenirs qu’une grosse santé dominante rendrait impossible. De ce qu’il a vu et entendu, l’écrivain revient les yeux rouges et les tympans percés.

“Maintenant supposez qu’un personnage se trouve dans une situation, quotidienne ou extraordinaire, qui déborde toute action possible ou le laisse sans réaction. C’est trop fort, ou trop douloureux, trop beau. Le lien sensori-moteur est brisé. Il n’est plus dans une situation sensori-motrice, mais dans une situation optique et sonore pure. C’est un autre type d’image. Soit l’étrangère dans *Stromboli* : elle passe par la pêche au thon, l’agonie du thon, puis l’éruption du volcan. Elle n’a pas de réaction pour cela, pas de réponse, c’est trop intense : «Je suis finie, j’ai peur, quel mystère, quelle beauté, mon Dieu...» [...] C’est cela, je crois, la grande invention du néo-réalisme : on ne croit plus tellement aux possibilités d’agir sur des situations, ou de réagir à des situations, et pourtant on n’est pas du tout passif, on saisit ou on révèle quelque chose d’intolérable, d’insupportable, même dans la vie la plus quotidienne. C’est un cinéma de Voyant. P74

3

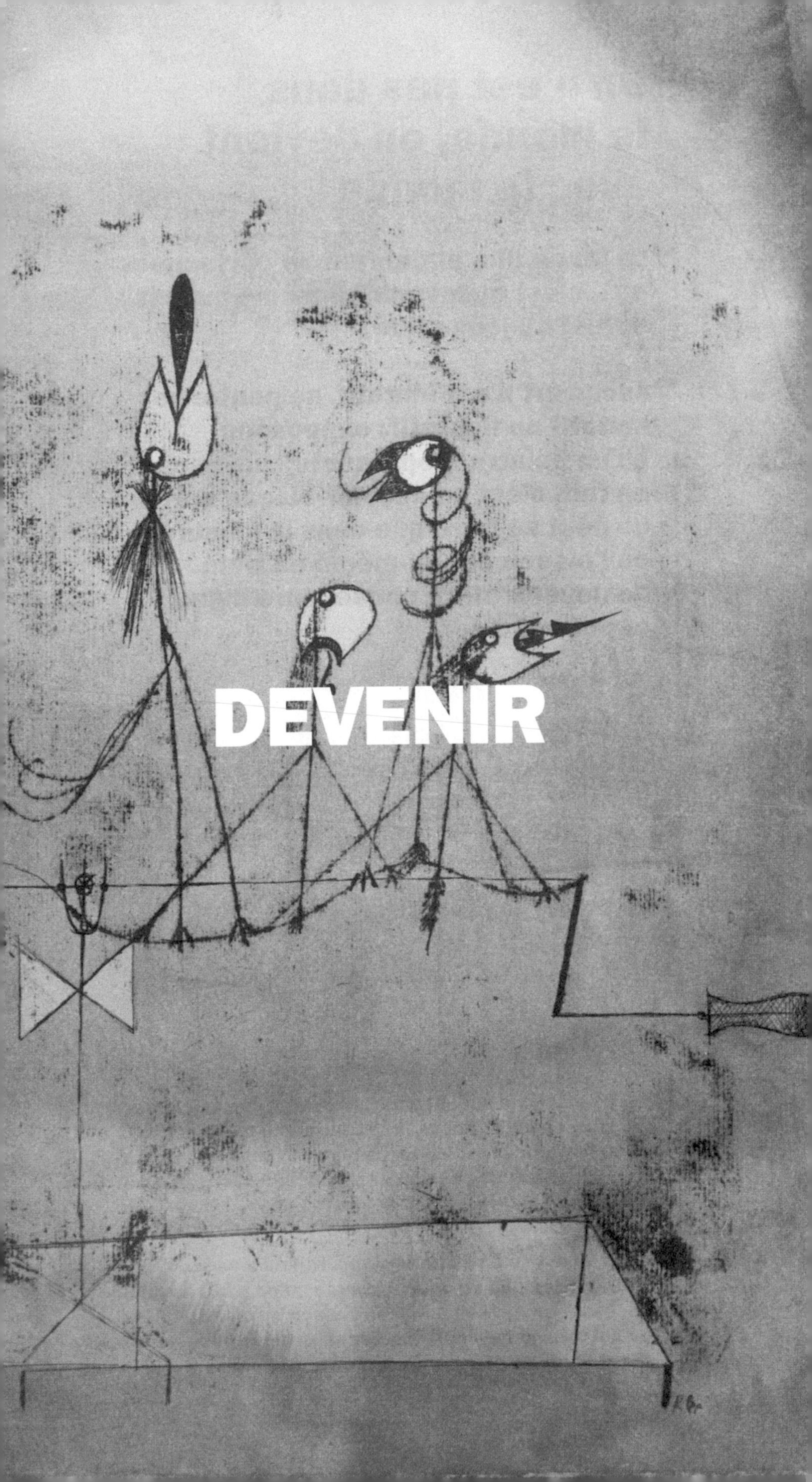
DEVENIR

QLP160 « On n'est pas dans le monde, on devient avec le monde [...].

MP340 « La jeune fille et l'enfant ne deviennent pas, c'est le devenir lui-même qui est enfant ou jeune fille.

MP374 « Aucun art n'est imitatif, ne peut-être imitatif ou figuratif : supposons qu'un peintre « représente » un oiseau ; en fait, c'est un devenir-oiseau qui ne peut se faire que dans la mesure où l'oiseau est lui-même en train de devenir autre chose, pure ligne et pure couleur.

MP294 « Qui n'a connu la violence de ces séquences animales, qui l'arrachent à l'humanité ne serait-ce qu'un instant, et lui font gratter son pain comme un rongeur ou lui donnent les yeux jaunes d'un félin ? Terrible involution qui nous appelle vers des devenirs inouïs.

MP343-344 « Alors on est comme l'herbe : on a fait du monde, de tout le monde un devenir, parce qu'on a fait un monde nécessairement communicant, parce qu'on a supprimé de soi tout ce qui nous empêchait de nous glisser entre les choses, de pousser au milieu des choses.

“Les devenirs, c’est le plus imperceptible, ce sont des actes qui ne peuvent être contenus que dans une vie et exprimés dans un style. D9

“ La guêpe et l’orchidée donnent l’exemple. L’orchidée a l’air de former une image de guêpe, mais en fait il y a un devenir-guêpe de l’orchidée, un devenir-orchidée de la guêpe, une double capture puisque «ce que» chacun devient ne change pas moins que «celui qui» devient. La guêpe devient partie de l’appareil de reproduction de l’orchidée, en même temps que l’orchidée devient organe sexuel pour la guêpe. D8-9

“ **Le penseur n’est pas acéphale, aphasique ou analphabète, mais le devient. Il devient Indien, n’en finit pas de devenir, peut-être «pour que» l’Indien qui est Indien devienne lui-même autre chose et s’arrache à son agonie. On pense et on écrit pour les animaux mêmes. On devient animal pour que l’animal aussi devienne autre chose. L’agonie d’un rat ou l’exécution d’un veau restent présentes dans la pensée, non par pitié, mais comme la zone d’échange entre l’homme et l’animal, où quelque chose de l’un passe dans l’autre. C’est le rapport constitutif de la philosophie avec la non-philosophie.** QLP105

“ **Or quelle est l’affaire de la musique, quel est son contenu indissociable de l’expression sonore? C’est difficile à dire, mais c’est quelque chose comme: *un* enfant meurt, un enfant joue, une femme naît, une femme meurt, un oiseau arrive, un oiseau s’en va. Nous voulons dire qu’il n’y a pas là des thèmes accidentels de la musique [...] quelque chose d’essentiel. Pourquoi un enfant, une femme, un oiseau? C’est parce que l’expression musicale est inséparable d’un devenir-femme, d’un devenir-enfant, d’un devenir-animal qui constituent son contenu.** MP367

4

LIGNES

– Ma ligne de chance.
– Ta ligne de hanche.

D151-152 **“La première sorte de ligne qui nous compose est segmentaire, à segmentarité dure (ou plutôt il y a déjà beaucoup de lignes de cette sorte); la famille-la profession; le travail-les vacances; la famille-et puis l’école-et puis l’armée-et puis l’usine-et puis la retraite.[...] Bref toutes sortes de segments bien déterminés qui nous découpent en tous sens, des paquets de lignes segmentarisées.**

[...]

En même temps, nous avons des lignes de segmentarité beaucoup plus souples, en quelque sorte moléculaires.[...] Elles tracent de petites modifications, elles font des détours, elles esquissent des chutes ou des élans.[...] Mais plutôt que des lignes molaires à segments, ce sont des flux moléculaires à seuils ou quanta.[...] Il se passe beaucoup de choses sur cette seconde sorte de ligne, des devenirs, des micro-devenirs, qui n’ont pas le même rythme que notre «histoire».[...] Un métier, c’est un segment dur, mais aussi qu’est-ce qui passe là-dessous, quelles connexions, quelles attirances et répulsions qui ne coïncident pas avec les segments, quelles folies secrètes et pourtant en rapport avec les puissances publiques.

[...]

En même temps encore, il y a comme une troisième sorte de ligne, celle-là encore plus étrange: comme si quelque chose nous emportait, à travers nos segments, mais aussi à travers nos seuils, vers une destination inconnue, pas prévisible, pas préexistante. Cette ligne est simple, abstraite, et pourtant c’est la plus compliquée de toutes, la plus tortueuse: c’est la ligne de gravité ou de célérité, c’est la ligne de fuite et de plus grande pente.

“Individus ou groupes, nous sommes faits de lignes, et ces lignes sont de nature très diverse. D151

“Tout ce qui devient est une pure ligne, qui cesse de représenter quoi que ce soit. D89

“Trois lignes, dont l’une serait comme la ligne nomade, l’autre, migrante, l’autre sédentaire [...]. D165

5

LIGNES DE FUITE

ZETA

MP602 “Il y a non seulement d’étranges voyages en ville, mais des voyages sur place : nous ne pensons pas aux drogués, dont l’expérience est trop ambiguë, mais plutôt aux véritables nomades. C’est à propos de ces nomades qu’on peut dire, comme suggère Toynbee : *ils ne bougent pas*. Ils sont nomades à force de ne pas bouger, de ne pas migrer, de tenir un espace lisse qu’ils refusent de quitter, et qu’ils ne quittent que pour conquérir et mourir. Voyage sur place, c’est le nom de toutes les intensités.

“À chaque moment, qu’est-ce qui fuit dans une société ? MP250

“La grande erreur, la seule erreur, serait de croire qu’une ligne de fuite consiste à fuir la vie ; la fuite dans l’imaginaire, ou dans l’art. Mais fuir au contraire, c’est produire du réel, créer de la vie, trouver une arme. D60

“Alors que le migrant quitte un milieu devenu amorphe ou ingrat, le nomade est celui qui ne part pas, ne veut pas partir, s’accroche à cet espace lisse où la forêt recule, où la steppe ou le désert croissent, et invente le nomadisme comme réponse à ce défi. Bien sûr, le nomade bouge, mais il est assis, il n’est jamais assis que quand il bouge (le Bédouin au galop, à genoux sur la selle, assis sur la plante de ses pieds retournés, « prouesse d’équilibre »). Le nomade sait attendre, et a une patience infinie. MP472-473

“Nous disons plutôt que, dans une société, tout fuit, et qu’une société se définit par ses lignes de fuite qui affectent des masses de toute nature (encore une fois « masse » est une notion moléculaire). [...] Les grandes aventures géographiques de l’histoire sont des lignes de fuite, c’est-à-dire de longues marches, à pied, à cheval ou en bateau : celle des Hébreux dans le désert, celle de Genséric le Vandale traversant la Méditerranée, celle des nomades à travers la steppe, la longue marche des Chinois – c’est toujours sur une ligne de fuite qu’on crée, certes pas parce qu’on imagine ou qu’on rêve, mais au contraire parce qu’on y trace du réel, et que l’on y compose un plan de consistance. Fuir, mais en fuyant chercher une arme. D164

6

DÉSIR

A-Œ59 “[...] **au lieu de participer à une entreprise de libération effective, la psychanalyse prend part à l'œuvre de répression bourgeoise la plus générale, celle qui a consisté à maintenir l'humanité européenne sous le joug de papa-maman, et à *ne pas en finir* avec ce *problème-là*.**

A-Œ34-35 “**Les pauvres ou les dépossédés** [...] **savent qu'ils sont proches de l'herbe, et que le désir a «besoin» de peu de choses, *non pas ces choses qu'on leur laisse, mais ces choses mêmes dont on ne cesse de les déposséder*** [...]**. Les révolutionnaires, les artistes et les voyants se contentent d'être objectifs, rien qu'objectifs: ils savent que le désir étreint la vie avec une puissance productrice, et la reproduit d'une façon d'autant plus intense qu'il a peu de besoin** [...].

MP191-192 “**Chaque fois que le désir est trahi, maudit, arraché à son champ d'immanence, il y a un prêtre là-dessous. Le prêtre a lancé la triple malédiction sur le désir: celle de la loi négative, celle de la règle extrinsèque, celle de l'idéal transcendant. Tourné vers le nord, le prêtre a dit: Désir est manque (comment ne manquerait-il pas de ce qu'il désire?).** [...] **Puis, tourné vers le sud, le prêtre a rapporté le désir au plaisir. Car il y a des prêtres hédonistes et même orgastiques.** [...] **Le plaisir-décharge: le prêtre opère le second sacrifice nommé masturbation. Puis, tourné vers l'est, il s'écrie: Jouissance est impossible, mais l'impossible jouissance est inscrite dans le désir. Car tel est l'Idéal, en son impossibilité même, «le manque-à-jouir qu'est la vie».** [...] **La figure la plus récente du prêtre est le psychanalyste avec ses trois principes, Plaisir, Mort et Réalité.**

A-Œ8 “**Partout des machines productrices ou désirantes, les machines schizophrènes, toute la vie générique: moi et non-moi, extérieur et intérieur ne veulent plus rien dire.**

D95 “**Contre la psychanalyse nous n'avons dit que deux choses: elle casse toutes les productions de désir, elle écrase toutes les formations d'énoncés.**

“Le désir ne manque de rien...

D95

chapitre 1
les machines désirantes

Ça fonctionne partout, tantôt sans arrêt, tantôt discontinu. Ça respire, ça chauffe, ça mange. Ça chie, ça baise. Quelle erreur d'avoir dit *le* ça. Partout ce sont des machines, pas du tout métaphoriquement : des machines de machines, avec leurs couplages, leurs connexions. Une machine-organe est branchée sur une machine-source : l'une émet un flux, que l'autre coupe. Le sein est une machine qui produit du lait, et la bouche, une machine couplée sur celle-là. La bouche de l'anorexique hésite entre une machine à manger, une machine anale, une machine à parler, une machine à respirer (crise d'asthme). C'est ainsi qu'on est tous bricoleurs ; chacun ses petites machines. Une machine-organe pour une machine-énergie, toujours des flux et des coupures. Le président Schreber a les rayons du ciel dans le cul. *Anus solaire.* Et soyez sûrs que ça marche ; le président Schreber sent quelque chose, produit quelque chose, et peut en faire la théorie. Quelque chose se produit : des effets de machine, et non des métaphores.

La promenade du schizophrène : c'est un meilleur modèle que le névrosé couché sur le divan. Un peu de grand air, une relation avec le dehors. Par exemple la promenade de Lenz reconstituée par Büchner.[1] C'est différent des moments où Lenz se retrouve chez son bon pasteur, qui le force à se repérer socialement, par rapport au Dieu de la religion, par rapport au père, à la mère. Là au contraire, il est dans les montagnes, sous la neige, avec d'autres dieux ou sans dieu du tout, sans famille, sans père ni mère, avec

1. Cf. le texte de Büchner, *Lenz*, tr. fr. Ed. Fontaine.

7

CORPS SANS ORGANES

MP187 “Est-ce si triste et dangereux de ne plus supporter les yeux pour voir, les poumons pour respirer, la bouche pour avaler, la langue pour parler, le cerveau pour penser, l'anus et le larynx, la tête et les jambes? Pourquoi pas marcher sur la tête, chanter avec les sinus, voir avec la peau, respirer avec le ventre[...].

MP187 “Là où la psychanalyse dit: Arrêtez, retrouvez votre moi, il faudrait dire: Allons encore plus loin, nous n'avons pas encore trouvé notre CsO, pas assez défait notre moi.

D75-76 “De même que vous ne savez pas ce que peut un corps, de même qu'il y a beaucoup de choses dans le corps que vous ne connaissez pas, qui dépassent votre connaissance, de même il y a dans l'âme beaucoup de choses qui dépassent votre conscience. Voilà la question: qu'est-ce que peut un corps? de quels affects êtes-vous capables? Expérimentez, mais il faut beaucoup de prudence pour expérimenter.

MP198 “Défaire l'organisme n'a jamais été se tuer, mais ouvrir le corps à des connexions qui supposent tout un agencement, des circuits, des conjonctions, des étagements et des seuils, des passages et des distributions d'intensité, des territoires et des déterritorialisations mesurées à la manière d'un arpenteur.

“Il y a désir dès qu’il y a machine ou «corps sans organes». D173

“Nous vivons entre deux dangers: l’éternel gémissement de notre corps, qui trouve toujours un corps acéré qui le coupe, un corps trop gros qui le pénètre et l’étouffe, un corps indigeste qui l’empoisonne, un meuble qui le cogne, un microbe qui lui fait un bouton; mais aussi l’histrionisme de ceux qui miment un événement pur et le transforment en fantasme, et qui chantent l’angoisse, la finitude, la castration.[...] Entre les cris de la douleur physique et les chants de la souffrance métaphysique, comment tracer son mince chemin stoïcien, qui consiste à être digne de ce qui arrive, à dégager quelque chose de gai et d’amoureux dans ce qui arrive, une lueur, une rencontre, un événement, une vitesse, un devenir? D80

“Toute une vie non organique, car l’organisme n’est pas la vie, il l’emprisonne. [...] Aussi la sensation, quand elle atteint le corps à travers l’organisme, prend-elle une allure excessive et spasmodique, elle rompt les bornes de l’activité organique. En pleine chair, elle est directement portée sur l’onde nerveuse ou l’émotion vitale... Contrairement à une peinture misérabiliste qui peint des bouts d’organes, Bacon n’a cessé de peindre des corps sans organes, le fait intensif du corps. FB33

8

VISAGE

P40 “[...] nous croyons que le visage est un produit, et que toutes les sociétés ne produisent pas du visage, mais que certaines ont besoin d'en produire. Dans quels cas et pourquoi?

MP212 “Pas un visage qui n'enveloppe un paysage inconnu, inexploré, pas de paysage qui ne se peuple d'un visage aimé ou rêvé, qui ne développe un visage à venir ou déjà passé. Quel visage n'a pas appelé les paysages qu'il amalgamait, la mer et la montagne, quel paysage n'a pas évoqué le visage qui l'aurait complété, qui lui aurait fourni le complément inattendu de ses lignes et de ses traits?

❝Ton secret, on le voit toujours sur ton visage et dans ton œil. Perds le visage. D59

❝[…] comment défaire le visage, en libérant en nous les têtes chercheuses qui tracent des lignes de devenir ? Comment passer le mur, en évitant de rebondir sur lui, en arrière, ou d'être écrasés ? Comment sortir du trou noir, au lieu de tournoyer au fond, quelles particules faire sortir du trou noir ? Comment briser même notre amour pour devenir enfin capable d'aimer ? Comment devenir imperceptible ? IM127

❝Á un visage, il y a lieu de poser deux sortes de questions suivant les circonstances : à quoi penses-tu ? Ou bien : qu'est-ce qui te prend, qu'est-ce que tu as, qu'est-ce que tu sens ou ressens ? […] En tant qu'il pense à quelque chose, le visage vaut surtout par son contour enveloppant, son unité réfléchissante qui élève à soi toutes les parties. Tantôt, au contraire, il éprouve ou ressent quelque chose, et vaut alors par la série intensive que ses parties traversent successivement jusqu'à un paroxysme, chaque partie prenant une sorte d'indépendance momentanée. MP107

❝Nudité du visage plus grande que celle des corps, inhumanité plus grande que celle des bêtes. IM141

❝[…] taches de rousseur qui filent à l'horizon, cheveux emportés par le vent, yeux qu'on traverse au lieu de s'y regarder, ou de les regarder dans le morne face-à-face des subjectivités signifiantes. MP209

9

ÉNONCER

MP468-469 “Gagner du temps, et puis peut-être renoncer, ou attendre. Nécessité de ne pas avoir le contrôle de la langue, d’être un étranger dans sa propre langue, pour tirer la parole à soi et «mettre au monde quelque chose d’incompréhensible».

MP97 “Le langage ne se contente pas d’aller d’un premier à un second, de quelqu’un qui a vu à quelqu’un qui n’a pas vu, mais va nécessairement d’un second à un troisième, ni l’un ni l’autre n’ayant vu. C’est en ce sens que le langage est transmission du mot fonctionnant comme mot d’ordre, et non communication d’un signe comme information.

MP107 “Écrire, c’est peut-être amener au jour cet agencement de l’inconscient, sélectionner les voix chuchotantes, convoquer les tribus et les idiomes secrets, d’où j’extrais quelque chose que j’appelle Moi. JE est un mot d’ordre.

“Il y a beaucoup de passions dans une passion, et toutes sortes de voix dans une voix, toute une rumeur, glossolalie : c'est pourquoi tout discours est indirect. MP97

“Il y a des mots de passe sous les mots d'ordre. Des mots qui seraient comme de passage, des composantes de passage, tandis que les mots d'ordre marquent des arrêts, des compositions stratifiées, organisées. La même chose, le même mot, a sans doute cette double nature : il faut extraire l'une de l'autre – transformer les compositions d'ordre en composantes de passages. MP139

“Le langage n'est même pas fait pour être cru, mais pour obéir et faire obéir.[...] On s'en aperçoit dans les communiqués de police ou de gouvernement, qui se soucient peu de vraisemblance ou de véracité, mais qui disent très bien ce qui doit être observé et retenu. MP96

“Il n'y a pas d'énoncé qui ne présente ce lien, directement ou indirectement. Une question, une promesse, sont des mots d'ordre. Les mots d'ordre ne renvoient donc pas seulement à des commandements, mais à tous les actes qui sont liés à des énoncés par une « obligation sociale ». MP100

“Le langage n'est pas la vie, il donne des ordres à la vie ; la vie ne parle pas, elle écoute et attend. MP96

10

TERRITOIRES

MP393

“Le territoire, c’est d’abord la distance critique entre deux êtres de même espèce : marquer ses distances. Ce qui est mien, c’est d’abord ma distance, je ne possède que des distances. [...] Au besoin, je prendrai mon territoire sur mon propre corps, je territorialise mon corps : la maison de la tortue, l’ermitage du crustacé, mais aussi tous les tatouages qui font du corps un territoire.

“ I.

Un enfant dans le noir, saisi par la peur, se rassure en chantonnant. Il marche, s’arrête au gré de sa chanson. Perdu, il s’abrite comme il peut, ou s’oriente tant bien que mal avec sa petite chanson. Celle-ci est comme l’esquisse d’un centre stable et calme, stabilisant et calmant, au sein du chaos. [...]

MP382-383

“ II.

Maintenant, au contraire, on est chez soi. Mais le chez-soi ne préexiste pas : il a fallu tracer un cercle autour du centre fragile et incertain, organiser un espace limité. [...] **Voilà que les forces du chaos sont tenues à l’extérieur autant qu’il est possible, et l’espace intérieur protège les forces germinatives d’une tâche à remplir, d’une œuvre à faire.** [...] **Or les composantes vocales, sonores, sont très importantes.** [...] **Un enfant chantonne pour recueillir en soi les forces du travail scolaire à fournir. Une ménagère chantonne, ou met la radio, en même temps qu’elle dresse les forces anti-chaos de son ouvrage.** [...]

“ III.

Maintenant enfin, on entrouvre le cercle, on l’ouvre, on laisse entrer quelqu’un, on appelle quelqu’un, ou bien l’on va soi-même au-dehors, on s’élance. On n’ouvre pas le cercle du côté où se pressent les anciennes forces du chaos, mais dans une autre région, créée par le cercle lui-même. Comme si le cercle tendait lui-même à s’ouvrir sur un futur, en fonction des forces en œuvre qu’il abrite. Et cette fois, c’est pour rejoindre des forces de l’avenir, des forces cosmiques. On s’élance, on risque une improvisation. Mais improviser, c’est rejoindre le Monde, ou se confondre avec lui. On sort de chez soi au fil d’une chansonnette. [...]

“ **Ce ne sont pas trois moments successifs dans une évolution. Ce sont trois aspects sur une seule et même chose, la Ritournelle.**

I.

Un enfant dans le noir, saisi par la peur, se rassure en chantonnant. Il marche, s'arrête au gré de sa chanson. Perdu, il s'abrite comme il peut, ou s'oriente tant bien que mal avec sa petite chanson. Celle-ci est comme l'esquisse d'un centre stable et calme, stabilisant et calmant, au sein du chaos. […]

II.

Maintenant, au contraire, on est chez soi. Mais le chez-soi ne préexiste pas : il a fallu tracer un cercle autour du centre fragile et incertain, organiser un espace limité. […] Voilà que les forces du chaos sont tenues à l'extérieur autant qu'il est possible, et l'espace intérieur protège les forces germinatives d'une tâche à remplir, d'une œuvre à faire. […] Or les composantes vocales, sonores, sont très importantes. […] Un enfant chantonne pour recueillir en soi les forces du travail scolaire à fournir. Une ménagère chantonne, ou met la radio, en même temps qu'elle dresse les forces anti-chaos de son ouvrage. […]

11

III.

Maintenant enfin, o[illegible] le cer[illegible]vre, on laisse entrer quelq[illegible]n, on appelle [illegible]qu'un, ou bien l'on va soi-même au-de[illegible], on s'élan[illegible]n n'ouvre pas le cercle du côté où [illegible]ssent les a[illegible] forces du chaos, mais dans [illegible] autre région [illegible] par le cercle lui-même. Com[illegible] à s'ouvrir sur un futur, en[illegible] qu'il abrite. Et cette fois, c'est pour rejoindre des forces de l'avenir, des forces cosmiques. On s'élance, on risque une improvisation. Mais improviser, c'est rejoindre le Monde, ou se confondre avec lui. On sort de chez soi au fil d'une chansonnette. […]

Ce ne sont pas trois moments successifs dans une évolution. Ce sont trois aspects dans une seule et même chose, la Ritournelle.

PENSER

IT221 “L’impuissance à penser [...] appartient à la pensée, si bien que nous devons en faire notre manière de penser, sans prétendre restaurer une pensée toute-puissante. Nous devons plutôt nous servir de cette impuissance pour croire à la vie, et trouver l’identité de la pensée et de la vie [...].

DR192 “Penser, c’est créer, il n’y a pas d’autre création, mais créer, c’est d’abord engendrer «penser» dans la pensée.

QLP197-198 “C’est le cerveau qui pense et non l’homme, l’homme étant seulement une cristallisation cérébrale. On parlera du cerveau comme Cézanne du paysage : l’homme absent, mais tout entier dans le cerveau…

MP467 “Mettre la pensée en rapport immédiat avec le dehors, avec les forces du dehors, bref faire de la pensée une machine de guerre [...].

DR181 “En vérité, les concepts ne désignent jamais que des possibilités. Il leur manque une griffe, qui serait celle de la nécessité absolue, c’est-à-dire d’une violence originelle faite à la pensée, d’une étrangeté, d’une inimitié qui seule la sortirait de sa stupeur naturelle ou de son éternelle possibilité : tant il n’y a de pensée qu’involontaire, suscitée, contrainte dans la pensée, d’autant plus nécessaire absolument qu’elle naît, par effraction, du fortuit dans le monde. Ce qui est premier dans la pensée, c’est l’effraction, la violence, c’est l’ennemi. [...]

“La logique d’une pensée est comme un vent qui nous pousse dans le dos, une série de rafales et de secousses. P129

“Toute pensée est déjà une tribu, le contraire d’un État. MP467

“On reconnaît volontiers qu’il y a du danger dans les exercices physiques extrêmes, mais la pensée aussi est un exercice extrême et raréfié. Dès qu’on pense, on affronte nécessairement une ligne où se jouent la vie et la mort, la raison et la folie, et cette ligne vous entraîne. On ne peut penser que sur cette ligne de sorcière, étant dit qu’on n’est pas forcément perdant, qu’on n’est pas forcément condamné à la folie ou à la mort. P141

“De l’intensif à la pensée, c’est toujours par une intensité que la pensée nous advient. DR188

12

RÉSISTER

QLP104 **“Nous ne manquons pas de communication, au contraire nous en avons trop, nous manquons de création. *Nous manquons de résistance au présent*.**

MP293 **“Qu’est-ce qu’un cri indépendamment de la population qu’il appelle ou qu’il prend à témoin?**

QLP103 **“La honte d’être un homme, nous ne l’éprouvons pas seulement dans les situations extrêmes décrites par Primo Levi, mais dans des conditions insignifiantes, devant la bassesse et la vulgarité d’existence qui hantent les démocraties, devant la propagation de ces modes d’existence et de pensée-pour-le-marché, devant les valeurs, les idéaux et les opinions de notre époque. L’ignominie des possibilités de vie qui nous sont offertes apparaît du dedans. Nous ne nous sentons pas hors de notre époque, au contraire nous ne cessons de passer avec elle des compromis honteux. Ce sentiment de honte est un des plus puissants motifs de la philosophie. Nous ne sommes pas responsables des victimes, mais devant les victimes. Et il n’y a pas d’autre moyen que de faire l’animal (grogner, fouir, ricaner, se convulser) pour échapper à l’ignoble : la pensée même est parfois plus proche d’un animal qui meurt que d’un homme vivant, même démocrate.**

P239 **“Croire au monde, c’est ce qui nous manque le plus; nous avons tout à fait perdu le monde, on nous en a dépossédé. Croire au monde, c’est aussi bien susciter des événements même petits qui échappent au contrôle, ou faire naître de nouveaux espaces-temps, même de surface ou de volume réduits.[…] C’est au niveau de chaque tentative que se jugent la capacité de résistance ou au contraire la soumission à un contrôle.**

QLP105 **“L’artiste ou le philosophe sont bien incapables de créer un peuple, ils ne peuvent que l’appeler, de toutes leurs forces. Un peuple ne peut se créer que dans des souffrances abominables, et ne peut pas plus s’occuper d’art ou de philosophie. Mais les livres de philosophie et les œuvres d’art contiennent aussi leur somme inimaginable de souffrance qui fait pressentir l’avènement d’un peuple. Ils ont en commun de résister, résister à la mort, à la servitude, à l’intolérable, à la honte, au présent.**

“Ce système où nous vivons *ne peut rien supporter* : d’où sa fragilité radicale en chaque point, en même temps que sa force de répression globale.

ID291

13

CRÉER

P182 **“La création se fait dans des goulots d’étranglement. Même dans une langue donnée, même en français par exemple, une nouvelle syntaxe est une langue étrangère dans la langue. Si un créateur n’est pas pris à la gorge par un ensemble d’impossibilités, ce n’est pas un créateur. Un créateur est quelqu’un qui crée ses propres impossibilités, et qui crée du possible en même temps.**

“Il faut parler de la création comme traçant son chemin entre des impossibilités. P182

“Créer n’est pas communiquer, mais résister. Il y a un lien profond entre les signes, l’événement, la vie, le vitalisme. C’est la puissance d’une vie non organique, celle qu’il peut y avoir dans une ligne de dessin, d’écriture ou de musique. Ce sont les organismes qui meurent, pas la vie. Il n’y a pas d’œuvre qui n’indique une issue à la vie, qui ne trace un chemin entre les pavés. P196

“On dirait que la lutte *contre le chaos* ne va pas sans affinité avec l’ennemi, parce qu’une autre lutte se développe et prend plus d’importance, *contre l’opinion* qui prétendait pourtant nous protéger du chaos lui-même. [...] Le peintre ne peint pas sur une toile vierge, ni l’écrivain n’écrit sur une page blanche, mais la toile ou la page sont déjà tellement couvertes de clichés préexistants, préétablis, qu’il faut d’abord effacer, nettoyer, laminer, même déchiqueter pour faire passer un courant d’air issu du chaos qui nous apporte la vision. QLP191-192

“Les signes renvoient à des modes de vie, à des possibilités d’existence, ce sont les symptômes d’une vie jaillissante ou épuisée. Mais un artiste ne peut pas se contenter d’une vie épuisée, ni d’une vie personnelle. On n’écrit pas avec son moi, sa mémoire et ses maladies. Dans l’acte d’écrire, il y a la tentative de faire de la vie quelque chose de plus que personnel, de libérer la vie de ce qui l’emprisonne. L’artiste ou le philosophe ont souvent une petite santé fragile, un organisme faible, un équilibre mal assuré [...]. Mais ce n’est pas la mort qui les brise, c’est plutôt l’excès de vie qu’ils ont vu, éprouvé, pensé. P195-196

P48-49

“Créer de nouvea
qui aient une né
ça a toujours ét
de la philosophi
c’est plein d’une
politique et de li

P4e Couv.

“N’étant pas une puissance, la philosophie ne peut pas engager de batailles avec les puissances, elle mène en revanche une guerre sans bataille, une guérilla contre elles. Et elle ne peut pas parler avec elles, elle n’a rien à leur dire, rien à communiquer, et mène seulement des pourparlers. Comme les puissances ne se contentent pas d’être extérieures, mais aussi passent en chacun de nous, c’est chacun de nous qui se trouve sans cesse en pourparlers et en guérilla avec lui-même, grâce à la philosophie.

MP466

“Moins les gens prennent la pensée au sérieux, plus ils pensent conformément à ce qu’un État veut. En effet, quel homme d’État n’a pas rêvé de cette toute petite chose impossible, être un penseur ?

x concepts
essité,
a tâche
...] Un concept,
orce critique,
erté.

DELEUZE ET SON ŒUVRE

Gilles Deleuze et Félix Guattari

“À la Libération, on restait bizarrement coincé dans l’histoire de la philosophie. Simplement on entrait dans Hegel, Husserl et Heidegger; nous nous précipitions comme de jeunes chiens dans une scolastique pire qu’au Moyen Âge. Heureusement il y avait Sartre. [...] Reste que je ne me sentais pas d’attrait pour l’existentialisme à cette époque, ni pour la phénoménologie, je ne sais vraiment pas pourquoi, mais c’était déjà de l’histoire quand on y arrivait, trop de méthode, d’imitation, de commentaire et d’interprétation, sauf par Sartre.” D18-19

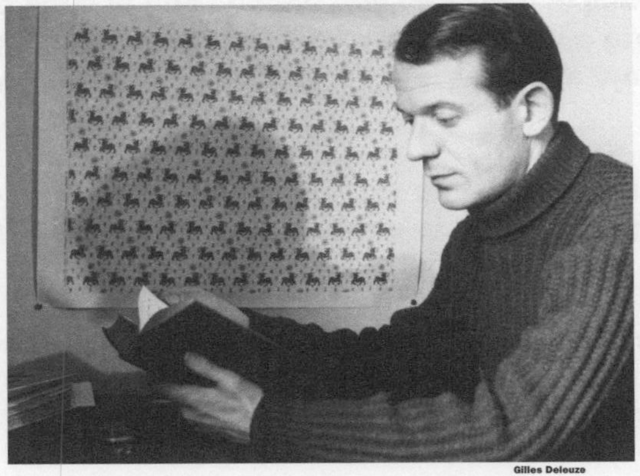

Gilles Deleuze

1953 Premier ouvrage Empirisme et subjectivité **“Si vous voulez m’appliquer les critères bibliographie-biographie, je vois que j’ai écrit mon premier livre assez tôt, et puis plus rien pendant huit ans. [...] C’est comme un trou dans ma vie, un trou de huit ans. C’est cela qui me semble intéressant dans les vies, les trous qu’elles comportent, les lacunes, parfois dramatiques, mais parfois même pas. Des catalepsies ou des espèces de somnambulisme sur plusieurs années, la plupart des vies en comportent. C’est peut-être dans ces trous que se fait le mouvement.”** P188-189

1962 Nietzsche et la philosophie **“J’ai commencé par des livres d’histoire de la philosophie, mais tous les auteurs dont je me suis occupé avaient pour moi quelque chose de commun. Et tout tendait vers la grande identité Spinoza-Nietzsche. L’histoire de la philosophie n’est pas une discipline particulièrement réflexive. C’est plutôt comme l’art du portrait en peinture. Ce sont des portraits mentaux, conceptuels.”** P185-186

1964 Proust et les signes
1966 Le bergsonisme **“Hume, Bergson, Proust m’intéressent tant parce qu’il y a chez eux de profonds éléments pour une nouvelle image de la pensée. Il y a quelque chose d’extraordinaire dans la manière dont ils nous disent : penser ne signifie pas ce que vous croyez.”** ID193

1967 Présentation de Sacher Masoch **“Ce qui me plaisait chez Masoch et Sade, c’était leur conception tout à fait tordue du contrat selon Masoch, de l’institution selon Sade, rapportés à la sexualité.”** P229

1968 Spinoza et le problème de l’expression **“C’est sur Spinoza que j’ai travaillé le plus sérieusement d’après les normes de l’histoire de la philosophie, mais c’est lui qui m’a fait le plus l’effet d’un courant d’air qui vous pousse dans le dos chaque fois que vous le lisez, d’un balai de sorcière qu’il vous fait enfourcher.”** D22

“Ensuite, j’avais payé mes dettes, Nietzsche et Spinoza m’avaient acquitté. Et j’ai écrit des livres davantage pour mon compte.” D22-23

“J’ai donc commencé à faire deux livres en ce sens vagabond, *Différence et répétition*, *Logique du sens*. Je ne me fais pas d’illusion : c’est encore plein d’un appareil universitaire, c’est lourd, mais il y a quelque chose que j’essaie de secouer, de faire bouger en moi, traiter l’écriture comme un flux, pas comme un code.” P16

1969 Différence et répétition
1969 Logique du sens

“Et puis il y a eu ma rencontre avec Félix Guattari, la manière dont nous nous sommes entendus, complétés, dépersonnalisés l’un dans l’autre, singularisés l’un par l’autre, bref, aimés. Ça a donné *L’Anti-Œdipe*.” P16 **“*Une* philosophie, ce fut donc pour moi comme une seconde période qui n’aurait jamais commencé et abouti sans Félix.”** P187 **“À deux, nous voudrions être l’Humpty Dumpty ou les Laurel et Hardy de la philosophie.”** DRF

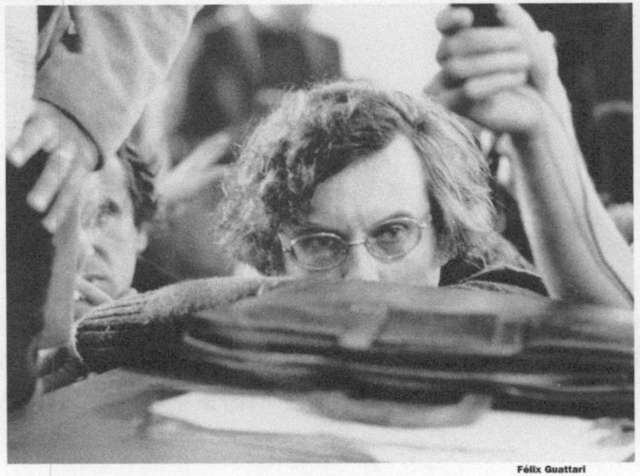
Félix Guattari

1972 L'Anti-Œdipe – Capitalisme et schizophrénie 1 **avec Félix Guattari**

"*L'Anti-Œdipe*, c'est une rupture qui se fait toute seule, à partir de deux thèmes: l'inconscient n'est pas un théâtre, mais une usine, une machine à produire; l'inconscient ne délire pas sur papa-maman, il délire sur les races, les tribus, les continents, l'histoire et la géographie, toujours un champ social." P197

1975 Kafka, pour une littérature mineure **avec Félix Guattari**
1977 Dialogues **avec Claire Parnet**
1980 Mille plateaux– Capitalisme et schizophrénie 2 **avec Félix Guattari**

"Les concepts, ce sont des singularités qui réagissent sur la vie ordinaire, sur les flux de pensée ordinaires ou quotidiens. Il y a beaucoup d'essais de concepts dans *Mille Plateaux*: rhizome, espace lisse, heccéité, devenir-animal, machine abstraite, diagramme, etc. Guattari invente beaucoup de concepts, et j'ai la même conception de la philosophie." DRF

“Ensuite, supposons que ce soit une troisième période où il s’agit pour moi de peinture et de cinéma, d’images en apparence. Mais ce sont des livres de philosophie. C’est que le concept, je crois, comporte deux autres dimensions, celle du percept et de l’affect.” P187

1981 Francis Bacon : logique de la sensation
1983 Cinéma 1 – L’image-mouvement
1985 Cinéma 2 – L’image-temps **“Le cinéma procède à un auto-mouvement de l’image, et même à une auto-temporalisation : c’est ça la base, et ce sont les deux aspects que j’ai essayé d’étudier. Mais justement, qu’est-ce que le cinéma va ainsi nous révéler de l’espace et du temps, que les autres arts ne nous révèlent pas ?”** P83

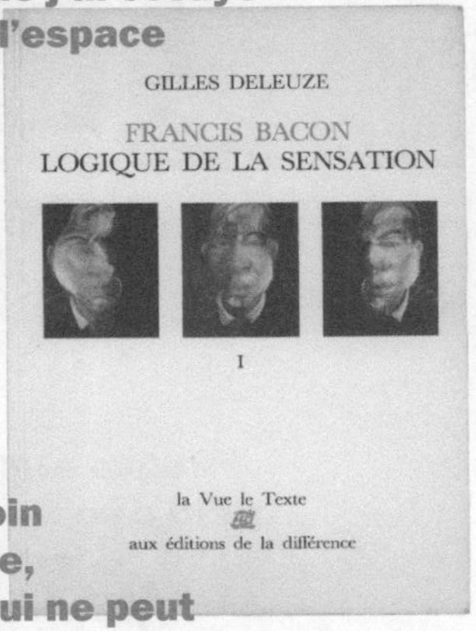

1986 Foucault **“Quand quelqu’un meurt qu’on aime et qu’on admire, on a parfois besoin de faire un dessin de lui. Pas pour le glorifier, encore moins pour le défendre, pas pour la mémoire, mais plutôt pour en tirer cette ressemblance ultime qui ne peut venir que de sa mort, et qui fait dire « c’est lui ».”** P139

1988 Le Pli – Leibniz et le baroque **“Il y a pourtant une unité concrète du concept, une opération ou construction qui se reproduit sur ce plan, le Pli, les plis de la terre, les plis des organismes, les plis dans l’âme. Tout se plie, se déplie, se replie chez Leibniz [...].”** P 211

1990 Pourparlers
1991 Qu'est-ce que la philosophie ? **avec Félix Guattari**

“Peut-être ne peut-on poser la question *Qu'est-ce que la philosophie ?* que tard, quand vient la vieillesse, et l'heure de parler concrètement [...] C'est une question qu'on pose dans une agitation discrète, à minuit, quand on a plus rien à demander. Auparavant on la posait, on ne cessait pas de la poser, mais c'était trop indirect ou oblique, trop artificiel, trop abstrait, et on l'exposait, on la dominait en passant plus qu'on n'était happé par elle [...] On n'avait pas atteint à ce point de non-style où l'on peut dire enfin : mais qu'est-ce que c'était, ce que j'ai fait toute ma vie ?” QLP 7

1993 Critique et clinique
1996 Abécédaire **vidéo avec Claire Parnet**

«Abécédaire de Gilles Deleuze par Claire Parnet»
Dir. Pierre-André Boutang, 1996
Éditions Montparnasse

2002 L'île déserte et autres textes
2003 Deux régimes de fous

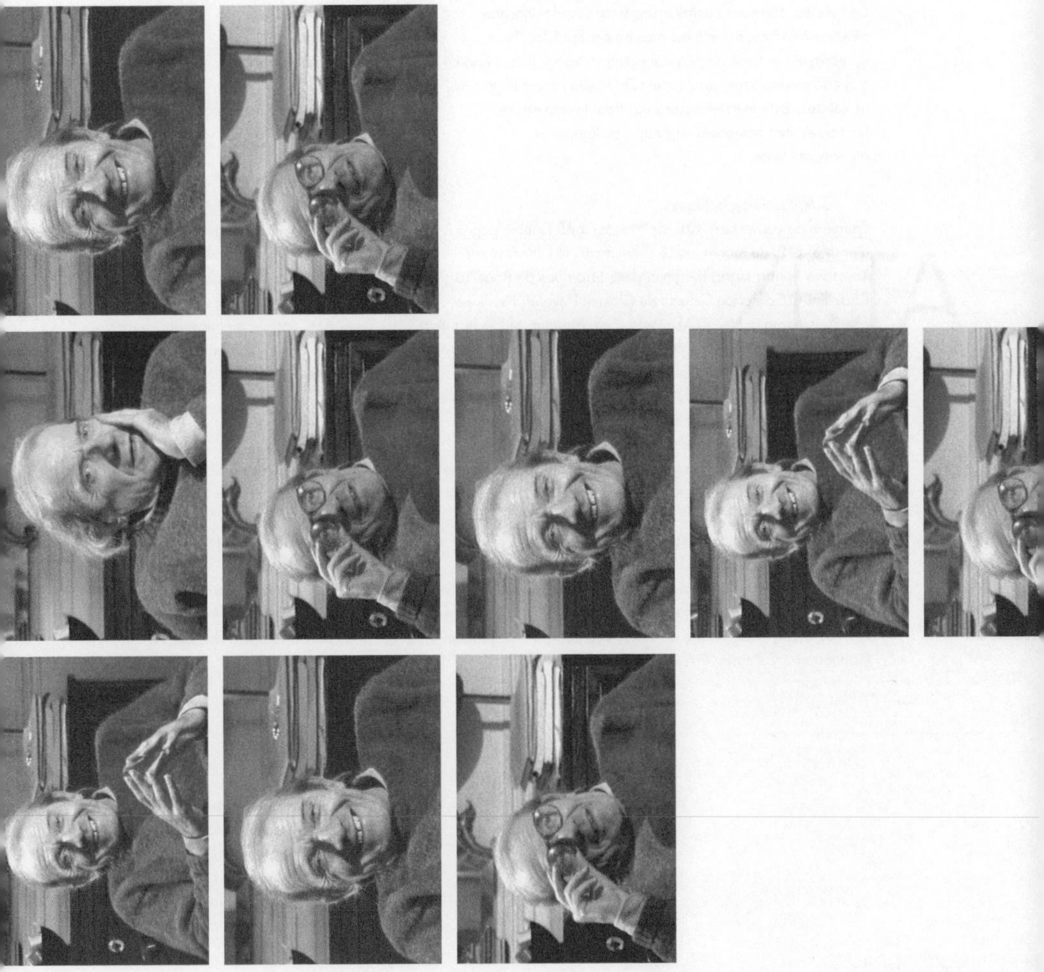

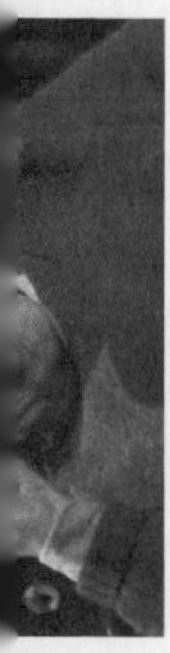

Ce livre est édité par l'**adpf** association pour la diffusion de la pensée française ● Il est dessiné par SpMillot, Paris, et fabriqué par Cent pages en septembre 2003. Il est imprimé à 12500 exemplaires, sur Zanders Zeta velin nature et gris 80, et Zanders Zeta martelé nature 150 pour la couverture. Les textes sont composés en Architype Renner et Monotype Dante.

Crédits iconographiques

Première de couverture: © B. de Monès, 1988 Double page d'entrée: © B. de Monès, 1988 Événement: © L'Illustration/ Keystone Sentir: Ingrid Bergman dans *Stromboli* de Roberto Rossellini © Collection Cahiers du Cinéma Devenir: Paul Klee, *Die Zwitsher-maschine* © Akg Paris. Coll. Museum of Modern Art, New York Lignes: H. © Zepha Hoaqui B. Anna Karina et Jean-Paul Belmondo dans *Pierrot le fou* de Jean-Luc Godard © Bifi, P. Georges, Périphéria production Lignes de fuite: H. © LL-Violet B. © R. Depardon/Magnum © LL-Violet Désir: Laurel et Hardy dans *La Maison à construire* de Leo McCarey © Collection Cahiers du Cinéma Corps sans organes: Francis Bacon *Turning Figure*, 1962 © A. R. Zepka © Mnam, Bibliothèque Stravinsky Énoncer: Gilles Deleuze à l'Université de Vincennes, 1975 © H. Gloaguen/Rapho Résister: © M. Monteaux, 2003 Créer: Gilles Deleuze à Big Sur © J.-J. Lebel Deleuze et son œuvre: Gilles Deleuze et Félix Guattari © Fonds Félix Guattari/Archives Imec • Portrait de Gilles Deleuze © M. Tournier • Félix Guattari © Frilet/Sipa • «Abécédaire de Gilles Deleuze» © Sodaperaga Productions/ C. Parnet, P.-A. Boutang